Melancholia's Dog

Melancholia's Dog

ALICE A. KUZNIAR

The University of Chicago Press   Chicago and London

ALICE A. KUZNIAR is professor of German and comparative literature at the University of North Carolina, Chapel Hill. She is the author, most recently, of *The Queer German Cinema* (2000).

The University of Chicago Press, Chicago 60637
The University of Chicago Press, Ltd., London
© 2006 by The University of Chicago
All rights reserved. Published 2006
Printed in the United States of America

15 14 13 12 11 10 09 08 07 06   1 2 3 4 5
ISBN: 0-226-46578-0 (cloth)

Library of Congress Cataloging-in-Publication Data

Kuzniar, Alice A.
  Melancholia's dog / Alice A. Kuzniar.
    p. cm.
  Includes bibliographical references and index.
  ISBN 0-226-46578-0 (cloth : alk. paper)
    1. Dogs in art. 2. Dogs in literature. 3. Human-animal relationships. I. Title.

  NX650 .D63K89 2006
  700'.4629772—dc22

                                    2005034633

Contents

Illustrations

Acknowledgments

My deepest gratitude goes to David Clark who not only from the start encouraged me to pursue the writing of this book but also has inspired me with his brilliant and sensitive writing on animals in philosophy. He was the sole friend to read the entire manuscript. I should also like to thank the several colleagues, friends, and students who directed me to the sources discussed in this book: Nico Beger, Deb Booth, Rich Cante, Stanley Corngold, Eric Downing, Maria de Guzman, Graydon Ekdahl, Sue Gustafson, Yvonne Ivory, Clayton Koelb, Dick Langston, Carol Mavor, Fatima Naqvi, Ann Marie Rasmussen, Meg Rich, Jonathan Risner, Gregor Thuswaldner, and Christopher Wild. I have benefited from the insights of the perceptive, enthusiastic students I taught over the years in my first-year seminar "Canine Cultural Studies" and wish to acknowledge my gratitude to them here. The University of North Carolina at Chapel Hill College of Arts and Sciences provided me with leave time to finish the book and with ample research funds that permitted me to call upon my assistants David Smith and Catherine Mainland for trips to the library. Without their help this manuscript could never have been completed. The additional funding offered to me while I was teaching at Rutgers University as the Charlotte Craig Distinquished Professor in the spring of 2002 allowed me to take advantage of the resources at the American Kennel Club Library in New York, where Barbara Kolk led me to some wonderful finds. I also wish to thank Jennifer Pournelle for sharing with me her experiences in publishing. Alan Thomas at the University of Chicago Press has been a supportive, prompt editor, who solicited extraordinarily perceptive and helpful readings from two anonymous readers, whom I should like very much to thank here. Finally, I could not have been more fortunate to have in Yvonne Zipter a copyeditor whose own writing—her poetry on greyhounds—is as elegant and spirited as her dogs must be. And, at the penultimate stages of the book's preparation, the University of Minnesota graciously provided additional funds; my thanks go to Alison Guenther-Pal for compiling the index with such fine attention to detail.

Karen Lee, Chris Strom, and Karin Yates entrusted me with the care of the animals, so lovely and graceful, that they brought into this world. My two whippets have sweetly accompanied me during the writing of this book, in their physical presence and in every thought put to paper. This book is dedicated to the memory of my beautiful Tania, who, with a heart literally too big for this world, passed away this very month.

CHAPEL HILL, OCTOBER 2005

Introduction

To write on the exquisite ways in which the visual and literary arts contemplate and reassess the human-canine relationship is, alas, an exercise in mortification. The subject of dogs is presumed to be unfit for serious scholarly investigation: it is held to be sentimental, popular, and trivial, both by the academic and by the general lay population. Whenever I had to explain and justify to what I was devoting years of research and writing, I felt embarrassed. What kind of artistic works did I have in mind? Was I investigating children's illustrated books or juvenile novels? Was I approaching my studies through the culture of TV commercials, articles in *Dog Fancy*, or Disney films? Had I seen the exhibition of dog painting by a local artist at such-and-such a restaurant? Had I read the most recent book on the popular psychology of pet owners? Was I writing a coffee table book devoted to stylish black-and-white photography of dogs? Or a collection of anecdotes and poems by contemporary authors? These inquiries always left me depressed that I could not answer them in a sunny affirmative. How could I counter politely that this was precisely the kind of book I was *not* writing? That I was focusing instead on the vicissitudes of interspecial communication and the sadness that they brought on?

Echoing in my mind, too, were the questions left unvoiced but that I easily could imagine, edged with derision and dismissiveness. I feared my project would be received as an indulgence held impermissible in our pragmatic society, proving just how useless we literary scholars were. I am sure my colleagues and graduate students were skeptical, for this venture strayed far from my previous publications on German literature and cinema. Furthermore, my new endeavor was an anomaly not just in my field but completely out of step with research interests in the humanities and social sciences, which focused on race, class, gender, and ethnicity. Pet keeping in Victorian England or France, as in the work of Harriet Ritvo and Kathleen Kete, or in contemporary society, as in Marc Shell, John Berger, and Yi-Fu Tuan, was an acknowledged and acceptable object of study, but since I concentrated on such literary figures as Turgenev, Kafka, Mann, and Coetzee, I could hardly be analyzing pet keeping as a social phenomenon (which is not to say their work is without social criticism). Whereas my colleagues in cultural theory despised the sentimental projections of human emotion onto the pet, my lay acquaintances conceived of my endeavors solely in those terms. Both parties shared the inability to envisage the representation of the dog outside the confines of the lowbrow, popular media and arts.

It occurred to me that perhaps the problem resided in the strictly codified way in which we speak about dogs, which is why, like the weather, they are a safe object of chitchat but not of scholarly reflection. In other words, it is difficult to think outside the box when it comes to dogs. In our society the canine companion is just irresistibly cute; or its value is determined by how closely it matches AKC breed standards; or it is the subject of strict obedience class prescriptions, even if it is the gentle modeling of behavior in the clicker method. Dogs must be trained to listen to us, not the other way around. I thus felt the need to quiet the din in my head—to escape from the clamor of the automatic, unreflective phrases about dogs that pervade our society. It was the stillness I sought and what it meant. It is not the dog who cannot speak and must learn our language (sit, down, stay), but we who cannot speak properly about it, whereby this speaking would not include the pretense of making it think silly human thoughts, as so often happens in cartoons, which actually belittle the dog for its lack of speech. What was needed was not how to project into human words what the dog was thinking but how to preserve, respect, and meditate on its muteness and otherness. From the outset, then, my project was a melancholic one— to probe the boundaries, however expansive they may be, to human-canine communication. I wanted to find an apt language for our attachment to the dog, and it was this appropriate representation, in all its richness and attentiveness, that I set out to discover and explore.

But where was it to be found? Local library and bookstore shelves are lined with countless popular collections of cute poems and short stories on dogs that parcel out sentimental wisdom in little excerpts or anecdotes.

Dog cartoons pepper the pages of the *New Yorker*. *Bark* magazine advertises "16 Pages of GREAT LITerature" on the cover of its summer 2004 issue. And then there are the children's books and films on canine adventures and canine companions. The popular culture industry capitalizes on this need to come closer to the dog; indeed it sustains it. This present book, by contrast, wants to address the reader who senses that, in this surfeit of dearth, we are not thinking adequately about our close companions. For the reader who wants to expand the vocabulary and imagery with which we voice and picture our relation to the dog, I offer suggestions as to where she can turn to find the intelligence, creativity, and intensity she seeks—be it in the writings of Virginia Woolf, Tibor Dery, or Rebecca Brown or in the artwork of Paula Rego, Sue Coe, or Sally Mann.

At the crux of this present inquiry lies, then, not an expansion of an academic, historical approach to the social function of the pet but what the latter tends to disparage, namely, the affective, immediate ties between man and the four-footed. These bonds involve such difficult concepts as intimacy, compassion, propinquity, and mourning over their death. I investigate the awareness of separation from the companion animal and identification with what is then perceived as its abandonment, forlornness, and sadness. I want to examine what occurs when these affective feelings are disavowed and when the identification with the dog becomes the object of shame. I want to inquire whether acknowledgment of empathic sensibilities might permit us to circumvent the condescension and cruelty that can often dominate relations with animals. Mindful that we cannot fully eradicate the power relations that determine our dealings with the creature dependent on our care, can we nonetheless try to rethink our attachment to it in terms of reciprocity and responsibility? And how would it be possible to do so without falling into sentimentality? How, in thinking through our similarities with animals, can we resist anthropomorphization? I aim to inquire into how the literary and visual arts explore shifting, unsure divisions and alliances between man and beast and how they do so based on the uniqueness of each animal life. This artistic intervention takes as its imaginative task how to reassess these bonds.

And what better example among living creatures to investigate interspecial commonalties than the dog, bred, by refining its traits as a pack animal, to adapt to human companionship. Because of its need for human direction and because of our emotive sharing with it, the dog is best suited as a test case to explore the philosophical, ethical, and imaginary connections and impasses between the self and other, between the human and animal world. Or, as the theologian Stephen Webb cogently put it: "Dogs are, literally and figuratively, what we have made of them, but it is precisely that fact that gives the question of otherness its urgency and difficulty. Can the closeness of dogs enable us to see their very otherness? Can their similarity shed light on difference? Can dogs be both our 'best friends' and an intrusion of something persistently other, demanding respect and attention on their own terms?" (6).

To ask what "respect and attention" to animals "on their own terms" would mean has been a question markedly avoided in cultural studies on pet keeping and, in raising it, this present investigation differs significantly from them. The cultural historians Kathleen Kete and Harriet Ritvo, for instance, have interpreted nineteenth-century dog fancy through the lens of class and gender struggles. Similarly, John Berger, Marc Shell, and Yi-Fu Tuan have exposed the compensatory struggles for dominance and control over the pet in contemporary society, as if consideration of the warm-blooded animal in and of itself must be bracketed from debate. This reluctance to tackle the "urgency and difficulty" of animal otherness can even be seen in Marjorie Garber's *Dog Love*. For all her affection for her topic, she coyly distances herself from the seriousness of pet love and pet death through her sprightly compendium and witty commentary on dogs in culture—from the literary highbrow to popular legend.

These scholars are not alone, though, in being deeply suspicious of the tradition of pet keeping or in making light of it. A gamut of other contemporary thinkers have interpreted the desire for closeness to a pet as redolent of bourgeois sentimentality and narcissistic identification with the animal Other. Steve Baker notes, for instance, that postmodern artists tend either to ironize the pet (Jeff Koons, Thomas Grünfeld, Jordan Baseman) or to take animals such as sharks (Damien Hirst, Olly and Suzi) as objects of representation, as if wary of sentimentality. He terms this mistrust of pets the "fear of the familiar" (*The Postmodern Animal* 166–90). In the field of philosophy, Gilles Deleuze and Félix Guattari in *Kafka: Toward a Minor Literature* and *A Thousand Plateaus* speak of "becoming animal," fetishizing the wild, indecipherable creature that would represent the opposite of tame social norms and thus promise liberation from them.[1] Consequently, they shun "family pets, sentimental, Oedipal animals each with its own petty history, 'my' cat, 'my' dog. These animals invite us to regress, draw us into a narcissistic contemplation. . . . *Anyone who likes cats or dogs is a fool*" (*A Thousand Plateaus*, 240). Surprisingly, from a very different camp, animal rights philosopher Tom Regan has warned against the sensibilities of empathy for animals because they are insufficient for enacting change. Human logic must drive reform and press for taking responsibility for rationally less capable beings.[2]

One of the most prominent contemporary philosophers, Jacques Derrida, however, provides an exception to this wariness toward the pet. As will be evident in subsequent chapters, time and again I have taken inspiration from his article entitled "L'animal que donc je suis" where he analyzes the denigration of the animal in Western philosophy and the resulting chasms between man and beast.[3] The beginning of Derrida's essay is significant because the premise from which he launches into his analysis of the loss incurred by the scientific, philosophical, and religious separation of man from beast is his own immediate interaction with his pet: he describes the moment when he catches the gaze from his cat. Derrida insists on the peculiarity of this moment and on the irreplaceable singularity of *this* creature (he isn't speaking of a symbolic or imaginary cat). Its illegible, enigmatic look signifies the secret of a unique, total Other whose proximity is unbearable. This mindfulness of closeness, mysteriousness, and individuality are crucial for Derrida because he warns against thinking of the animal in the grammatical singular, as if all living beings (humans excepted) could be subsumed under one category. He observes how their manifold differences are ignored in order to posit and uphold the apartness of mankind, "a humanity that is above all careful to guard, and jealous of, what is proper to it" (383). Through this one word, "animal" (which Derrida rewrites as "animot," signifying the confinement of the plural[istic] "animaux" to the singular), man reserves the right to control and dominate other living creatures: "The animal is a word, it is an appellation that men have instituted, a name they have given themselves the right and the authority to give to another living creature [*à l'autre vivant*]" (392). To the reductive unitariness of this name, Derrida juxtaposes the uniqueness of his cat and, to the naming, the facticity or thereness of this particular living being with whom he stands face to face.[4]

Because Derrida sees the Western philosophical and theological tradition as insisting on demarcating the division between man and animal so as to define what is quintessentially human, he wants to complicate the notion of such a unitary border: "Whatever I will say is designed, certainly not to efface the limit, but to multiply its figures, to complicate, thicken, delinearize, fold, and divide the line precisely by making it increase and multiply" (398).[5] In the spirit of Derrida, then, I too wish to call into question this divide, though precisely via the animal with which the human has the closest contact, namely, the dog. I want to probe the interstices where, in trying to distinguish himself from the dog or, the opposite, to extol the dog's uniqueness among species, man actually confuses boundaries. I want to see how artists and writers "complicate, thicken, delinearize, fold, and divide the line" between canine and human beings, whether it be in the mute intimacy that can arise between them or, conversely, in the shame such attachment evokes. Resisting the trap of a mawkish, sentimental anthropomorphism, such artists are aware of the arduousness of breaching the gap between the species. Yet at the same time they deconstruct the simplistic binary that would pit man against animal. In fact, they soberly realize that this very binary is what makes guilt inescapable vis-à-vis the animal dependent on human care; but it also makes possible empathetic shame, the sharing of vulnerability, and the mourning of pet loss, for these all operate along the fault plane of this very division.

To illustrate how fraught close contact with the dog can be, consider how mimetic resonance between the canine and human is generally taken for granted and left unquestioned. The dog is said to represent the fantasy of perfect communication, indeed of unalloyed love. Our communication with it runs the gamut from "What does it imagine I am saying?" to "What do I understand it as saying?" Yet how can we presume to know that it can be so attuned to our feelings? Similarly, the dog is said to embody the virtues of trust, faithfulness, empathy, and loyalty. Yet to what extent can the best of so-called human traits properly be called "human" when they apply quintessentially to the dog? How appropriate is it for animal being to be used in representing human rectitude? Are human desiderata here merely anthropomorphized, or is the accusation of anthropomorphism itself a quick means of denying animals emotional sensibilities? Such questions probe the ontological certainty of the divisions between mankind and the so-called brute.

It is when such borders threaten to dissolve that one encounters the abject, defined as that from which one wants to distance oneself because it conjures up an uneasy or repulsive association and thus threatens firm ego boundaries. For however much the dog is said to possess human virtues, it is also, as Sigmund Freud remarked, repugnant to man because of its lack of shame about its excrement and sexual functions (14:459). Even admittance of emotional reliance on the pet can be shame inducing, for it can be regarded as an improper, unclean object of love. Julia Kristeva, in *Powers of Horror*, has called the abject a "border" (9) and the borderline case a situation "where identities (subject/object, etc.) do not exist or only barely so—double, frizzy, heterogeneous, animal, metamorphosed, altered, abject" (207). She observes that "the abject confronts us . . . with those fragile states where man strays on the territories of *animal*" (12). If Derrida has examined how Western philosophy wishes to ratify the boundaries between human and animal—the territories proper to each—I want to set about investigating how multiple examples from art and literature explore the borderline confusions between the species, indeed, how they either acknowledge or repudiate identification with the loathsome in the dog. And, because I am interested in issues of empathetic resonance and emotive oneness in the companionship with the pet, I take recourse to another concept that Kristeva examined in her subsequent and companion work to *Powers of Horror*—namely, the psychoanalytic concept of melancholia.[6] Because the melancholic individual struggles with the intractable, unacknowledged indivisibility of self and other, the intensity of the canine-human bond warrants special interrogation under this rubric.

At least until depression began to be preferably treated with drugs, Sigmund Freud's 1915 essay "Mourning and Melancholia" was the most significant foray into twentieth-century explorations of melancholy, with reverberations in the work of Melanie Klein, Nicolas Abraham and Maria Torok, and Judith Butler, as well as Julia Kristeva. Freud describes the melancholic as interiorizing and hiding an unavowed affection for or bond to another human being. If one refuses to acknowledge the importance of this individual, his or her loss will go unmourned. Indeed, someone who is depressed often cannot say why. Freud attributes this speechlessness to the forfeited beloved having secretively become an integrated part of the self: melancholia signals a silent identification with the person who has disappeared. Consequently, instead of designating the loss as that of something residing outside the self, the subject regards itself as depleted and injured, itself an object meriting bereavement. In the terms of psychoanalysts Nicolas Abraham and Maria Torok, the Other lies buried, encrypted, and sealed up within the Self: although never identified and acknowledged as lost, it remains lodged, silenced, and hidden away at the core of one's being. Were the melancholic to pinpoint the source of her mourning and psychic pain, she would cease to brood; otherwise she mourns without end and falls into protracted depression.

How, then, does this disavowal of loss manifest itself when the ambivalently regarded Other is an animal, especially the one to whom humans have the most empathetic bond, namely, the dog? Paradoxically, although the dog belongs to another species, as a pet that is thoroughly integrated into daily human life and companion to one's quietest moments, it fills one's psychic space. The melancholic pet owner longs for complete rapport and to know that the dualisms between animal and human are untrue. Yet she is saddened by the inevitable disjointedness and nonsimultaneity between herself and the extimate species, extimacy being that which is exterior to one yet intimately proximate. At the same time, it is precisely the intimate nature of this affiliation that remains unspoken, in fact, at times unutterable, verging on a social taboo, because the dog is often considered an inferior replacement for human love. In addition, as the passage from Freud suggests, the dog is often regarded as an unclean being. Given this repudiation of ties to the animal, despite overproximity to it, it comes as a surprise that psychoanalytic theories on melancholia address neither the dilemma of pet loss nor the fervency of pet love. Yet however much pet keeping calls out for melancholic analysis, because pet keeping is generally ridiculed as trivial and sentimental, and the animal held to be a lesser being, psychoanalysis has dismissed the powerful implications of canine-human relations.[7]

The following chapters, although not constantly referencing the workings of melancholia, are nonetheless deeply informed by them. In these chapters, and in contrast to Sigmund Freud, I am treating melancholia neither as a mental disease nor even as an abnormal condition or disorder. Rather, I emphasize the subjective distress and sorrow, the mood of sadness, that arise both from separation from animal being and from ambivalent identification with it. This said, I also need to make clear that, although psychoanalytic views at times help nuance and animate my discussion of the literary and visual text, by invoking such theory I by no means claim to offer a coherent psychoanalytic explanation of pet keeping, an investigation into possible psychoanalytic positions on it, or even a series of applications of psychoanalysis to dog love, which would entail weighing competing views. If psychoanalysts themselves have shied away from this difficult topic, far be it from me to fill the gap. I furthermore can only invoke a psychoanalytic vocabulary in terms of our ambivalent attachment to dogs, for can it say anything at all to us about the canine mind? We cannot know about their secret inner life or, even, whether what we call "secret inner life" is something presumed by an anthropocentric psychoanalysis and that would perforce exclude animals from possessing it.[8] When making reference to psychoanalytic insights, I thus turn to them not as truth claims but as probings and experiments, as evocations and provocations.[9] Psychoanalysis provides us, next to the arts themselves, with our most richly textured vocabulary for affective conditions.

In the first chapter I examine how muteness is transferred onto the animal in a process whereby it is disavowed in the human. As Derrida has remarked, Western humanist philosophy, for its own purposes, has rendered animals silent: if animals are supposed to be devoid of language, then man can assure himself of his superiority, proof of which is in his naming the other dumb. Indeed, as I shall show, not only is the animal said to be deprived of speech, its taciturnness is even interpreted as a token of its sadness. Yet perhaps the question should be not "do *they* have language?" but "do *we* have an adequate language to speak to them and about them?" To interrogate the clear-cut divisions between mankind and beast, then, is to address the limits of representation. I thus look at how various writers and artists acknowledge the melancholic longing for perfect communion with the pet and reflect on the silences that arise from two species inhabiting different orders of discourse. Here I take recourse to Kristeva's analysis of the depressive's faltering language. Yet not only are these writers and artists cognizant of what lies beyond word and image, they also critically interrogate the compensatory moves designed to fill the unsettling gap between man and brute. This capacity of the arts to interrogate their own means of communication offers insight into the controversies raised by animal rights philosophy, which explores precisely these tensions between animal inarticulateness and human morals, between the silent or silenced animal and a human compassion that responds to a glimmer of identification with the suffering brute.

To imagine blurring the distinctions between human and beast is to enter into the territory of shame. Identification with the dog can prove unsettling and either entail feelings of embarrassment and disgrace or convert into angry disavowal of such feelings. But in the case of what psychologists call "empathetic shame," it can also lead to vicarious feeling for another's mortification. It is here that the roots of compassion lie. In the chapter on shame I examine what occurs when one's own poverty is disowned as being dishonorable and then displaced onto the dog who now becomes the repository of shame and is believed to merit cruel rebuke, so that one's own self-esteem can be reclaimed. By contrast, one can also openly identify with the shamelessness and abjection of dogs and thereby resist self-censorship and self-loathing. I thus also look at works that hypothesize a human-canine hybrid, resulting in the representation of a contaminated, impure being. Female artists, in particular, use this bastardized creature to flaunt indecorousness and counteract the humiliation women can be made to experience. As they know, a painful self-consciousness, the awareness of one's visibility, presupposes the gaze of a judging Other. I then take this centrality of the gaze in shame theory to ask what happens when the camera is set before the face of an animal. If its visage is said to be open and undissimulating, what does it mean for the photographer and viewer to capture it before an intrusive camera? How would embarrassment be registered either by the canine sitter or the human viewer, when the dog in the portrait is made fun of? These issues and questions, too, arise from empathy and identification with the canine species.

One of the most unutterable aspects of closeness to pets is the shamefulness about intimacy with them, as if it might be construed as bordering on bestiality or as if to love dogs betrayed an inability to love humans. In chapter 3 I examine how, contrary to such internalized feelings of shamefulness, closeness to the companion animal actually serves as an antidote to emotions of self-unworthiness and depression. Women writers, time and again, record how the dog serves to restore moments of centeredness and equilibrium to the wounded, melancholic self. In being alone with one's pet companion, these women experience what the novelist Elizabeth von Arnim called *recueillement*, the regathering of one's self in peace and quietude. But is the dog thereby instrumentalized as a therapeutic aide? Rather than seeing in the responsiveness of the dog a prop to one's narcissism, such writers both acknowledge the separateness and uniqueness of the animal Other as well as testify to the complexity underlying the workings of intersubjectivity between species.

Given the intense closeness to one's pet and that the extent of transference with it largely goes unacknowledged, its death can be devastating without its owner being able to say why. Once again melancholic, unavowed identification and attachment make recognition of the loss difficult and amplify its magnitude. Early twentieth-century suffragette, composer, and dog-lover Ethel Smyth, for instance, spoke of her "inordinate affection" for her Old English Sheepdog and, on its death, of her "constant brooding over the companion of the last years whose presence [she] saw everywhere, everywhere, everywhere" (83–84). The inability to articulate or measure one's bereavement is why one grieves so intensely for departed pets; it seems unfathomable how, in their short lives, they could have come to mean so much to one. In her inability to abandon mourning, the melancholic person is faithful to the lost object, so faithful, as if she were, so to speak, a dog herself: she wishes, in her mourning, to be as faithful to the pet as it was to her in life. Although numerous novels either fearfully anticipate or work through the death of a beloved pet, other examples can also be found where one's kinship to animals is denied and their death left unacknowledged. Mourning the dog—and the failure to do so—are the topics of the final chapter.

In this book I try to align and blend many voices. In addition to Freud and Kristeva on depressive illness, I consult such psychologists as Silvan Tomkins and Jack Katz on the affect of shame and psychoanalyst Jessica Benjamin on intersubjectivity. Alongside Derrida, I examine the philosophers Walter Benjamin, Ludwig Wittgenstein, Emmanuel Levinas, and Thomas Nagel on the muteness of animals. Ecofeminists Carol Adams and Josephine Donovan help clarify the role of sympathy in the ethics of care for animals. Above all, I focus on the attempt of the arts to address and repair melancholia; in other words, they rescue the animal made abject from silence and death. I look, for example, at the photography of Pentti Sammallahti, Keith Carter, and Sally Mann, at paintings by Lucian Freud, David Hockney, Paula Rego, and Sue Coe, and films by Ulrich Seidel and Alejandro González Iñárritu. The writers I examine range from Turgenev to J. M. Coetzee and include the modernists Michael Field, Franz Kafka, Thomas Mann, R. M. Rilke, D. H. Lawrence, and Virginia Woolf, as well as a panoply of current authors, including Rhoda Lerman and Rebecca Brown. In the years I have been researching this project, these were the most profound works on the dog that I discovered; their complexity demanded an investigation for the most part denied them in academic scholarship.

A final word, then, on the importance of art to melancholia: to speak in terms of a redemption of loss through representation is to invoke a different tradition of melancholia in juxtaposition to the Freudian one that robs the depressed patient of consciousness of her loss and the ability to voice it. This tradition, too, informs this study and, ultimately, counteracts the Freudian legacy. Stretching back to Aristotle, the prepsychoanalytic theory of melancholia as one of the four humors maintains that the melancholic is keenly aware of not being able to attain an ideal and is dejected because of this heightened knowledge.[10] This temperament is associated with the genius, the prophet, and the scholar, all of whom engage in a metaphysical pursuit, while knowing that their goal is a transcendent, unattainable one. Cast in terms of my present study, melancholia means that, however close we are to the canine pet, that closeness can never be enough and we are always conscious of the obliqueness and imperfection that govern our communion with it and, hence, of a fundamental muteness. But the ideal of crossing that barrier motivates the writers and artists to whom I referred above: they attempt to come closer to the animal, all while melancholically despairing at not being able to do so. Most important, their art reflects on this impasse. They reach for the impossible in their art because they know that the unvoiced lies at the heart of pet love.

In addition, the humoral theory holds the belief that one can compensate for loss through art however inexactly it may capture the object of its longing. Hence one speaks of sweet melancholy: the impossibility of regaining a lost object is aestheticized, and poetic gains from sustaining melancholy are reaped. Kristeva, in particular, has theorized in contrast to Freud how artistic and literary expression can symbolize unsymbolizable loss. She observes that sublimation and idealization are the gifts of "beauty, the depressive's other realm" (*Black Sun* 95). Indeed, explicitly linking her study to the pre-Freudian tradition, Kristeva entitles it *Black Sun*, after an iconographic detail from the most famous artwork devoted to the humor, Dürer's etching *Melencolia I* (1514). Evoking the same metaphor of a resplendent blackness, Jean Starobinski has written: "Melancholia turned into ink becomes the tain thanks to which the image shines. The deepest darkness opposes to light a surface from which it springs forth again, luciferian, as from a second source" (423). John Keats, too, alluded to the aestheticizing influence of the humor when he wrote in "Ode on Melancholy": "She dwells with Beauty—Beauty that must die" (209).

In turning to the beauty and pathos in the art and literature on the dog, I want to acknowledge indebtedness to this prepsychoanalytic tradition of melancholia, this tradition of artistic redemption and illumination. The separation from this other species, causing a yearning for closeness and communion, becomes the subject for idealization in work after work I discuss and transmutes into the desire to perfect a representation of it, to particularize, circumscribe, nurture, and preserve one's relationship to the dog in a language as true and comely as possible.[11] But first I want to study this humoral tradition in three works in which its iconography appears and is intimately tied to the dog. All three cases lead us to reflect melancholically on limits—on the inadequacies of language and representation and hence on the loneliness between man and beast.

An Excursus on Melancholia's Dog (Three Examples)

In a painting, a woman in a somber blue dress sits on a bed, her tiredness betrayed by how she props herself up: she is slouched into a pillow to brace her back, while her head is supported by her hand as she gazes ahead (fig. 1). Staring off into space, she fails to perceive what is before her. Instead her thoughts preoccupy her. The rags piled up in abstract randomness behind her seem to represent the convolutedness of her cogitation, and her face is darkened by shadow as if to suggest a lack of

1   Lucian Freud, *Triple Portrait*, 1986–87. Oil on canvas. 120 × 100 cm. Private Collection. Courtesy Bridgeman Art Library, London.

inner clarity. The physiognomy and pose are thus ambiguous, signifying either fatigue or reflection, resignation or intensity, lethargy or creativity. In contrast to this brooding wakefulness, two whippets lie deep asleep at her feet and at her side. Although the woman seems remote and alone, the canines press up against her, reminding her of their humble presence. They are loyal companions to her thoughts.

The artist of this remarkable painting is Lucian Freud, the grandson of Sigmund Freud. Lucian Freud often included his whippets in his studio portraits, *Triple Portrait*, being the title (1986–87) of the above painting. In an earlier work, *Double Portrait* (1985–86), the same woman is depicted asleep, her arm shielding her eyes, as if the world were too much for her and might even disturb her dreams. Asleep as well, the whippet rests its head on her shoulder and open palm, while its front leg dangles over her other, outstretched arm. One notices the weary physicality of both their bodies, in both the well-formed muscles. The woman's veins parallel the brindle markings on the hound, while its thin fur makes it appear naked. So close, lying side by side, human and canine are truly doubles of each other. The dog is not just in the portrait of a woman, it is equally the subject of portraiture. Conversely, the human sitter in Freud's works is portrayed in his or her animal heaviness, frequently naked. Freud said of his models in a radio interview, "I'm interested, really interested in them as animals."

Yet however much Freud's figures connect via touch, each is lost in its own world; each signifies apartness. As the double, the dog in its dormancy mirrors human withdrawal from the world. Sandra Miller beautifully captures this tension in Lucian Freud's work "between closeness and distance, encounter and isolation . . . Animals . . . have as much personality and as much strong presence as the humans they accompany. . . . He keeps the sense of individual presence, and therefore, with the togetherness, we cannot forget their separateness, the space between them even when they are in contact" (118). In addition, the shared rest between woman and dog in Freud's paintings means silence, for closeness replaces other forms of communication. Paradoxically, then, the repose that comes from the companionship with animals, because it is mute, also evokes solitude.

Let us now go back almost 500 years to the work that Lucian Freud's, in so many of its details, richly evokes. In Albrecht Dürer's 1514 copper etching *Melencolia I*, a woman sits with her head resting heavily on her clenched fist (fig. 2). Her other hand idly holds a compass, while various construction and geometric tools lie discarded at her feet. Mindful of the vanity of all human endeavor, Melencolia is incapable of action.[12] Although she bears wings, her flights of fancy do not take her into idyllic realms: like Lucian Freud's sitter, she stares sullenly and intently before her, lost in her own thoughts. Her face is likewise somber reflecting her spiritual state, but the dark complexion is also symptomatic of illness from the black bile. The word melancholy is the Latin transliteration of the Greek word for black bile, *atra bilis*. The magical square as well as the wreath around her head function as talismans against her mental and physiological sickness.

2　Albrecht Dürer, *Melencholia I*, 1514. Engraving. Courtesy of the Ackland Art Museum, The University of North Carolina at Chapel Hill, Gift of W. P. Jacocks.

The four temperaments or humors (the others being phlegmatic, sanguine, and choleric) were said to determine not only the health but also character of an individual. Melencolia's inert pose signifies a compendium of characteristics associated with the depressive humor— sadness, exhaustion, indifference, as well as meditation. Downcast, the melancholic cannot say why: she experiences a sense of loss but her spirits are too torpid to identify what she lacks. Although her wings suggest that she longs for the ideal, pessimistically she knows it cannot be attained.[13] She is aware that she cannot step beyond the limits of the imagination. The bat that hovers in the air signifies both wakefulness and work during the midnight hours as well as the twilight of the spirit: even after rumination, Melencolia cannot reach clarity. The cherub, busily scribbling, marks a striking contrast to her inactivity: while she represents idle thought, he represents unthinking vitality. Her disinclination to exertion and her overwhelming sense of tedium has led melancholy to be associated with *acedia* or sloth, one of the seven deadly sins.

But as Lucian Freud also intimated, Melencolia's propped up head can signify not just tiredness over the *taedium vita* but also its opposite, creative intensity. Ever since Marsilio Ficino, melancholy has been associated with the genius, who is said to translate loss into gain, emotion into art. The melancholic individual is gifted with a heightened sensitivity and creativity. Its despair can also metamorphose into exultation, dejectedness into sublimation. These two opposites underlie the reason for the presence of the dog in Dürer's engraving.

Traditionally, the dog in art has been associated with loyalty (in friendship), fidelity (in marriage), envy (for the other dog's bone), or lasciviousness (once in the lady's lap). Dürer was the first, though, to link the dog to the melancholy habit. It will then reappear in other Renaissance depictions by Lukas Cranach, Domenico Fetti, and Giovanni Benedetto Castiglione and in the twentieth-century variations, George Grosz's *Die Liebeskranke* (The love-sick girl [1918]), Dieter Kraemer's *Melancholie* (1970), and conceivably even Joseph Beuys's *Coyote: I Like America and America Likes Me* (1974).[14] Walter Benjamin also took up the connection of the dog to melancholy in his *Origin of the German Tragic Drama*: melancholy is "the most truly creaturely of the contemplative impulses, and one has always noticed that its power need be no less in the gaze of a dog than in the attitude of the brooding genius" (1.1:324).

The dog quintessentially stands for the animalistic heaviness and weariness that beset the humor. The German word for melancholy is, incidentally, *Schwermut*, a heavy spirit. Of the four elements, melancholy is associated with the earth, and her earth-boundedness is signified by the dog sleeping on the ground (in Lucian Freud, on the earthen-colored blanket). Curled in on itself, this dog is oblivious to its surroundings, for the dispirited temperament regards all appearances as false and misleading and thus prefers to ignore the world; hence Melencolia herself stares off into space. The greyhound appears old, having lost muscle mass, and is dormant and hungry. It illustrates the stupor of creation, delivered over to its unconscious suffering or contentedness.

Yet the dog does not represent only torpor or dullness. Like many of the other allegorical objects in Dürer's engraving it carries layered meaning. One of the dangers of depression is that it can switch into mania: considered to be the most gifted and sensitive of animals and because of its serious nature, the dog indicates how the melancholic individual could fall prey to insanity. It is associated with scholars and prophets, for like them, it is always hunting after things, doggedly sniffing out the truth. Dürer hence depicted the dog lying down next to the lion in Saint Hieronymous's study (1514).[15] It is one's companion in meditation. Linking these very opposites of the madman and prophet, Benjamin writes apropos the hound in Dürer:

> According to old tradition "the spleen dominates the organism of the dog." This he has in common with the melancholic. If the spleen, an organ believed to be particularly delicate, should deteriorate, then the dog is said to lose his vitality and become rabid. In this respect he symbolizes the darker aspect of the melancholy complexion. On the other hand the shrewdness and tenacity of the animal were borne in mind, so as to permit its use as the image of the tireless investigator and the brooder [*Grübler*]. "In his commentary on this hieroglyph Pierio Valeriano says explicitly that the dog that *facem melancholiam prae ferat* [bears a melancholy face] would be the best at tracking and running." In Dürer's engraving, especially, the ambivalence of this image is enriched by the fact that the animal is depicted asleep: bad dreams come from the spleen, but prophetic dreams are also the prerogative of the melancholic. (1.1:330)[16]

Double, melancholic portraits, then, lie here next to each other—Lucian Freud next to Albrecht Dürer, woman next to hound. What arises from this peculiar doubling? In other words, how can one read Freud and Dürer through each other? And what is one to make of the resemblances between Melencolia and her dog? First, one notes with Benjamin the ambivalence governing this resemblance: the dog reflects the divergent tendencies of the melancholic—madness *and* prophecy, inertia *and* metaphysical reflection, earth-boundedness *and* sky-borne musings. As the paragon of animals sensitively attuned to human companionship, many of its traits are idealized, but yet it is given over to stupor and suffering. Conversely, the human is associated with the brute, yet at the same time creatureliness is repudiated in the attempt to sublimate it. Thus, although they mirror each other, Melencolia's dog is nonetheless set apart from her. Each is lost in his or her own dream world. They become an image of two solitudes. Nietzsche captured this tension between introversion and communion with the animal when he wrote: "His love of animals—men have always recognized the solitary by means of this trait" (10:426).

The frozen stillness of Melencolia and her mute attendant can also be seen as a sign of silence. In Lucian Freud the very physicality of sinews, bones, and the heavy limbs points to the absence of verbal discourse, as if, in this example of "still life," he were reflecting on the essence of painting—its stillness or speechlessness. Likewise self-reflexively, Dürer's iconographic work seems to suggest that, with the failure of the verbal, the emblematic needs to signify instead. Since Melencolia cannot speak of her dejection, her body displays her affect and the objects around her tell her story. Scholar Hartmut Böhme proposes that, in its multivalent meaning, Dürer's work even reflects back on the subject who realizes the limits of interpretation. Melencolia herself represents this impasse: she has scattered about her all the geometric tools of measurement, but unused, they cannot lead her to gauge boundaries correctly.

Melencolia's own dullness and torpor, stemming from her incessant brooding and inactivity, thus lend her proximity to the dormant hound. Aware of her own ineffectuality, she is trapped in self-deprecation, which brings her close to the shame of animal creatureliness. As Benjamin said, melancholy was the "most truly creaturely of the contemplative impulses" (1.1:324). Most important, however, if Melencolia is aware of her own inarticulateness and becomes taciturn, she further resembles the dumb animal lying at her feet. Not only can her language not truly speak for the animal, out of its consciousness, but because of this limitation she also mirrors the dog's inability to command human speech. Instead of regarding the animals as mute, the melancholic here discovers and probes the implications of her own silences.

Thus in solitude, mute, Melencolia longs for the ideal. In the depression of not being able to realize it, I shall read her unfulfillable desire to understand her intimate companion. For, could it be that among all the imponderables on which she broods is that of the radical alterity of animal being, despite its embodiment in the mundane hound at her feet or despite its physical immediacy as it presses up against her body? And might she, in fact, be preoccupied by the thought that this companion, who lies so heavy and lifeless next to her, may all too easily slip away into infinite otherness and never awake from its sleep? The barriers, confines, and encumbrances that Melencolia faces are multiple, but they are epitomized by death as the ultimate limit and as allegorized in the hourglass above her head that reminds her of mutability. Mortality, of course, is what Melencolia shares most with the animal.

And now to my third example. If Melencolia and her dog are indeed double, mirror portraits of each other, what would it mean to coalesce human and animal into the same being? This is the project or experiment attempted time and again by that astonishing, perplexing author of talking animals, Franz Kafka. For instance, in "The Metamorphosis" (1915), Gregor Samsa, the mute (and mutant) melancholic beast par excellence, on hearing his sister play the violin, poses an arresting question about his transformation into a bug: "War er ein Tier, da ihn Musik so ergriff?" (Was he an animal, that music should so move him?") (*Sämtliche Erzählungen* 92). The query raises a host of subsequent ones in the reader's mind: What distinguishes man from beast? Is the beast closer than the human to beauty? Does animality reside in a higher sensitivity for music? Is there in the nonverbal expression of music the confirmation of muteness? Is it because the animal cannot speak that it is especially attentive to a musical form of expression? And is the beast closer to the beauty in music because he is a melancholic, mourning the failure of language?

Kafka's phrasing of the question also interrogates what it *is* to be an animal. Paradoxically, in this sole question Gregor ever poses of his existence—what it means to be an animal (and not a human being)—he finally transcends his beastly condition. Yet, to assume that animality is defined by being moved by music implies a fundamental lack on the part of the human being—the inability to be so moved. Thus, in being gripped by music, Gregor also seems to surpass the human condition. Kafka thereby queries where the distinctions lie between human and animal being, and whether, paradoxically, in the most lowly form of existence there lies the capacity for transcendence.

Gregor is divided, then, between his melancholic stupor or *acedia* and his glimmer of transcendence. His body, too, is that of the melancholic: it literally transforms into an ever hollow shell in which is entombed, buried away from the light of investigation, an unnamable loss. The melancholic, according to Freud, takes himself as the object of loss; and it is indeed the body of Gregor that withers away. Beauty, in his sister's violin playing, is the food, he realizes at the end, with which he could have nourished himself.

Franz Kafka frequently endows animals with human thought and speech: there is the mouse in "Josephine the Singer, or the Mouse People" (1924), the nesting creature in "The Burrow" (1923), the ape in "Report from an Academy" (1917), the jackal in "Jackals and Arabs"

(1917), and the dog in "The Researches of a Dog" (1922). The basic questions these tales pose are: Why does Kafka turn to the animal to begin with? Wherein lie the barriers to signification if an animal is used to convey human dilemmas? And what silences arise as a consequence of the rift between the species? As these fundamental questions also guide this present study, I want to close the introduction with Kafka. Yet he also leads back to Albrecht Dürer. If the enigma of Kafka's dark allegories is not enough to link him to the 1514 engraving, then the disposition of the first-person narrator in "The Researches of a Dog" would seal the tie. Here Kafka fashions the truly melancholic hound, depressed and uncertain over the inadequacies of communication, relentlessly brooding over his own nature, consternated by the inaccessibility of other species, and yet idealistically pursuing his metaphysical quest.

"The Researches of a Dog" is a late, unfinished work that conveys the bizarre musings of a dog who obtusely and confusedly relates to the world around him. Dürer included the hound in his engraving because of its association with the doggedness of scholarly pursuit. Kafka's canid stubbornly pursues his speculations—he is, indeed, manically obsessed by them ([*ihnen*] *verfallen* [*Sämtliche Erzählungen* 325]). Yet true to the reasons that cause the humoral despondency, his scholarly ambitions concentrate on the immanent, beyond which he cannot see. His primary, relentless investigation—where does food come from?—is prosaic and earthbound and testifies to the limitations and sense of futility that the melancholic encounters. He mechanistically attempts to solve his questions by testing whether or not starving brings forth food, displaying a fundamental misunderstanding of what sustains life. Although it could be argued that it is both a material and spiritual nourishment that he seeks—and he does expect food to fall from the sky—he seems to confuse the phenomenal with the spiritual. Can he even access the spiritual by focusing on, even denying himself, the former, namely, food? Literally he becomes the hungry dog of Dürer's engraving; he becomes so weak and lethargic that he cannot raise himself off the ground.

Thus, although Kafka's dog tries to find meaning, it eludes him. He recognizes the uselessness of his questioning (340) and despairs (330). It is hopeless (342). Among the last words of the text are those that deprecate his research, his "lack of propensity for science, scanty intellectual power, poor memory and, above all, inability to focus consistently on a scientific goal" (354).[17] The dog thus participates in the self-conscious brooding of the melancholic, whose own hypothesizing become the object of scrutiny. Melencolia's gaze may be intent, but she casts it into empty space, while her tools lie idle about her, as if she too were unable to stay focused on a goal.

Like English, the German language is replete with derogatory phrases that involve dogs. *Auf den Hund kommen* means to become physically, morally, and economically ruined; *jemanden wie einen Hund behandeln* has the direct English equivalent "to treat someone like a dog"; *Hunde-arbeit* denotes hard, difficult labor; *mir ist hundelend* signifies "I feel miserable"; and *hündisch* means blindly subordinate and submissive. Kafka's allusions to dogs are equally disparaging. Josef K's death in *The Trial* (1925) is the culmination of his senseless life, for he perishes "like a dog." The condemned man in "The Penal Colony" (1919) appears so submissive (*hündisch*) that one only needed to whistle for him to come to his own execution. In his *Kafka-Kommentar*, Hartmut Binder notes that dogs can refer to a directionless, stagnating, and futile-uncertain form of being: he quotes Kafka as referring to running around "so hündisch" (so slavishly) and confessing "Ich umlaufe und umbelle sie, wie ein nervöser Hund eine Statue" (I run around and bark at them, like a nervous dog around a statue [263]). And in the story "Blumfeld, an Older Bachelor," the title character resists getting a pet dog when he considers the drawbacks—dirtiness, fleas, sickness, and decrepitude in old age.

Despite Kafka's denigration of the dog and the self-deprecation of the narrator in "The Researches of a Dog," the latter's intense desire for illumination—be it solely regarding the source of nourishment—has a metaphysical dimension. He hungers after enlightenment; his questioning is a replacement for food. Or rather, food is a substitute for all his questioning: perhaps, he muses, one wanted to stop his mouth by filling it with chow. Kafka's hound also obsesses over the perplexing music he hears emanating from two sorts of dogs: the musical dogs and the hunter. As a young dog he encounters seven mysterious dogs, who, the reader would assume, are dogs performing to circus music. "They did not speak, they did not sing, in general they held their tongue with almost a certain doggedness [*Verbissenheit*], but they conjured forth music out of that empty space. Everything was music" (326). Similarly, later in life the dog encounters a strange hunter who suddenly begins to sing, although he too is silent, as if the source of the music comes from outside his chest. Presumably, although the reader cannot know for sure (trapped as he or she is within the canine narrative perspective), this overwhelming, sublime sound comes from hunting horns.

The dog's bewilderment thus becomes the reader's own, for it is impossible to evaluate the dog's limitations. Presumably it is stupid in its inability to recognize circus music or hunting horns as external sources of sound; yet it also has the marvelous capacity to transform this dyslexia into a sense of awe and wonder. Thus his investigations juxtapose a certain dogginess with intimations of the transcendent; they combine earth-boundedness with sky-borne musings. Perhaps in refusing the mundane (food), he hopes to attain the spiritual (another form of sustenance). It is the hope, so intense, to find answers to his impossible questions that renders his quest sublime. Thus he closes by admitting that, although his instincts hinder his research, nonetheless they make him long for freedom—freedom that would break the bonds within which he is trapped. Kafka's dog therewith illustrates the antitheses that characterize Dürer's melancholic: inertia versus obsessive fixations; dullness of spirit versus reflection; awareness of boundaries versus a longing for freedom. Ultimately, it is the impossibility of finding elucidation that casts the melancholic into depression, for even the intimations of a metaphysical realm are unpromising.

Kafka in fact uses the word melancholic in reference to the animal's depressed sense of isolation: the dog confesses that interactions with others confuse him and make him "melancholic" (343). He wants deliberately to disassociate himself from others. The story even starts by him admitting being "withdrawn, solitary, preoccupied only with my hopeless, dilettantish but for me, indispensable little researches" (324). He feels he is dying not from hunger but abandonment (350). And he senses his questions to other dogs about the nature of their existence are not taken seriously, so that others want to distract him from them. This melancholic loneliness derives in part from his fatalistic recognition of what he characterizes as the essence of the dog: the problem with canine nature is its *Verschwiegenheit*, meaning a reticence or taciturnity bordering on silence and secrecy. It could even be that the music he hears reflects such a *Verschwiegenheit*, for it is paradoxically silent, not emanating from the mouth. Because he cannot vocalize adequately, the dog-narrator falls into melancholic depression.

Kafka's melancholic hound sees meaning as extinguished, artificial, and absurd. The dog disparages his own language as exaggerated and misleading despite his contorted, long, qualifying sentences. He acknowledges the pointlessness of discussion with others (342) and is cognizant of the danger of misspeaking (*verreden* [329]) and the misrepresentation of a situation (329). He cannot impart to others what has occurred, as after the encounters with the circus dogs and the hunter; moreover, he knows that no one wants to listen. Yet true to the melancholic's inability to abandon the ideal, despite all these communicative setbacks, the dog longs for "the true word" (341). The dog states as his purpose or goal to reveal the essence of dogdom. This essence, however, proves to be its silence (334); consequently, because he too is a dog, he cannot impart what it is that dogs know. He is trapped within this circularity. Would his investigations, though, have been helped, were he to have stepped outside himself or his self-preoccupation with dogdom? How does he represent other species to himself? And what does the result say about K's representation of a narrative perspective outside the human?

The poet Rainer Maria Rilke bestowed loving praise on the dog, by imagining, from a divine perspective, what it would be like to reside within the creature's center:

I love gazing into things. Can you imagine with me how glorious it is, for example, to see into a dog, in passing—*into* him (I don't mean to see through him, which is merely a kind of human gymnastics, where one comes right back out on the other side of the dog, using him as a window to whatever human concerns lie behind him, no, not that)—but to ease oneself into the dog exactly at his center, the place out of which he exists as a dog, that place in him where God would, so to speak, have sat down for a moment when the dog was complete, . . . that he lacked nothing, that no better dog could be made. (*Rilke and Benvenuta* 77)

Rilke imagines how glorious it would be to gaze into the dog. But how, even though it is "man's best friend," can one possibly represent the mind of the dog to the human? Kafka attempts this very feat—to peer inside the mind of a foreign, enigmatic creature. Paradoxically, though, the narrative perspective, by inhabiting the dog's consciousness, only reveals that the essence of the dog is to be mute, hence unfathomable. Thus, when Kafka tries to narrate from within this consciousness of the dog, the point of view is perplexing, lacking in the divine clarity that Rilke envisioned.

In "Terzinen über Vergänglichkeit" (Terza rima on mutability) yet another contemporaneous German-speaking writer, Hugo von Hofmannsthal, referred to the dog as being mute and foreign (*stumm und fremd* [*Gedichte und Lyrische Dramen* 17]). Kafka uses the exact same words to describe—not the dog—but how other species appear to him: they are "poor, meager, mute beings, whose speech is limited only to certain cries" [stumm und fremd, nur auf gewisse Schreie eingeschränkt (324)]. Kafka's dog parallels human anthropocentrism, in other words, man's tendency to take himself as the measure and arbitrator of all living things and to regard those who do not possess human language as expressing themselves in mere cries. Indeed, the dog not only regards other species as inarticulate, he goes so far as to not recognize them at all: "For what else is there besides dogs?" (333). He assumes his reader is likewise a dog in referring to "dogs like you and me" (326). Moreover, he obdurately refuses—conceivably to retain his freedom—to see humans as the source of his food.[18]

That Kafka can place himself within the mind of another initially contrasts with the dog's inability to recognize others. Or does it contrast? Is not such a narrative perspective bound to lead to skewed, incoherent results? Kafka uncovers the limits of trying to fathom another's consciousness, for to occupy its center of being creates discord. Clearly this is an unlikely dog in its metaphysical meditations—a creature of contrary qualities and bizarre aspirations, neither doglike nor humanlike but an unsettling hybrid.[19] Because the reader cannot successfully place himself in the perspective of this dog, the point of his musings remains only vaguely decipherable. The reader thereby senses his own creatureliness, his own constraints in his inability to conjecture the precise referent of the dog's perceptions. Although exposed to the ontology of another being, Kafka demonstrates the boundaries of access to it. Thus, just as the dog fails to recognize species outside his own, so too does Kafka illustrate—as if through a reversed mirror image—human *méconnaissance* vis-à-vis another species.

Kafka's lesson would then be that one must learn to "deanthropomorphize," an act that would entail the loss of language when one communicates across species. When Gregor loses the ability to speak in words, he is open to music. The dog, too, encounters music as not being uttered through the mouth. What would it mean to escape from language in order to communicate with another species? Can muteness speak? Kafka quintessentially illustrates the major aporia that literature and art on the dog faces: silence lies at the heart of representation of the dog. For how does one make the mute dog speak? How can one enter its consciousness? How does one listen to its muteness? If the dog's voice cannot be understood and if the hunter and the circus dogs are not even voicing their own song, then what does issue out of the mouth—is one with it—is hunger itself. Hunger here can be understood as the expression of the desire for articulateness: "In reality we were utterly painfully one, and when I said to myself, 'That is hunger,' it was really the hunger that was speaking" (348). This is where the reality of communication with the other species lies: in the hunger for communication and understanding. There is a connection, in other words, between the hunger of Melencolia's dog and her own falling silent. And it is to the silences in the representation of the dog that I now turn.

ONE

Muteness

In his *Sonnets to Orpheus* (1923), a cycle devoted to the difficult beauty of poetry, Rainer Maria Rilke addresses his sixteenth sonnet to his friend, a dog. It begins: "Du, mein Freund, bist einsam, weil . . . / *Wir* machen mit Worten und Fingerzeigen / uns allmählich die Welt zu eigen" (*Werke* 497). [You, my friend, are lonely, because . . . / *We*, with words and finger-pointings, / gradually make the world our own (47).] Although befriended by the poet, the dog is lonely. And although, given the ellipsis at the end of the first line, the reason for this isolation seems to elude the poet, Rilke immediately juxtaposes the dog to the human being who makes the world his own by familiarizing himself with it through words: hence the dog is presumably lonely because, unlike man, it is without the means of representation.[1] Rilke here joins a long tradition of ascribing muteness, isolation, and hence melancholy to animals. Heidegger in his Freiburg seminar lectures of 1929–30, for instance, speaks of the animal as being poor in the world (*weltarm*), resulting in its sadness. In explicating Heidegger, Derrida sees him as attributing this despondency to the animal's banishment from the world of man, which includes the realm of speech: the animal exudes the "impression of sadness . . . as if [he] remained a man enshrouded, suffering, deprived on account of having access neither to the world of man that he nonetheless senses, nor to truth, speech, death, or the Being of the being as such" ("Eating Well" 111–12).[2] What separates man from beast is the latter's muteness, which is also a dumbness or dullness that mourns for what it senses yet cannot articulate.

Another early twentieth-century German writer whom Derrida discusses in conjunction with animals, sadness, and the lack of language is Walter Benjamin. In his 1916 essay "On Language as Such and on the Language of Man," Benjamin speculates that after the Fall nature is engulfed by a deep sadness and muteness (*Stummheit* [2.1:155]).[3] Were nature to be endowed with language she would raise her voice in lament (*klagen*). But such a lament would still be an inarticulate utterance, a physical exhalation (*sinnlichen Hauch*), it being in the nature of the plaint that it is the most undifferentiated, powerless expression (*der undifferenzierteste, ohnmächtige Ausdruck der Sprache*). Such a pure lament would be unable to designate its causes. Thus even while with voice, nature is deemed voiceless. One is reminded of Nietzsche's aphorism in "On the Uses and Abuses of History": "The human may well ask the animal one day, 'Why do you not talk to me of your bliss and only look at me?' The animal really wants to answer and say: 'It comes of always forgetting right away what I wanted to say.' Thereupon it forgot even this answer and fell silent so that the human could only wonder" (2:101). Here too the animal in beginning to speak immediately becomes speechless.[4] Moreover, its forgetting can be attributed not to a pure bliss but to a profound sadness, it being in the nature of melancholy to be unable to locate and articulate the cause of its helplessness.

Precisely because melancholy is characterized by this tendency to fall silent, Benjamin comes to question his initial postulation that it is her speechlessness that lies at the root of nature's sadness. He in fact reverses the order of causation: it is not her powerlessness, her speechlessness that renders nature melancholic, but her melancholy that makes her silent, suggesting that there is another reason for her despondency. Nature, Benjamin then proposes, is dejected because she feels misrecognized in the act of being named by human language.[5] The naming is a form of recognition, but it falsely labels what is essentially unidentifiable (*Unerkennbaren* [2.1:155]). As if resigned to her sorry fate, nature realizes that there would be no point in participating in this language, a language that needlessly, superfluously, and disproportionately squanders itself in what Benjamin calls overnaming (*Überbenennung*). If nature is solemnly mute, then human speech immoderately babbles. *Überbenennung* suggests a dissipation of words and disregard for them. More fundamentally and inescapably, postlapsarian signification sets up an incongruous relation between word and thing; language overshoots the mark. Benjamin thus implies that nature's muteness is a deliberate reticence, a notion to which I shall return shortly.

Although Benjamin casts doubt on human language, which ends up diminishing what it designates, Derrida nonetheless positions Benjamin squarely within the Western philosophical practice that elevates man over animals. According to this tradition, Derrida notes, the single, indivisible limit that separates man from animal is consistently determined by knowledge of the word and the voice that can name. Stated explicitly, the animal is defined as that being that lacks the word. Thus, in its efforts to define the quintessentially human, Western philosophy has sought to bolster human uniqueness and superiority by abrogating to itself the sole command of speech. Indeed, "animal" is the designation that man has reserved for himself to bestow in order to maintain his sole proprietary right over language: "*Animal* is a word that men have given themselves the right to give, . . . reserving for them, for humans, the right to the word, the name, the verb, the attribute, to a language of words, in short to the very thing that the others in question would be deprived of, those that are corralled within the grand territory of the beasts: the Animal. All the philosophers we will investigate (from Aristotle to Lacan, and including Descartes, Kant, Heidegger, and Lévinas), all of them say the same thing: the animal is without language" ("The Animal" 400).[6] Another major contemporary philosopher, Giorgio Agamben, has joined Derrida in this critical analysis of Western philosophy's strategic and persistent denigration of the animal by observing that man "must recognize himself in a non-man in order to be human" (27). This maneuver is accomplished primarily via an exclusionary self-assignation of language: "In identifying himself with language, the speaking man places his own muteness outside of himself, as already and not yet human" (35).

Confronting this philosophical tradition, Derrida questions, during his long meditation on what his cat's gaze means to him, whether there is any sign whatsoever of the creature's linguistic inferiority, for his cat does not exhibit the need for words. Instead it is he, the philosopher, who, *in his "own melancholy"* (387, emphasis mine), desires to lend the cat a voice and to interpret what the creature would say to him. Echoing Benjamin's "*Über*benennung," this fantasy would indulge in an overinterpretation ("*sur*interpréter" [269, emphasis mine]). Thus, in a fascinating reversal of Benjamin's and Rilke's position, it is now the human being who is melancholic. Derrida leads us to question whose melancholy we are then dealing with. Whose longing and for what? Whose loneliness? Above all, whose muteness? What are the reasons and implications for this projection of one's own melancholy onto the animal? It is this reversal, this folding in on itself, of who is deemed silent and sad that I want to investigate more closely in this chapter. Where indeed can the distinctions between man and animal be upheld if they so collapse on themselves? And if Derrida's cat demonstrates no need for words and Benjamin suggests that human words are invariably an *Überbenennung*, what would it mean to bestow language on the dog? Can one find such critical reflection on language, even repeal of it, precisely in literary works that narrate from a canine perspective? The question then becomes not "do *they* have language?" but "do *we* have an adequate language to speak to them and about them?" Furthermore, how would one represent the vocal reticence of the animal and how can it signify something beyond lack or deficiency? I want to address the question of "whose muteness" from the philosophers Ludwig Wittgenstein to Emmanuel Levinas, from the novelists Ivan Turgenev to Charles Siebert, and from visual artists David Hockney to Pentti Sammallahti.

However much one resists, as does Derrida, denying animals the gift of language and however open one is to other means of communication, whether these be physical or extrasensory, animal stillness is not therefore any less pressing, especially for the devoted pet lover. I have spent hours trying to penetrate the minds of my whippets and despair of ever understanding them fully. Because they are such dear companions, not knowing what they think creates an ache, a yearning that is at times a daily affliction. My fascination and attraction are amplified by their silence, untranslatability, and detachment. The intimacy between us is even enhanced by their silence, for with the failure of words, I encounter instead the loveliness of their bodies and mien, the thereness of their secretive being. My dogs are thus both intimate and distant, and, because I want to be closer to them, I fall prey to a sweet melancholy.

The questions run through my mind: What do they suppose I'm saying? What do I understand them as communicating? In the midst of my attempt to escape my anthropocentrism, I feel I sink more deeply into it by the unavoidability of projection. And even when their sighthound eyes are deeply expressive and responsive, I am still lost. I want to know the true desire of this enigmatic Other and say to their gazes: What do you want? What are you aiming at with your look? In *A Lover's Discourse* Roland Barthes explores these imaginary monologues conducted by the one secluded in love, and he observes in words that aptly fit the longings of the passionate dog owner: "I cannot decipher you because I don't know how you decipher me" (134). And, "The amorous subject suffers anxiety because the loved object replies scantily or not at all to his language" (167). In our incessant specular reflections, we wonder if the dog, too, would frustratingly accuse us of responding "scantily or not at all to his language," failing to match his attention and devotion.[7] Or does the dog cheerfully assume his barking and tail wagging are transparent and will be immediately comprehended? Is it only we who are melancholic over the gap in communication between us?

But what if they could speak in human tongue? The literary tradition of the dog gifted with human speech goes back to Lucian's *Dialogues of the Dead* and counts among its writers such luminaries as Cervantes ("Colloquy of the Dogs" [1613]), E. T. A. Hoffmann ("Account of the Most Recent Fortunes of the Dog Berganza" [1813]), Gogol ("The Diary of a Madman" [1833–34]), Franz Kafka ("The Researches of a Dog" [1922]), Mikhail Bulgakov (*The Heart of a Dog* [1925]), and Paul Auster (*Timbuktu* [1999]).[8] In addition, the fantasy of the talking dog has spawned countless sentimental poems and trite stories. In popular visual culture it has inspired cute comic strips from Charles Schultz's *Peanuts* to Gary Larson's *Far Side* and the animated mutt from Pluto to the computer-generated figures in *Cats and Dogs* (2001).

But, although commonplace, either how innocent or high-minded are such attempts to endow the dog with language? The historian of contemporary art Steve Baker coined the word "disnification" to express the dissonance and misleading signification in current Hollywood practice; Disney only makes non-sense of the animal (*Picturing the Beast* 174–75). No less kind to literary forays into the talking dog genre, Roger Grenier, author of *On the Difficulty of Being a Dog*, acerbically observes that "worst of all is a writer who makes animals talk, as Colette does in her *Creature Conversations*. Anyone trying to write like a dumb animal writes like a dumb animal" (73). Perhaps for this reason Virginia Woolf disparaged her novel *Flush* (1933), where she whimsically expressed the feelings of Elizabeth Barrett Browning's spaniel: she called it a "silly book . . . a waste of time" (*Diary* 153). Clearly the imaginative leap into the dog's thoughts arises from the desire to supply what is missing; it is compensatory for both the animal's silence and human incomprehension. But so often the attempt to bring animals to life fails to capture their very presence and, as Baker and Grenier suggest, descends into banality and insipidness. Especially in the humorous genres such as cartoons, the anthropomorphizing gesture reduces the animals to the silliness of humans.

Making animals talk, moreover, betrays the supposition that they don't otherwise communicate. And it presupposes that human verbal communication always is efficacious and direct. John Muir, founder of the Sierra Club, challenges both presumptions in *Strickeen* (1897), a novel on a dog by the same name: "We know about as little of [animals] in their inner life and conversation as we do of the inhabitants of other stars. . . . 'If they could talk' we say. But they do in a universal language no Babel has ever confused; and the gift to them of articulate speech would probably leave us about as far apart as before. How much do we make of speech in knowing each other[?]" (108). The most sarcastic critic of such ventriloquistic chatter is cultural sociologist Jean Baudrillard, who detects in contemporary oversaturation with media signs a nervousness and discomfort with the taciturnness of real-live animals: "In a world bent on doing nothing but making one speak, in a world assembled under the hegemony of signs and discourse, their silence weighs more and more heavily on our organization of meaning. . . . Nowhere do they really speak, because they only furnish the responses one asks for. It is their way of sending the Human back to his circular codes, behind which their silence analyzes us" (137–38).[9]

In the face of such *Überbenennung* (as Benjamin so cogently assessed, as if anticipating today's pervasive "disnification") is it possible to conceive of an alternative? Derrida, in fact, offers an ever so brief and tentative response that I should like to pursue further: "It would not be a matter of 'giving speech back' to animals but perhaps of acceding to a thinking, however fabulous and chimerical it might be, that thinks the absence of the name and of the word otherwise, as something other than a privation" ("The Animal" 416). As an answer to the purported muteness of animals, he points out that it is not a question of endowing them with speech—we recall that his cat demonstrates no need of words. But how could his goal of reconceptualizing what the absence of words would be other than as privation be accomplished? What would it look like?[10] To answer this question I first want to turn to various philosophers who have rethought animal silence, reticence, reserve, and self-containment. I then want to examine how various literary and visual artists reconceptualize the silence in nature alongside man's own pauses, whether these be in his own linguistic hesitation or in deference toward the animal and its enigma. I turn to the literary and visual arts out of the conviction that, precisely because they operate in the realm Derrida calls the "fabulous and chimerical," they can provide remarkable imaginative insight into ways in which this rethinking of animal wordlessness can occur so that it is not regarded as poverty or privation. Art is where the longing to come into contact with the mystery of animal being expresses itself.

Hearne, Wittgenstein, Kierkegaard, and Levinas

One contemporary author who has responded eloquently and forcefully to the philosophical assumption that animals are deficient in language is Vicki Hearne. An obedience trainer herself, she testifies to the elegant understanding that can arise between an accomplished handler and her dog: they are "obedient to each other and to language" (*Adam's Task* 56). Her paradoxes are just and to the point: "A well-trained dog or horse may be said to have a greater command of language than a human being whose code is infinitely more complex" (*Adam's Task* 42). This communication goes beyond verbal commands to include unmediated bodily response. In her novel *The White German Shepherd* (1988) she encourages her reader to envisage the scenario of a dog "standing by your side, so that you and the dog are both looking ahead, . . . and there is, for the moment, no Gap. The Gap is everywhere, between lovers, between friends, between the world and God, between the mind and what you say. In dog training you go for the right posture, ruthlessly, and then there is no Gap, things fit together, and when they fit, they move" (20).

Among her essays is one that challenges Wittgenstein's claim in *The Philosophical Investigations* that, if a lion could talk, we wouldn't be able to understand him (223). In accordance with his famous dictum from the *Tractatus Logico-philosophicus*, "Whereof one cannot speak, thereof one must be silent," Wittgenstein argues that only language gives us access to certain concepts and, hence that, if we do not share the same linguistic system with, say, a lion or horse, we cannot know such things about them as, for instance, their state of being. Moreover he states: "There is nothing astonishing about certain concepts' only being applicable to a being that e.g. possesses a language" (*Zettel* 91, no. 520). Hence he rhetorically asks, "Why can a dog feel fear but not remorse? Would it be right to say 'Because he can't talk'?" (*Zettel* 91, no. 518). Repeatedly, Wittgenstein uses the inaccessibility of the dog, a creature otherwise close to us, in order to illustrate what lies outside the realm of empirical certainty because outside the confines of our language, which structures how we think. Such questions that we cannot answer include, Can a dog simulate pain? (*Philosophical Investigations* 90, no. 250) and Can it experience hope? (*Philosophical Investigations* 174). In another analogy that illustrates this dependency on a shared language or what he calls language games and the misunderstandings arising from assuming even common bodily codes, he writes: "We don't understand Chinese gestures any more than Chinese sentences" (*Zettel* 40, no. 219). He thus also asks what grounds we have to ask if a dog means something by wagging its tail (*Zettel* 91, no. 521).

Hearne's response is that Wittgenstein incorrectly presumes that a lion and human couldn't understand each other, for as any lion tamer knows they must come to mutual understanding.[11] Inattentive to the subtleties of animal communication, Wittgenstein likewise fails to "consider the possibility that the lion does not talk to us because he knows we could not understand him" (*Adam's Task* 170). In thus grammatically rearranging Wittgenstein's sentence, Hearne proposes that in his "vast self-containment" the lion may be "reticent, but not languageless" (170). Could, then, this reticence or renunciation of speech serve as a model and antidote to human *Überbenennung*? Could one uncover, although I can only begin to do so here, a different genealogy in philosophy, theology, and the arts that acknowledges a sovereign reserve in nature rather than her sad muteness? Her forbearance rather than the passive resignation of her silence? Would ascribing virtues such as reserve to nature fall into precisely the error Wittgenstein tries to isolate, in other words, unreflectingly anthropomorphize nature? Or, rather than a heedless projection of human assumptions, would such an attempt be an attentive listening and observation, as in the case of Hearne? Can one adopt an attitude of respect toward the animal's reserve? And how would this reconceptualization of the absence of language form the basis of a critique of human disregard for language?

Søren Kierkegaard and Emmanuel Levinas are two philosophers who, however briefly in their writing, reevaluate animal silence, both invoking the Judeo-Christian tradition on the holiness in nature, all while addressing the immediacy of the secular world. Although in his essay "The Lilies of the Field and the Birds of the Air," Kierkegaard refers to the silence in nature, it is not a muteness arising from a fallen condition as in Benjamin. On the contrary, the peacefulness in nature is beatific and shows nature living in a state of grace. Kierkegaard cites from the Sermon on the Mount: "Look at the birds of the air: they neither sow nor reap nor gather into barns, and yet your heavenly Father feeds them. . . . Consider the lilies of the field, how they grow; they neither toil nor spin; yet I tell you, even Solomon in all his glory was not arrayed like one of these" (Matt. 6:26–29; also Luke 12:24–27). Kierkegaard takes Christ's exhortation to man not to be anxious about the future as a parable on the eloquent silence and reverent waiting in nature: "This silence thou canst learn from the lilies and the birds" (324). Nature is meditatively attentive to the moment; its stillness is a "reverence before God" (328): "Only by keeping silent does one hit upon the instant, while one is talking, though one says only a word, one misses the instant" (349). Levinas, too, admittedly in a vastly different context, recalls a biblical episode of animal silence in worship before divine presence. In a short essay entitled "The Name of a Dog, or Natural Rights" and published in 1975, he recalls how in Exodus 11, during the night Israel is released from its house of bondage and the first-born of Egypt are struck dead, the dogs do not growl. Levinas writes: "With neither ethics nor *logos*, the dog will attest to the dignity of its person. This is what the friend of man means. There is a transcendence in the animal! . . . It reminds us of the debt that is always open" (152).

The context into which this reflection is placed has been a contentious one, for Levinas sets up troublesome parallels between dissimilar horrors. In the first half, he begins by discussing Exodus 22:31, where carrion is proscribed as meat to be "cast to the dogs." Levinas argues that, if only wild animals are seen to "half-devour one another," then man can sublimate his own war games and, on par with them, his own carnivorous practices. In the second half of his essay, he then moves from biblical references to a real canid who involuntarily resurfaces in his memory, one named Bobby who wandered into the Nazi labor camp where Levinas was interned during the war. In always delighting to see the prisoners, Bobby was the sole creature to treat them as humans. If one aligns the two halves of the essay, Levinas, as John Llewelyn tersely states, "all but proposes an analogy between the unspeakable human Holocaust and the unspoken animal one" (235). Bracketing aside for the moment the pressing questions that scholars such as Llewelyn and David Clark have courageously tackled in light of this juxtaposition (Is the animal an Other to whom one owes responsibility? Why does the animal not have a face for Levinas? What are the implications of not distinguishing between atrocities committed against humans and the mass slaughter of animals?), I should like to argue that the answer to such questions must be channeled through how Levinas discusses the implications of the figurative use of the animal. Disparaging references to "dog"—such as in Exodus 22—must be seen in the light of another predisposition against animals, namely, the onto-theological tradition of denying them access to "ethics and *logos*."

Following the passage from Exodus 22, Levinas lists various commonplace derogatory usages of the word "dog," such as "a dog's life" and "raining cats and dogs." Such turns of phrase are suspect to him, for they are heedless of the implications of "what comes out of the mouth," namely, the disparagement of both humans ("Someone who is given

the dirtiest work—a dog's life") and animals themselves ("the crouch-
ing, servile, contemptible dog"). As David Clark asks: "Figuring animals,
we *config*ure the human. But at what cost to animals?" (169).[12] Joining
such rhetorical commonplaces are the theological and philosophical
traditions that deny animals power over the word. I would propose that,
rather than necessarily ascribing to this tradition (as Clark maintains),
Levinas mocks it, as if to say, precisely the creature deemed to be "with
neither ethics nor *logos*" testifies to command over both by remaining
silent at the moment of the divine act so that the Jews can safely flee
Egypt. If language can all too easily silence others, then here the inverse
occurs: the dogs' silence provides testimony and witness to God's purpose. The episode reminds Levinas as well of our debt to animals,
which—as he so strongly exhorts, evoking the immeasurable responsibility we hold toward animal life in general—remains open.

The dogs on the banks of the Nile, Levinas continues, are the ances-
tors of Bobby, who would "bark in delight" when the prisoners assembled. Although lacking the ability to "universalize maxims and drives,"
Bobby was Kantian in his ethics, in fact, "the last Kantian in Nazi Germany" (153). In contrast to his friendly vocalizing, then, is the Nazis'
treatment of the Jews as "beings without language" who jabber "mon-
key talk." In the camp the Jews are treated as deserving to be "depriv[ed]
of expression" (153). Levinas suggests that undergirding the Nazis'
labeling of the Jews as "subhuman, a gang of apes" is a tradition that
metaphorically debases animals, a tradition, he has just argued, that has justified animal slaughter for meat. By the same token, denying animals language becomes contorted into denying a certain category of humans
voice because they are deemed to be merely animals—and hence also
worthy of slaughter. That is, Levinas attacks the abusive, violent power
of language to "name" both animals and humans heedlessly, with
impunity, and without the respect that each are separately due. The
problem therefore of ascribing muteness to animals is that it regards
them as dumb, savage beasts, as if only man should be granted language. Such reasoning is blind to how language actually gags the other,
as in calling Jews apes. The dog, too, is not so much without *logos* as, in
Clark's impeccable phrasing, "the site of an excess against which one
might measure the prescriptive, exclusionary force of the *logos*, the ways
in which the truth of the rational word muffles, strangles, and finally
silences the animal" (191). As in Benjamin, naming not only dimin-
ishes, it silences the other. For Levinas, moreover, it kills.

Levinas concludes by saying that Bobby's "friendly growling, his animal faith, was born from the silence of his forefathers on the banks of

the Nile" (153). Levinas thereby suggests that, whether it be in a friendly greeting or in deliberate silence and reticence, the dog does command language, perhaps more honestly than do humans, who choose to disregard its rhetorical implications. Moreover, the dog is gifted with its animal faith. But is to ascribe to the dog the capacity for faith, ethics, language, testimony, and transcendence not a dangerous anthropomorphization? Does Levinas back away from such claims, as Clark maintains, by redrawing the line between human and animal in saying, for instance, that the dog cannot universalize maxims or that it is without *logos*? Is Levinas speaking "only" figuratively (using Bobby, like the dogs in Egypt, as "a figure of humanity"), although he has just instructed us to be attentive to the unspoken assumptions of analogies? In other words, if elsewhere in this essay the confusion of man and animal in rhetorical speech has led to the unspeakable in the Holocaust, is Levinas not now intimating the opposite, that, as his own usage of terms such as transcendence implies, man and beast cannot and should not be so tidily separated—that language can help us imagine the dog otherwise? Indeed, the references to faith and transcendence seem far too weighty to be classified as mere sentimentality.[13] Could the powerful ascription of wisdom and judgment to the animal signify instead, rather than anthropocentric pathos, a humility on the part of the human who usually reserves such attributes for himself? Ultimately, Levinas leaves the answer to these questions open, but he does suggest that such a recognition of the animal would mark the first step toward reciprocation—toward meeting the unfulfilled debt to it.

In sum, then, in the reticence of Hearne's lion, the silence of Kierkegaard's lilies and birds, and the reverence of Levinas's dogs, the absence of language is conceived other than as deprivation. Moreover the silence of the beasts becomes a model for the human; it inspires deference in reply. To put it another way, I have endeavored to trace a 180 degree turn: rather than project poverty onto the animal, as Heidegger does in his term *weltarm*, human discourse can be seen as needing to recognize the imperative to reticence, circumspection, and awareness of its own moments of muteness. Such a discourse would grieve over its own impasses. As the early nineteenth-century German writer Jean Paul Richter observed, addressing the questions "Whose muteness?" and "Whose poverty?": "Language. In the impossibility of bringing the animal voice into words I see the poverty of the letter" (173, no. 355). Thus, it would be the human response to animals that needs to be assessed in terms of melancholy, for which purpose I now turn to Julia Kristeva's analysis of different forms and manifestations of depressive language. If the sign of human melancholy after the Fall is a compensatory *Überbenennung*, then Benjamin's essay merits alignment with Julia Kristeva's *Black Sun*. In turning, at this juncture, to psychoanalysis, I aim to develop a heuristic vocabulary that would help us think through and articulate what is at stake in our melancholy, our sadness over animal loss and animal silence. I then want to see how various literary and visual artists via their minimalist, collapsed, melancholic language reflect on their own unsureness as how best to represent the animal.

Julia Kristeva

According to Sigmund Freud in "Mourning and Melancholia" (1917), one of the main features of the melancholic personality is that it cannot name its loss and falls speechless because the lost object has become such an integrated part of the self. If it cannot separate the ego from the object with which it identifies, it cannot name it. Unless the melancholic can pinpoint the source of her mourning, she mourns interminably. Taking her cue from Freud, French psychoanalyst Julia Kristeva, in her book *Black Sun: Depression and Melancholia*, notes that the melancholic, who unconsciously yet loyally adheres to the beloved lost object, proves the failure of the Symbolic realm. Because she cannot identify or verbalize the loss from which she suffers, the melancholic's primary characteristic is her silence. Although language falters when it cannot adequately measure the impoverishment, how the melancholic individual preserves the object is nevertheless characterized by her language use—the departed is invariably wrapped up in words, even when they are halting. Kristeva captures this predicament of language—its silences yet also its exuberant compensations.

Kristeva isolates three successive depressive categories, three stages of dysfunctional language, each an enhanced response to the one that preceded it, each a different form of repression. Relying on Freud's terminology, Kristeva names them *Verneinung*, *Verleugnung*, and *Verwerfung*. She begins with the negation (*Verneinung*) of loss. It is the state where the subject on some level acknowledges the forfeiture of an essential object only to claim to recover it in signs. In his 1925 essay "Die Verneinung," Freud writes that it "results in a kind of intellectual acceptance of the repressed [*des Verdrängten*], while at the same time what is essential to the repression persists" (14:12). Representation is allowed on the condition of denying loss, which it amply papers over. What characterizes such language is its proliferation of signs and a signifying exaltation. Because of its linguistic overproduction in the face of loss, it is the mode most comparable to Benjamin's postlapsarian *Überbenennung*. What is peculiar to Kristeva, however, is that language is a compensatory pleasure that is counterpoised to privation and soothes with the creation of loveliness. *Verneinung* is the realm of sublimation. "Beauty is consubstantial with it. Like feminine finery concealing stubborn depressions, beauty emerges as the admirable face of loss" (99). The lost object is retrieved in images and words.

Verneinung, however, can be disavowed by depressed persons, such that they fall back on the "Thing" of their loss and remain painfully riveted to it. Here language, less exalting, breathes sadness; it is "an artificial, unbelievable language, cut out of the painful background that is not accessible to any signifier and that intonation alone, intermittently, succeeds in inflecting" (44). Words seem extinguished, absurd, and delayed. "That is what one deciphers in the blanks of discourse, vocalizations, rhythms, syllables of words that have been devitalized and need to be restored by the analyst" (26). This is the state of the denial or disavowal (*Verleugnung*) of negation (*Verneinung*).

The most enhanced state of depression is total catatonia. Psychosis in the form of repudiation (*Verwerfung*) occurs when even the representative function of repression is halted and linguistic signs are denied in mutism. In the milder stages of *Verwerfung*, *Verleugnung* prevails over *Verneinung*; but repudiation can develop fully into asymbolia. As an extreme case, it demonstrates the converse—why language is so crucial to the healing of depression. Kristeva writes: "Naming suffering, exalting it, dissecting it into its smallest components—that is doubtless a way to curb mourning" (97). Language, of course, cannot always be so perfunctorily manipulated, which is why melancholia is so protracted and, on final account, is associated with artistic expression, which knows the complexities of representation.

The pet dog in today's culture is granted the extravagant, intense value that marks it as compensatory for an originary loss. In this capacity, the dog fits into the category of *Verneinung*.[14] As the metonymy of pleasure, the dog serves as a replacement for the archaic Thing, which Kristeva locates in the maternal. It offers an idealizing comfort and, indeed, the historical rise of the pet dog starting in the latter part of the eighteenth century coincides with the development of the bourgeois family, whose investment in the mother Freud exposed. The soft, warm closeness of the pet, together with its fixed, loving gaze is evocative of maternal proximity and reassurance. To own a pet, then, means refusing to give up the lost object; it is a shield against recognition of forsaken-ness; and it allows for an intimacy that would otherwise be forbidden with the pre-oedipal object of desire. The dog, of course, is a remarkably efficient substitute, who always exists in the immediate present in its companionship, love, and capacity for affection.

Not unsurprisingly, given the surrogate yet immediate pleasure the dog provides, it spawns its own metonymic, fetishistic signs, as if the dog were "the Thing" itself to which Kristeva alludes and that generates the desire for other proxies, in other words, for substitutive erotic com-pensations.[15] Serving as objects of reverie, dog collectibles are a case in point. Imitation and proliferation in the form of family photographs, porcelain figurines, even handsome coffee table books on dogs function as safeguards or antidotes against their loss. The collectibles sentimen-talize the pet and hence evoke a pleasurable but imprecise nostalgia, a melancholic dwelling on reminiscences of the pet. Conceivably it could even be the realm of silence—the canine lack of speech—that requires this plethora as compensation.[16]

More contemplative, overtly melancholic and artistic works return to the domain of loss and demonstrate, in contrast to *Verneinung*, the workings of *Verleugnung*. This is the mode where language hesitates, thereby dampening manic *Überbenennung* and revealing its depressive underside. Given its tendency to reflect on its own sparseness, poetry in particular can link the dog to wordlessness and to affect, which arises in the absence of words. Paring down its language, poetry wants to res-onate with the animal's own lack of speech. Take, for example, "Les hurleurs" (The howlers [1855]) by the French nineteenth-century poet Leconte de Lisle. He writes of a night by the sea, where the moon is silent, casting its sepulchral reflection on the ocean. Along the beach, "De maigres chiens, épars, allongeant leurs museaux, / Se lamentaient, poussant des hurelements lugubres" (151). [Emaciated dogs, straggling, lifting their muzzles, lamented and howled mournfully.] The paroxys-mal lament of crying dogs, the sheer giving voice to despondency without the capacity to verbalize what it is that they lack, evokes melan-choly's tendency to asymbolia. The lonely cry evokes some unnamable, inaccessible trauma, resistant to translation into words. The speaker then addresses the emaciated, lamenting dogs with the question: "Quelle angoisse inconnue, au bord des noires ondes, / Faisait pleurer une âme en vos formes immondes?" (What unknown suffering, at the edge of the black waves, made a soul weep in your impure forms). The question will never be answered, for however powerful the cry, it remains opaque to human comprehension. Leconte de Lisle calls the dogs specters, and indeed they evoke his own confused past, encrypted away beyond recovery. In its place remains, forever present, the harrowing affect or cry. Because of its inarticulateness, he names this sorrow feral (*douleurs sauvages*).

As with Leconte de Lisle, there is something of the suffering animal in the inability of another nineteenth-century French poet, Alphonse de Lamartine, to name his pain. Even the joyful greeting by his whippet after a long absence brings forth cloying emotion that can express itself only in the affect of sadness. A passage in *Jocelyn* (1836) recounts this solitary reunion and contains numerous references to the sighthound's silent gaze: "tes yeux sur les miens, / Le silence comprend nos muets entretiens" (195). [Your eyes on mine, silence understands our mute dialogues.] Affect is thus paired with the absence of words, for the melancholic compensates for his halting language primarily by reliance on bodily signifiers. Generally speaking, in its somatic communication, in its display of pure affect, the dog can be said to appear quintessentially sad. In words seemingly meant for the canid, Kristeva writes: "Unbelieving in language, the depressive persons are affectionate, wounded to be sure, but prisoners of affect. Affect is their thing" (14).[17] Lamartine thus focuses on the physical expressions of their love: "Oh! viens, dernier ami que mon pas réjouisse, . . . Lèche mes yeux mouillés! mets ton cœur près du mien, / Et, seuls à nous aimer, aimons-nous, pauvre chien!" (196). [O come, the sole friend who rejoices at my footstep. . . . Lick my moist eyes! Put your heart close to mine, and alone in our love, let us love each other, poor dog!] The designation "poor dog" underscores the abjection that the species face and from which Lamartine empathetically suffers. His poetry tries to redeem an affection so deep that it reads as an affliction.

Rather than on *Verneinung*, which overcompensates for animal muteness, tries to paper over the gap of absence, and denies its own melancholy, I want to focus in the rest of this chapter on the implications of *Verleugnung*. Briefly put, I look at works that meditate on silence and, in their own meditation, fall silent. They exemplarily mourn the loss of the animal to human beings and the communicative gap between them and are cognizant of their own melancholy. Aware of the dangers of *Überbenennung*, they reflect on their own symbolic limitations and are reticent, halting, and minimalist in their descriptions. They point to what lies beyond signification—an ephemerality, an expectancy of what is about to happen, an elsewhere that intimates a realm beyond the human senses, and even a self-contained wholeness in the dog that has no need of words. Coming to the brink of abandoning the attempt at representation, such artistic expressions resist falling into the total asymbolia of *Verwerfung* and ultimately countervail against their own latent depression.[18] The following pages examine the contemporary canine photography of Keith Carter, Otmar Thormann, and Pentti Sammallahti, political allegories involving the dog by Ivan Turgenev and Tibor Dery, a cynomorphic novel by Charles Siebert, and the paintings of his pet dachshunds by David Hockney.

Keith Carter, Otmar Thormann, and Pentti Sammallahti

Documentary photographers and photojournalists have been keen observers of canine life in the twentieth century, as testified in such recent collections as *A Thousand Hounds: The Presence of the Dog in the History of Photography, 1839 to Today* and *The Dog: 100 Years of Classic Photography*. Notable dog photographers in the realist tradition include Frank Hurley, Henri Cartier-Bresson, Robert Capa, Robert Doisneau, Jacques-Henri Lartigue, André Kertész, William Eggleston, Richard Billingham, Elliott Erwitt, Michel Vanden Eeckhoudt, Josef Koudelka, Baylón, Jill Freedman, Ralph Gibson, Robin Schwartz, Keith Carter, and Pentti Sammallahti. Wherein lies, one wonders, the affinity of photography for dogs? Is it the thereness of the dog—its living in the present moment that the shutter catches? Is it the insouciance and openness of the dog before the camera—its lack of self-consciousness? Does its omnipresence in the city attract the street photographer's eye? Or does the dog's attentiveness lend itself to the intimacy of portraiture? I want to follow a different tack from these questions, however, and suggest a peculiar link between the dog and what the photograph cannot capture, in other words, its resistance to signification. Paradoxically, then, a realist mode of representation ends up partaking of the randomness, intermittence, and indifference to meaning that Kristeva finds haunting melancholic language.

In *Camera Lucida* Roland Barthes writes: "I cannot penetrate, cannot reach into the Photograph. I can only sweep it with my glance, like a smooth surface. . . . I have the leisure to observe the photograph with intensity; but also, however long I extend this observation, it teaches me nothing" (106–7). In *A Lover's Discourse* he likewise records his visual concentration: "I catch myself carefully scrutinizing the loved body (like the narrator watching Albertine asleep). *To scrutinize* means *to search*: I am searching the other's body, as if I wanted to see what was inside it" (71). Our fascination with canine photography, especially of a breed that we love, I would suggest, derives from this desire to wrest a secret from the animal being, as if we longed for the photograph to be somehow magically revelatory in its documentary capacity. Rather than recording mundane actuality, photography inversely promises to capture that for which there can be no proof, for it is, after all, an art that arrests ephemerality. Although the photo cannot spell out the mystery it apprehends, it nonetheless can intimate it, leading us to scrutinize it fixedly, though ultimately in vain. To gaze at my whippets, too, is to sweep my eyes over their smooth fur, to study them in their perfection, namely, to dwell with their muteness.

In his canine portraiture, Texan photographer Keith Carter excels in intimating that which lies beyond signification. In the introduction to his collection entitled *Bones* (1992), he writes: "Is it too improbable a leap to suppose [the dogs] might also have a spiritual life? One not defined by human sensibilities? . . . At times I have felt both a sentient power and a spiritual presence in the dogs I have photographed" (n.p.). How, though, would one read for this spiritual presence, especially if it is not "defined by human sensibilities"? How can photography express that which is ineffable? Can it be possible paradoxically because the animal is mute? Indeed by pointing to that which lies outside the viewer's grasp, Keith Carter imbues his photos with a sense of both melancholy and sublimity. The techniques at his disposal are as varied as they are ingenious. For instance, the dog's ears may be pricked up, signaling that its concentration is directed at a source the camera cannot capture. Or, the dog may turn its head, so that it looks outside the margins of the photo, alerting the viewer to an unseen, enigmatic presence. Insofar as it ignores the camera, it also seems to be preoccupied with thoughts focused elsewhere. In its very keenness and attentiveness the dog seems to be on the verge of saying something that we know it never will; it remains inaccessible to us in its silence, but a silence not born of dullness. Yet despite this distance, Carter's photography creates a thusness, a being in its own world—via the loveliness of the fur, the large, dark eyes, and the unique contours of the canine body. Carter thus ultimately plays between immediacy and thereness, on the one hand, and absence and elsewhere, on the other.

One particular photo entitled "Lost Dog" (1992) illustrates how Carter signifies an elsewhere that lies outside representation. He trains his camera on a close-up of an older dog (fig. 3). The graying muzzle becomes blurred as the camera focuses on its large black eyes that look past the photographer. Due to the reflection in the dog's eyes of light and shadow from a landscape in front of it but that the viewer cannot

3   Keith Carter, "Lost Dog," 1992. Gelatin silver print. 15 × 15 inches. Copyright Keith
Carter, Beaumont, Texas.

see, the dog seems somewhere else in its mind, even confused. The ears
are pinned back so as to be invisible and to indicate its fear or trepidation. The absence of the ears accentuates the dome of the head and the
eyebrows that frame the worried eyes and thus draw attention back to
them. The neck and head are lifted as if the dog were searching for
something in the distance or longing for it. It tries to apprehend something but is cautious at the same time. As the background fades to black,
the viewer notices the empty space that engulfs the dog. Despite the
close-up, the hound is lost to the viewer, as its muzzle, ears, and the rest
of its body recede into darkness.

Christian Metz has written on photography: "The spectator has no
empirical knowledge of the contents of the off-frame, but at the same
time cannot help imagining some off-frame, hallucinating it, dreaming

the shape of this emptiness" (87). Oddly enough, what Metz describes in reference to the viewer also applies to Carter's lost dog: the hound seems to imagine and to long for what lies beyond its ken. Again in Metz's words, the photograph is "haunted by the feeling of its exterior, of its borderlines, which are the past, the left, the lost" (87). The helplessness that "Lost Dog" conjures is thus twofold. However long we scrutinize the photo, we cannot penetrate the thoughts and worries of the dog: it lives in an enigmatic world that we cannot perceive or read. Consequently, we are the ones who are lost. By the same token, the dog seems perplexed by human codes that it cannot interpret; hence it can neither find its way home nor understand why it seems to have been abandoned.

Keith Carter has also written: "Use the camera well, murmur the right words, and it is possible to conjure up proof of a dream" (n.p.) It is this manifestation of the dream that contemporary Austro-Swedish photographer Otmar Thormann alludes to in his photo collection *Dreaming Dogs* (1990). In this series he, too, conjures up the muteness and elsewhereness of the dog. For the gallery installation of the series, Thormann hung ten small snapshots of dogs sleeping on the ground under ten larger still life photos (fig. 4). The body of the dog takes up the whole frame of the photo, as it lies lost to the world on a beach of sand and rock. In some photos one can see traces in the sand of the legs having moved over it, indicating that the dog was dreaming and running in its sleep. The composition of the matching still life vaguely parallels the canine photo: it too is taken on a beach and features detritus from the sea—arrangements of rocks, shells, squid, a feather, or other washed up debris, some of which is indistinguishable. Shapes and lines that are common to each photo in the pair materialize before the viewer's eyes. The outline of a crumpled discarded paper, for instance, may mimic that of a curled up dog, or the stones resemble its spots. In fact, after noticing these formal similarities, one returns to the dreaming dog to see it, too, as a kind of still life, to whose organic form one now pays closer attention. Especially because there is not a one-to-one correlation in size between the photographic pairs, an imbalance is built into the arrangement, causing the viewer to shuttle between the two photos in an effort to make sense of their relation. Moreover, although the isolated objects suggest a concrete palpability and immediacy, they lack the precision of allegorical reference that characterizes baroque still life, making Thormann's photos seem drained of meaning. Although the relationship of the still life to the sleeping dog is tangential and strictly formal, one wonders what the dog could be dreaming. Could the image that forms beneath its eyelids be identical to the one before the viewer?

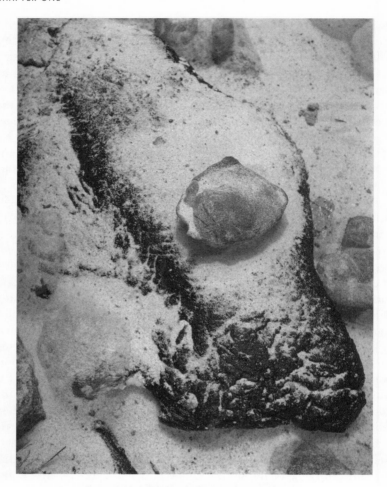

4 Otmar Thormann, from *Dreaming Dogs*, 1992. Black-and-white photographs on paper. 23 × 29 and 14 × 9 cm. Copyright Otmar Thormann. Courtesy Fotohof Gallery, Salzburg.

In all likelihood, Thormann is not trying to literalize what the dogs are dreaming, but he does set up corresponding enigmas. Insofar as the arrangements might subconsciously awaken symbolic associations for the viewer, they place her into the same oneric realm that the dogs inhabit. What one sees in the photo appears as if in a dream, that is, in enigmatic code. Its larger size intimates a reality grander than the actual world: it is a world magnified in close-up. The dreams rise up out of the same earth on which the dogs lie and, containing refuse from the sea, suggest memories of something resurfacing in altered, worn-out, extinguished appearance. The objects are evocative but undecipherable, seemingly erratic in their selection. As Kurt Kaindl writes in the introduction to the collection: "In these photos traces seem to be laid that point to what is absent in the photos" (n.p.; my translation from the German).

But there are also differences to the dream as commonly understood. Thormann's is a photography that challenges the assumptions of psychoanalysis, which claims to access and signify the dream world. Because we have no entry to canine memories, there is no hidden elsewhere to which one can trace back. Thormann's dream spaces do not have their source anywhere in a past but depict instead pure phenomena. The sheer visibility of the detritus thus paradoxically produces invisibility; the larger photograph withdraws from the world of representation as we see it in the smaller photograph of the sleeping dog and shows us something that cannot appear. Lest we forget the inaccessibility of the canine world, Thorman restores it here. We cannot even know if dogs possess a private inner life, since that too would be the construct of a humanist-centered psychoanalysis. Thormann's photography thus successfully imagines and embodies, in Derrida's words, the "fabulous and chimerical": it helps us accept the secrets of dogs and welcome their silence as an answer.

I want to look at one final example of a photography that tries to capture the mystery of the world in which the dog moves and that reminds us that the human cannot be the measure of this world. Pentti Sammallahti is a contemporary Finnish photographer who frequently incorporates the dog into his landscapes, whether they are shot in Karelia, Siberia, Buryatia, Wales, or Italy. The documentary realism of his landscapes demonstrates the randomness and arbitrariness of the signified that characterize melancholic language according to Kristeva. She describes how, for the melancholic personality, sublimity—which Sammallahti evokes through the use of a panoramic lens—"is already detached, disassociated, it has already integrated the traces of death, which is signified as lack of concern, absentmindedness, carelessness" (*Black Sun* 100). Within the limitless, desolate vistas he photographs, the dog seems to have suddenly materialized. It seems to have walked incidentally into the viewfinder, and the camera seems unintentionally to have captured it, an apparent lack of design and indifference that enhance the depressiveness of the black-and-white photography. Often shot at the edges of the frame or as a small object in a wider scene, the dog signifies the fragmentary. In its registering of the transience of light, moreover, this landscape photography appears inherently melancholic. In his beautiful, brief essay on Sammallahti's "The Russian Way," John Berger notes a "light in which there is no permanence, a light of nothing longer than a glimpse" ("Opening a Gate" 4).

Sammallahti also indexes the sign of time passing in the metaphor of the path. The roads he photographs seem to lead only to more vastness. A lone dog cuts across the path, having no intention to follow it and leaving the viewer to question what it sees or smells. Its isolation underscores the emptiness of the uniform landscape, especially in the snowy terrain and abandoned villages of Siberia where the winter light is dim. Through the panoramic lens, Sammallahti evokes the immensity of a world reaching endlessly and monotonously to the horizon. Moreover, his wide angle lens seems to want to capture something in the landscape but is not ample enough to do so. As opposed to *Überbenennung*, this sublimity and minimalism bespeak a stillness, and indeed Sammallahti travels to countries where the noise of the simulacra has not yet invaded or permeated.

The dogs in the landscapes seem outcast and half feral. Normally man's companion, here the dog is a sign of human absence, is man's metonym. Just as the road leaves a trace of the humans who made it but shows no figure traveling along it, so too does the dog appear as the remaining vestige of a living being. Like the huge truck tire left abandoned on the road, the dog is a lone object in the desolate landscape (fig. 5). Even when other dogs or people are present in Sammallahti's photography, they do not interact with each other. Moreover, despite his apparent loneliness, the dog does not care to approach the photographer, even notice him.

The avatar of the artist, the dog discovers the world. As John Berger muses, "Probably it was a dog who led the great Finnish photographer to the moment and place for the taking of these pictures. In each one the human order, still in sight, is nevertheless no longer central and is slipping away. The interstices are open" (5). But although the dogs "are the natural frontier experts of these interstices," the realm they open

5   Pentti Sammallahti, "Venehjärvi, Karelia," 1992. Gelatin silver print. 11.7 × 26.5 cm.
   Copyright Pentti Sammallahti. Courtesy Candace Perich Gallery, Katonah, N.Y.

also closes shut before the photographer. The dog lives and moves in his surroundings, indeed is at home in them and commands their vastness in a way the human never will. Not a part of this foreign world, Sammallahti remains melancholically detached from it in his observation. Hence, in Berger's words, "there is more solitude, more pain, more dereliction" (6). Not heeding the presence behind the camera, the dog thus signifies a lack of communication and the silence of the landscape. He is also the totem of its secretiveness.

In sum, if photography points to the imprint of what was but no longer is, Carter, Thormann, and Sammallahti point to yet another absence—what the photo cannot show at the moment when it was taken, a vastness of the world of the dog that it can never capture. All three remind us that dogs inhabit a realm foreign to us, an awareness that is cause for melancholic reflection but also a certain humility on our part. In other words, in their engrossing photography something hopeful countervails their melancholy, namely, an openness, a possibility, a limitlessness, or, in Berger's words, "an expectancy which I have not experienced since childhood, since I talked to dogs, listened to their secrets and kept them to myself" ("Opening a Gate" 6).

Ivan Turgenev and Tibor Dery

The questions, whose silence? and whose melancholy? lie at the crux of the political allegory involving the dog. Censorship, either internal or external, is a form of silencing, leading an author to take recourse to

allegorical indirectness, such that the injustices done the canid represent the oppression of the human being. The animal's mute, helpless
response to physical deprivation and senseless cruelty illustrate its master's forced silence. Since the latter cannot tell his story, the dog's story
must stand in for it. Because the focus is not on the human but a mere
pup, the author can feign that his topic is an innocent one and not a
subversive criticism of the state. However, the charade of naïveté actually serves to mock and taunt the political and social status quo. Such
irony and mockery, though, do little to mitigate the persistence of
melancholia—the listlessness and despair that result from being robbed
of direct critical speech. As in Ivan Sergeyevich Turgenev's story
"Mumu" (1854) and Tibor Dery's short novel *Niki: The Story of a Dog*
(1956), melancholia manifests itself in the presence of coerced silence.

Mumu is a spaniel; however, the muteness in Turgenev's tale belongs
to the main protagonist who is a deaf-and-dumb serf named Gerasim.
Like other realist narratives, such as Marie von Ebner-Eschenbach's tale
"Krambambuli" (1883), D. H. Lawrence's story "Rex" (1936), and Vitto-
rio de Sica's film *Umberto D* (1955), "Mumu" aligns the oppression of the
poor and voiceless with that of the dog. In more ways than one, then,
the muteness in "Mumu" pertains to the human. It is also intimately
connected with the loss of the spaniel, thus suggesting a Kristevean
descent into symbolic collapse.

The story runs as follows. A strong, massive peasant, Gerasim is sum-
moned to Moscow by his owner, an ailing old woman, to join her retinue of servants. There he falls in love with one of the laundresses,
Tatiana, and despite his physical handicap and shyness endears himself
to her. As fate would have it, though, one day the old lady decides to
promise Tatiana in marriage to Kapiton Klimov, the drunken shoe-
maker, in the hope that a wife will turn him from his vice. Fearing
Gerasim's wrath on hearing the news, the servants encourage Tatiana to
trick him by playing drunk so that he will despise her and fall out of
love. Hiding his feelings, Gerasim displays no sign of sadness at her loss,
apart from seeming somewhat more morose than usual. One day
Gerasim happens on a drowning puppy whom he rescues. She is a
pretty spaniel with large expressive eyes and long ears, and he passionately cares for her like a "little nursling" (379). Knowing that his "inarticulate sounds call the attention of others" (379), Gerasim names her
Mumu. The crotchety old lady, however, again intervenes in the burgeoning happy relationship when she comes to fancy that the dog's
barking keeps her awake all night. Though Mumu's delicate little voice
had only been raised to ward off an intruder, she must be disposed of.

Gersasim rescues her from the initial banishment and tries to sequester her away in his garret, but unbeknownst to him her cries for attention betray her hideaway. He then, tacitly resigned to the wishes of his mistress, takes it on himself to kill the dog, in the end wringing her neck and dropping her body into the river. Following this painful incident, Gerasim packs up his meager belongings and returns to the countryside.

Throughout the story, Gerasim is compared to various animals—a strong, young bull, a gander of the steppes, a bear, a lion, and, generically, a beast. In the final words of the story, he is implicitly compared to a dog: his fellow peasants observe that he needs no watchdog for no thief would dare go near his dwelling. With such similes, the divisions between human and animal are traversed and establish the basis for further comparisons. About Gerasim, Turgenev writes: "Like all deafmutes, he was very suspicious, and very readily perceived when they were laughing at him" (363–64). Animals are often considered deaf and dumb in that they do not seem to be on the same communicative level as humans, and dogs in particular can be hurt when made fun of. But a special sensitivity comes with this lack of communication and tightly bonds the giant and his dog. This tie, however, does not hold. Mumu's trusting eyes fail to meet his at her hour of death, for he turns his head away from her. Not only deaf and dumb, he chooses to be blind as well. His obliviousness to her suffering, symbolized by his lack of hearing and sight, thus embodies human stupefaction: he is not even an animal, he is, according to the observation of one character in the story, a block of wood (369), and his face seems turned to stone (389). Notwithstanding his apparent dullness and denseness, Gerasim garners the reader's sympathy because, like Tatiana and Mumu, he is the victim of serfdom. His animal silence contrasts with the irresponsible, careless orders of the old lady.

But what does his muteness signify? The name Mumu spells out a stuttering, in fact, an inability to name. His devotion to the spaniel is dumb both in the sense of besotted and in that it is so deep as to be inutterable. Moreover, because he is unable to communicate his forfeiture of Tatiana, the dog serves to cover up and to displace this prior loss. In its alliteration the name Mumu furthermore suggests a repetition. Just as Gerasim returns her to the waters from whence he rescued her, so too does he return home in the end. At the start, the narrative mentions that he was deaf and dumb from birth. Then at the close, in an uncanny moment out of place in the realist narrative, Turgenev describes him as hastening "as though his old mother were waiting for him at home, as though she were calling him to her after long wanderings in strange parts, among strangers" (403). Although Gerasim has no mother to return to, he does seem prompted to retrieve something at his birthplace, something doubly lost with first Tatiana and then Mumu, but ultimately left unuttered and unutterable, a traumatic parting that goes back to his birth and is connected with his mother. This loss, and with it an admission of love, seem to be repressed in the symbolic submerging of Mumu under water, which Gerasim cannot bear to watch. That is, perhaps it is not so much that he is born deaf and dumb and that these forfeitures occur subsequently during his life, but that inversely, on a symbolic level, separation precipitates his muteness and deafness. Words have lost for him their value in a devitalized world. He thus falls into Kristevean *Verwerfung*, refusing to admit his love and express his grief. Moreover, thrust into withdrawal, he fails to respond to or "hear" the world around him. Thus, in this repudiation, he goes back to his routine, as if nothing had happened. The only outward sign of his despondency is affective, that is, wordless, when two tears fall from his cheek as he gives Mumu her last meal.

Clearly, Gerasim's muteness also refers to a lack of voice under serfdom. The indenture reduces him to the level of an oppressed brute. To have no language means one has no power and means of protest despite one's massive size. Hence neither Gerasim nor any of the servants in sympathy with him can lift their voices in protest against the orders of the old lady. Turgenev's social criticism is thus strong but one that needs to be veiled through the poignant focus on the little bitch. "Mumu," in fact, belongs to a small but significant tradition of dog stories that are used as vehicles to express human muteness in the face of censorship.[19] What is prohibited from being uttered directly by a human being is represented via the dog, considered to be a creature without language. Over a hundred years later, Soviet writer Georgi Vladimov joins this tradition in *Faithful Ruslan: The Story of a Guard Dog*, which begins in the winter of 1956–57, after Khrushchev denounced Stalin and an estimated 8 million prisoners were released from the gulags. The novel, narrated from the perspective of the abandoned guard dogs from one such camp, tells of the dogs' incomprehension when the orders they were trained to enforce no longer hold. As we shall also see in *Niki*, here the dogs stand for human bewilderment and helplessness before arbitrary and perverse rule of law. Not surprisingly, although first conceived in 1963–65 as a short story entitled "The Dogs," *Faithful Ruslan* only saw print once its manuscript was smuggled out to the West in 1974. It first appeared with a German press in 1978 and was translated into English the following year.

Tibor Dery's *Niki*, although ostensibly about a dog, scathingly criticizes the repressive Stalinist regime in the author's native Hungary. Dery was prosecuted for writing this novel, dubbed "conspiracy against the state," and was sentenced for nine years, though released in 1960 due to international protest against his incarceration. His own gruesome fate is uncannily foreshadowed in *Niki*, where the dog's owner is imprisoned for five years for pointless reasons. The novel begins in spring 1948 with the fifty-year old engineer Janos Ancsa, a committed socialist, being posted to the directorship of the Mining Equipment and Tool Plant in Budapest at a time when Hungary's larger factories were being nationalized. Before he and his wife move to the city, a fox terrier mixed-breed bitch adopts them, preferring their gentle treatment to the rough handling and lack of care by its owner, a retired colonel. Mr. and Mrs. Ancsa come to realize that Niki's fear at raised voices "revealed and condemned the methods of intimidation of which she had formerly been the victim" (36). The novel is replete with such turns of phrase, which allude to the victimization of its citizens by the state. Indeed, although the subtitle reads *The Story of a Dog*, it is very much Ancsa's untold misery that Dery wants to impart, for the engineer is deposed from his position shortly after moving to Budapest, is arrested a year and a half later, and spends five years in prison, never informed of his crime, just as Mrs. Ancsa and Niki, through whose eyes the tale is told, barely hear news of him during this half decade. The very simplicity of the subtitle, then, characterizes the understatement and subtle irony that operate on all levels of the novel. The displacement of human aspirations, confusion, struggle, and grief onto the ordinary, simple-minded yet endearing mongrel lends to *Niki* a certain wistfulness, despite its bitter criticism of the communist regime. One is tempted to speak here of an ironic melancholia: Dery achieves distance from his painful subject matter via the displacement onto the bitch's story, whereby the necessity for this representational indirectness and inconspicuousness compounds his melancholia.

Tongue-in-cheek Dery admits that he reluctantly compares man to a dog, for "it would be blasphemous to draw a parallel between a soulless brute, and a man, with his sublime feelings and his vast intelligence" (68). On another occasion, Dery mimics the Communists' disparagement of the pet as a useless item of bourgeois luxury (30), implying, again in understatement, that his tale is insignificant. Yet such feigned self-deprecation actually functions to signal that its author is about to launch into trenchant comparisons between man and dog. As a domestic pet, Niki's liberty has to be kept in check, and discipline comes hard to a young dog, even though, unlike on Hungary's citizens, "no point-less constraint was placed on Niki's freedom" (38). Dery compares her to men whose "nerves can only stand [punishment] if the subtle mechanism is revealed to them, if it is all explained to them" (68). More unambiguously, Dery later writes: "In her total dependence on man, Niki was like those detainees who have no idea why they have been put in prison nor how long they will stay there" (114).

Niki's freedom is priceless to her. Given that she must be confined to the apartment during long hours, when her owners do play ball with her, "as if to revenge herself for her lost freedom, she would destroy, with blood-thirsty fury, the very object that, for brief minutes, gave her back the illusion of freedom" (72). Mrs. Ancsa concludes from this intense play that "nothing can replace freedom, nothing can possibly be superior to it" (73). A few pages later, Dery then makes explicit the connection to the human longing for liberty: "Was she trying to make up for the miseries of the body, inflicted on her by the long inertia of winter, by a heightened intensity of feeling, as do prisoners shut up in cells for many years?" (75). As the years pass and Niki grows bonier and her hair duller and thinner, Mrs. Ancsa is tempted to attribute her infirmity to worms or cardiac affliction. "But Mrs. Ancsa understood, or thought she understood, her bitch's ailment better than that. 'It's the want of liberty that's killing her,' she thought. The liberty which would have included the right to live with the engineer, the master she had adopted for herself of her own free will" (138). Her torpor, in a decline that mirrors her owners', indeed becomes symbolic for the melancholy of an entire nation: during these years of the early 1950s, general "public feeling was in a state of depression" (105). Yet however much Tibor Dery deploys the dog for the purposes of his political fable, he never abandons deference to the creature itself; Niki's own listlessness becomes all the more poignant and salient through a respectful analogy to human emotional grief. Conversely, human incarceration appears all the more unbearable insofar as Dery points out that all living creatures naturally long for health and liberty.

It is, however, on the issue of communication and silence that the interconnection—the convergence yet also scission—between human and animal becomes most complex. After Mr. Ancsa is incarcerated and Mrs. Ancsa must try to make ends meet on her own, Niki is left more frequently alone. Her depressed resignation to this treatment expresses itself most saliently in her silence: "What gave [Mrs. Ancsa] the most pain was the terrier's silence, the muteness of her whole body. The bitch neither cried, nor argued, nor protested, nor demanded explanations, and it was impossible to convince her. She simply resigned herself to her fate in silence. This silence, which resembled the ultimate silence of a prisoner broken in body and soul, was, for Mrs. Ancsa, like a violent protest at the nature of existence itself" (93–94). As Niki's health deteriorates, she becomes even more taciturn and remains mute for days at a time. "It was Niki's silence which made Mrs. Ancsa realise that the bitch was sick" (131). The fact that the creature knows not how to ask for help and withdraws into itself makes its suffering all the more painful for Mrs. Ancsa to watch.

Through Niki the reader is reminded that Mr. Ancsa, too, has become silenced: not only does the reader never hear his story but he is literally given no means of protest, even to inquire what his crime could have been, as the reader finds out on the last page when he suddenly appears before Mrs. Ancsa in the doorway:

> "Were you told why you were arrested?"
> "No," the engineer replied, "I was told nothing."
> "And you don't know, either, why you were released?"
> "No," the engineer replied, "I wasn't told." (144)

Of course, here silence is the prerogative of the state that exerts terror through being inscrutable and reducing its citizens to dogs in their utter dependency on its whimsical exercise of power. Niki, by contrast, however mute she might be, is beautifully transparent in her expression of both joy and sadness. Her body language is clear. On one issue, though, she cannot communicate to her mistress, and that is to tell her that she is still waiting for Mr. Ancsa to return home (107). Likewise Mrs. Ancsa is powerless to tell the terrier what she eventually does find out about her husband. "And even later when, three or four times a year, she was able to visit her husband in the Central Prison, she had no means whatever of telling the bitch about it. Yet Niki was in dire need of some such encouragement" (94–95). Is it then out of hopelessness, one wonders, that Niki finally dies?

The timing of Niki's death, or I should say, Ancsa's reappearance, comes as a shock to the reader: the dog dies hours before the husband walks in the door. Is it a senseless coincidence, mirroring the haphazard fate and pointless suffering to which the Ancsas are subject? Is her meager, short life intended to span and represent their most trying years? Does Dery wish to emphasize that Ancsa's ordinary story, an everyday occurrence in Stalinist Hungary, is not the heroic myth of Ulysses, whose dog Argos dies only after greeting his master on his return? Ultimately, the reason for the timing of Niki's death is another of the silences in the novel. What one can say is that Dery refuses to sentimentalize the Ancsas' story by having Niki live to see her master again. Mrs. Ancsa does not even have a photograph to remind her of the terrier, but keeps, in the final words of the novel, "by way of a souvenir, . . . a stone which she had recently found under the carpet" (144). During a time in which she had no play toy, a stone was Niki's sole joy, a substitute ball that she would bring home. How, one asks, is one to commemorate such a life of poverty and deprivation? The novel itself, of course, does attempt to recollect, assess, and protest postwar years for the Hungarians, but, given that human life and happiness were officially treated as worthless and insignificant at that time, such a tale is bound to be, so to speak, nothing but a meager stone, merely "The Story of a Dog."

Charles Siebert

Making the animal speak, as in *Faithful Ruslan*, or focusing on the dog, as in *Niki*, is a way of expressing one's own censorship and muteness—which brings us to the theme of stories that give the dog voice but in so doing also reflect on human muteness. Given all the talking-dog stories, comic strips, and movies, it is surprisingly rare to find those that take seriously the attempt to find an adequate voice for that which remains inaccessible. For how can one possibly capture the subjective character of an animal's experience in a language foreign to it? As mentioned previously, the real danger with such cynomorphic stories lies in their *Über-benennung*, in making the animal chatty, and therefore deliberately going to the opposite extreme from assuming it is mute.[20] Viennese writer Hugo von Hofmannsthal wrote that animals are "ciphers, which language is powerless to unlock" (*Prosa* 2:102) and that they "sense [*wittern*] that which goes beyond human comprehension" (*Prosa* 1:411–12). The challenge to which the poet would be drawn, her ideal, then, would be to grasp that which stretches beyond the confines of human thought. Accordingly, she would need to *wittern* precisely that which was foreign to her own perception of the world. In other words, the poet would take what Hofmannsthal called the animal's uncanny sensory capabilities as her own model.

Fundamentally motivating such writing would be the desire to escape anthropocentric limitations, which include those of human speech. To imagine becoming an animal, that is, holds the promise of breaking away from one's solipsistic self. A famous example of such ecstatic taking leave of oneself occurs in Hofmannsthal's "Letter," where Lord Chandos writes of watching poisoned rats die and finding himself being filled, not with compassion, but something far more intense, "a monstrous sympathy, a flowing over [*Hinüberfließen*] into those creatures" (*Prosa* 2:17). Chandos confesses a simultaneous breakdown in human language: words dissolve in his mouth like rotten mushrooms (*Prosa* 2:13). This *Hinüberfließen* into mute beings, even into repugnant dying rats, leads him not only to ecstatic self-abandonment but also a liberating asymbolia: he instinctively realizes that words would be too restrictive to describe his new elated state.

Hofmannsthal was influenced by the German Romantic writers and he could have been alluding to the process of self-alienation that Friedrich von Hardenberg (also known as Novalis) wrote about a hundred years earlier. Breaking with the eighteenth-century notion of the Great Chain of Being, which placed rational mankind at its pinnacle, Novalis envisaged the final development of his hero Heinrich von Ofterdingen as a metamorphosis into a plant, an animal, a stone, and a star (1:392). Even more audaciously, Novalis pondered whether God, since he could become man, could not also become a stone, plant, animal, even an element, thereby instigating an "ongoing salvation in nature" (2:826). At the basis of such interspecies reincarnation was Novalis's response to Fichte's ego philosophy, which claimed that the self posits itself and everything around it. Novalis rejected the solipsism Fichte's philosophy entailed and envisaged instead an eccentric pathway to self-knowledge that demanded taking leave of the self: he spoke of the necessity of springing over oneself (*sich selbst Überspringen* [2:345]) and traveling away from oneself in order to return there (*zu sich selbst wieder heraus* [2:224]). Hence, his ideal of a perfect protagonist for a novel was someone who was so infinitely open to all experience that he could be transformed unendingly.[21]

Theologically speaking, Novalis's theory of metamorphosis is indebted to a Spinozistic pantheism (*Deus sive natura*), whereby all of nature is infused with divinity. As in Spinoza, it is not an undifferentiated unity of substance that concerns Novalis but multiple concrete individuations. The infinite multiplicity present in each individual and interconnecting them is what comprises the One; an infinity of modifications pervades nature and is identical and extensive with the infinity of God. In his advocacy of the freedom of radical transformation, Novalis strikingly heralds Gilles Deleuze and Félix Guattari's concept of "becoming-animal," first mentioned in *Kafka: Towards a Minor Literature* and then more fully developed in their similarly jointly authored

A Thousand Plateaus: Capitalism and Schizophrenia. Like Novalis, Deleuze and Guattari are concerned not with identifying with the animal but with becoming it, again following Spinoza, not in a totality or unity of substance but in accidental forms and haecceities: "Not following a logical order, but following alogical consistencies or compatibilities, . . . because no one, not even God, can say in advance whether two borderlines will string together" (*Thousand Plateaus* 250). Here, too, the vision is to break loose from a false sense of groundedness in one's (for Deleuze and Guattari, bourgeois and oedipalized) subjectivity. If one pursues the implications of Novalis, Hofmannsthal, Deleuze, and Guattari for cynomorphic tales, to narrate from the animal's perspective would mean to shift one's locus suddenly into an entirely different being and picture identification as a leaving of oneself. Consequently, the imaginative leap into the consciousness of the animal would signify not the attempt to erase differences but precisely the contrary—to think through the differences in all their alogical complexity and thus to gauge the vast distance from animal being.[22]

Virginia Woolf yokes such contradictory impulses in her novel about Elizabeth Barrett Browning's spaniel Flush. She probes into Flush's thoughts yet acknowledges the difficulty of accessing the canine mind: "And yet sometimes the tie would almost break; there were vast gaps in their understanding. Sometimes they would lie and stare at each other in blank bewilderment. Why, Miss Barrett wondered, did Flush tremble suddenly, and whimper and start and listen? . . . Flush was equally at a loss to account for Miss Barrett's emotions" (36). The fact that they cannot communicate to each other in words leads Miss Barrett to ponder whether "words say everything? Can words say anything? Do not words destroy the symbol that lies beyond the reach of words?" (37–38). *Flush* is one of the most notable cynomorphic stories to reflect on the impasses of interspecies communication. What makes it stand apart from other examples of this literary genre is that, rather than blithely anthropomorphizing the dog, making it into a mirror in which human behavior is confirmed, the gap between the species is acknowledged and probed.[23]

To operate at the edges of poetic language can also mean exploring the place where language is assumed not to be, namely, in animal consciousness.[24] In O. Henry's short story "Memoirs of a Yellow Dog" (1906), the canine narrator is suspicious of the power of human speech and wittily reverses the terms of who is endowed with language: "But, of course, he [his master] couldn't understand. Humans were denied the speech of animals. The only common ground of communication upon which dogs and men can get together is in fiction" (99). In narrating from the consciousness of the dog and in their struggle to find an adequate voice for animal thought, Woolf and O'Henry thus explore the limits to human language.[25] Among cynomorphic tales the most extreme example of such self-reflection on language and the unbreachable gulf between species is Kafka's "The Researches of a Dog." As discussed in the introduction, the canine narrator, in failing to recognize species beyond his own, illustrates a profound *méconnaissance* vis-à-vis any being outside the confines of his own consciousness. In the bizarre creature that he invents, the Czech author illustrates the boundaries of access to the inner life of another being: this perplexing dog—neither humanlike nor doglike—embodies the failure of the writer's attempt to hypothesize him and to fashion a creature who makes sense. As with Lord Chandos, the attempt to imagine a *Hinüberfließen* into the mute animal entails the inability of human language to cohere.[26]

In his illuminating short history of the cynomorphic tale, Theodore Ziolkowski argues that what uniquely characterizes this literary tradition is how the canine narrator poses as a philosopher. I would add that it is most often about language and communication that the canine philosopher broods. A contemporary novel narrated from the perspective of a dog that sensitively reflects on the incommensurable gap in communication between species is Charles Siebert's *Angus* (2000). Its narrative structure alone is complicated. Angus is a Jack Russell terrier, who at the start lies dying, having been attacked by coyotes one night after his owners, on vacation in the woods of southern Quebec, let him out. But this very situation is itself unclear and only revealed in the course of the narrative that leads up to it. At the opening the reader can only discern that the narrating "I" has been wounded outdoors but does not know the circumstances. What is recounted from this starting point onward are the dog's last thoughts, comprising recollections from episodes in his brief life. The reader learns, for instance, of the warmth of the whelping den, how his owners arrive one stormy night to pick him out of the litter, of his constricted, frustrating existence in a London flat, his travel in the cargo hold to Brooklyn, and finally of the enticing outdoors at the cabin in Quebec. As he lays expiring, these past experiences and reflections on them flit by his consciousness, interrupted periodically by his owners calling "An-gus?" as they search for him in the dark. In fact, what makes this tale so intriguing is that it is rendered as the dog's stream of consciousness, with the staccato-like style, digressions, and self-questioning unique to this narrative technique.

The stream of consciousness allows Siebert to relay in prose the keen alertness and attentiveness to the moment that characterize the terrier breed. The narrative style itself is fragmentary and on edge, capturing the liveliness, intensity, and distractedness of the Jack Russell, who even in his last moments is "an urge, an instinct, trying to climb away from the consequences of responding to [the] last one" (113). This very rush of the senses leads Angus to find human responses slow and human lives full of incomprehensible tedium. He wonders, for instance, referring to the couple who own him, whether "sometimes the world doesn't move enough for you either" (59). Canine time thus contrasts with human time. Angus writes of his species: "We do sense things, the about-to-happen, the disposition of every day toward dishevelment. . . . We're tuned to the things you can't hear, to extremes. . . . There's no middle ground for us, no half measure. Again, your province, the lukewarm, the static sphere of hope, and doubt and worry" (86). Whereas the dog is attuned to a dynamic present, so much so that they can anticipate the "about-to-happen," humans are either beset by worries about the future or weighed down by remorse over the past. As Angus, the keen observer and philosopher of human life, remarks: "Deep sorrows, harbored grudges, regrets of the centuries? Your sphere, remember?" (79).

Charles Siebert thus inverts who is regarded as the dumb beast, in other words, which creature—dog or man—is deemed to be without the means to interact fully and immediately with the world. Through the dog's intense feeling and ability to communicate it directly, Siebert calls attention to the inarticulate human self. Only his mistress, whom Angus calls Sweet-Voice, is "restless, like me, impatient in her bones. She senses the unseen, the about-to-happen." "Her days, too, are sensory onslaughts, of textures and touch" (66). For instance, she is "just too impatient to hunt for the words" (105) to respond to her husband's empty chitchat, to his naive, offhand question about Angus, "What's he thinking?" (105). Indeed, Angus wonders if his humans are at all capable of imagining his world, at least to the extent that he tries to fathom theirs (33).

In his essay "What Is It Like to Be a Bat?" philosopher Thomas Nagel investigates how inexorably foreign the subjective consciousness of another being is to us. His example is that of the bat whose sonar capability, "though clearly a form of perception, is not similar in its operation to any sense that we possess, and there is no reason to suppose that it is subjectively like anything we can experience or imagine" (483). This conundrum is not unique to the divide between species, for he also says that it occurs between people. For example, "The subjective character of the experience of a person deaf and blind from birth is not accessible to me . . . nor presumably is mine to him. This does not prevent us each from believing that the other's experience has such a subjective character" (440). Nagel elaborates at length on how difficult it would be to imagine the subjective character of the experience of the bat: "I want to know what it is like for a *bat* to be a bat. Yet if I try to imagine this, I am restricted to the resources of my own mind, and those resources are inadequate to the task. . . . The best evidence would come from the experience of bats, if we only knew what they were like" (439). As the example of the deaf and blind person illustrates, however, it would be false to deny that person a subjective consciousness only because we cannot fathom what it would be like to be that person. Hence the same holds for other species: "The fact that we cannot expect ever to accommodate in our language a detailed description of . . . bat phenomenology should not lead us to dismiss as meaningless the claim that bats . . . have experiences fully comparable in richness of detail to our own" (440).

Charles Siebert's *Angus* is unusual in that, unlike most cynomorphic tales that have a dog straight-forwardly narrate its daily encounters, this novel attempts to render the phenomenology of the dog through the interior monologue, as it switches from registering present sensations to recollecting episodes from the past. In so doing, Siebert renders Angus's feelings, thoughts, and desires as "fully comparable in richness of detail to our own." Rather than, as one would initially think, contesting or disregarding Nagel's claims that we cannot imagine another's consciousness, he actually underscores their veracity by making us aware that we generally mistake a dog's lack of language to mean the absence of a complex interior life.[27] Angus himself challenges this false assumption in his rhetorical question: "Who deemed that . . . we be the dimmer ones who live so much more fiercely than you do?" (34). What is even more remarkable about *Angus* is that, not only does Siebert try to answer the question of what the subjective experience of the dog would be like (though the result is clearly fictional), he also has the dog ask this very question about humans. He then portrays the frustrating limitations Angus encounters in trying to comprehend the human world and adjust to it.[28]

Angus is a profoundly Lacanian dog who longs to reach the Other and who, though embodied in Angus's rather prosaic owners, still remains inaccessible and unfathomable.[29] Angus wants to understand, meet, and be the desires of Huge-Head and Sweet-Voice. If he could speak, his very first words would be "what is it that you want, and how can we get it for you?" (142; see also 79).[30] Unlike Kafka's dog, who obstinately and implacably refuses to acknowledge species outside his own, whether they be birds or humans, Angus knows that the very ground of his being is defined by dependency. Who he is relies on a similarity and correspondence to this supreme Other: "So who and what are we really, then, and have we, would you say, hearts like yours?" (35). This address to the "you," indeed its pleading invocation, performs this subjection. Indeed, it is a recurrent refrain in the novel (see also 33 and 104). Moreover, it is not enough for Angus to wonder whether his existence could be confirmed by having a heart that pulsates with emotions similar to a human's, he must petition his owners on the matter. Thus, instead of the animal being considered mute, its language and desire are presented as the entreaty for dialog, an open address to the human being.

The pathos of this plea lies in the dog's struggling against the accusation of its inferiority yet feeling it nonetheless: "What are we, I wonder, that we have, like you, deep emotions and yet can't ever really live up to the notions you have of us? . . . What are we that we don't live up to your notions and yet end up living entirely for you?" (33). The repetition and the grammatical use of the question rhetorically underscore the longing. Indeed, because of its servile reliance on the Other and because of its constant second-guessing of human behavior, the dog lives against its will in a state of perpetual benightedness: "We will remain forever in the dark, won't we, about your moves, about what moves you?" (108). Conventionally, an animal's thoughts are seen as inarticulate and opaque to human understanding. Siebert dialecticizes this presumption by making the dog unknowable precisely because it mirrors back to the humans their own lack of transparency.

The intensity of Angus's dependency and longing leads him to make the comparison: "Our devotion makes yours pale" (92). This attentiveness, worship, even guarding meet the human's own profound neediness. The full citation reads: "Every day is an open book of devotion to me. That's why you keep us. I know that now. You keep us because our devotion makes yours pale" (92). Even as a puppy the Jack Russell terrier notices the clinging hands of Sweet-Voice and her lips pressed against him as expressing such a depth of "will and want and longing" (143) that he wonders where they come from (44). It is this Lacanian desire of the Other that Angus wishes to fathom and respond to. Reversing the question humans so often ponder about dogs, namely, what do they dream, here Angus wonders the same of his humans (91), in other words, he craves to know the unconscious needs of his owners, of which they themselves are not even aware.

In writing from Angus's perspective, then, Charles Siebert does not so much anthropomorphize him, imputing canine similarity with the human mind, as he probes the gaps between the two that lie at the foundation of the profoundly melancholic desire of one species for the other.[31] In so doing, he does not have the dog serve merely as the blithe narrator of external events but tries to imagine or track the dog's own form of consciousness. The results, the kinds of yearnings that arise in Angus's mind, are startlingly unique in the canon of the cynomorphic narrative.

David Hockney

The modernist writer Elias Canetti pondered whether animals have less fear because they live without words (19). And early twentieth-century writer John Galsworthy postulated that the tranquility of dogs is tied to their muteness. For him, the essence of companionship with pets lies in the peacefulness and centeredness they can impart: "For it is by muteness that a dog becomes for one so utterly beyond value; with him one is at peace, where words play no torturing tricks. When he just sits, loving, and knows that he is being loved, those are the moments that I think are precious to a dog" (156). Such thoughts recall the silent meditation and calm Kierkegaard praised in nature. I had earlier positioned the Danish philosopher as offering a different way of conceptualizing the absence of language in animals, one that does not see it as lack. To regard the animal as dwelling beyond human language, then, can lead to two diametrically opposed views, both of which locate the animal as other to the human: animals may be either denigrated as inferior, dumb brutes or idealized as embodying an imaginary fullness of being that has no need of words. Such animal completeness and peacefulness are beautifully captured by American artist David Hockney in a series of oil paintings and crayon drawings that he made of his pet dachshunds. Hockney's collection *Dog Days* (1998) is a tribute to stillness, a reinterpretation of what animal muteness can be. If the best literature on the dog reflects on the impasses of communication with another species and hence on its own shortcomings and silences, what, one wonders, would be a comparable self-reflexive move in the visual arts? Like Thormann, Hockney suggests that the nonverbal art form can self-consciously gravitate to the representation of mute being—of the animal in deep sleep.[32] Indeed, his dachshunds' stillness makes Angus's thought seem voluminous.

Describing the genesis of his canine paintings, Hockney writes: "In order to draw them I had to leave large sheets of paper all over the house and studio to catch them sitting or sleeping without disturbance. For the same reason, I kept canvases and a fresh palette ready for times when I thought I could work" (5). The result is portraits of absolute calm and candor. Curled up together, their bodies pressed against each other, the pair of dachshunds lie in undivided repose and well being (fig. 6). Their warm russet figures sink into a lemony yellow pillow with sky-blue edging and demonstrate how color can set off form, the square cushion contrasting with their oval roundness. Hockney positions his canvas close to the dogs so that only enough of their surroundings—the pillow, wall, and floor—are depicted to frame them. This proximity and minimalism help to convey intimacy and simplicity. If Elaine Scarry has observed that "beauty always takes place in the particular," (18), then the beauty of these dachshunds seems to reside not in their generic dog-ness but in their specificity as Hockney's companions whom he so esteems and loves that he wishes to capture their perfection in his art. Some of the oils show one of the hounds preferring to sleep stretched out on its back; it is so trusting of its safe environment that it exposes its vulnerable belly. Beauty thus also lies in this arrested nature that the viewer can contemplate at ease, appreciating the dachshunds' self-containment and admiring the otherness of their rotund bodies and sleek coats. Complete and separate unto themselves, the dogs exist in their own serene world, without need of the addition or complementarity of words. Their perfection and apartness reinforce their muteness.

Hockney's canine portraiture is reminiscent of the German Expressionist painter Franz Marc, whose painting *The Blue Rider* gave the name to a school of painting centered in Munich before the First World War and to whom Wassily Kandinsky, August Macke, Paul Klee, Gabriele Münter, and Alexey von Jawlensky also belonged. Marc's numerous paintings of horses and deer share not only the same palette of primary colors as Hockney's (especially the redness of the animals) but also the striking juxtaposition of color. One of Marc's most famous works, *Dog before the World* (1912), depicts a seated white dog gazing intently into a distant landscape, its whiteness suggestive of its essential purity and simplicity.[33] Indeed, in an essay from the same year entitled "The New Painting," Marc spoke of the need to depict the "inner, spiritual side of nature" (102), and in "On the Animal in Art" (1910) he voiced that his goal was to "feel out the inner, quivering life of animals" (98). "Who is able to depict the soul of the dog?" (100), he asked, wanting to immerse himself in the essence or spirit of the animal in order to divine how it

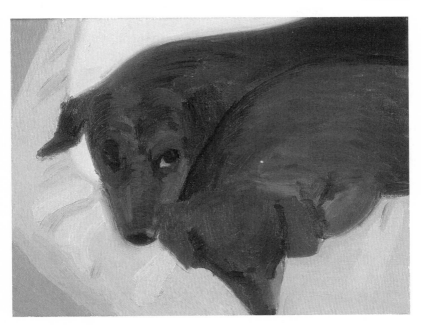

6 David Hockney, *Dog Painting 42*, 1995. Oil on canvas. 12 × 15 inches. Copyright David Hockney.

pictured the world (*um dessen Bilderkreis zu erraten* [99]). He guided his vision according to how he imagined nature would reflect itself in the eyes of an animal (99).[34]

Marc's utopian artistic program may be foreign to Hockney, but the postmodernist does capture how the dog exists in a realm of purity unto its own. One could say that, with their roundness and repose evoking an interiority, his dachshunds embody a materialized secret. However much they might evoke the closeness and intimacy one experiences with a pet, they are still shut off in their own dream world. Surrounded by an aura of pale gold, like icons they exist in a realm of purity unto their own. This transcendence in the animal marks an outer limit of accessibility to the viewer. We are fascinated and transfixed by this body of the animal, so perfect in its existence, as if before the dogs' self-containedness we didn't exist at all. We, then, are the ones on the outside, without the pure subjectivity that the animal possesses.

Several of the paintings show one of the dachshunds, while still motionless and ear flopped over the pillow, opening an eye to check on its surroundings. The single orb gives the impression of being pure "eye." Before it drowsily shuts again, it briefly registers the world but does not acknowledge it, as if the object it were registering (perhaps the viewer?) were not important but had vanished into thin air. In other words, this one open eye signifies a passive looking and not that the animal sees or acknowledges the human viewer. The languid gaze of Hockney's dachshunds, though, is not the profound, ideal recognition that the human longs to receive from the animal and that Maurice Maeterlinck, for instance, imagines seeing in his French bulldog's eyes: "He was there, studying, drinking in all my looks; he replied to them gravely, as from equal to equal, to inform me, no doubt, that at least through the eyes, the most immaterial . . . , he knew that he was *saying* to me all that love should say" (42). Rather, with Hockney's dogs, it is the look from the animal that is at one with itself and environment onto the human who doesn't possess that same groundedness, centeredness, and serenity. Contrast the gaze of Maeterlinck's dog, then, with J. R. Ackerley's Tulip's: "The look in hers disconcerts me, it contains too much, more than any beast may give, something too clear and too near, too entire, too dignified and direct, a steadier look than my own. I avert my face" (138). Unlike Maeterlinck, Ackerley notes the unsettling disjuncture between canine and human. Tulip looks back at the narrator, as if he were caught looking at himself, but her clear, steady gaze does not confirm him in his existence, rather he looks away in shame.[35]

I began this chapter with Rainer Maria Rilke, and I should also like to close with him. In his *Duino Elegies* (1923), Rilke addresses this precariousness and trepidation of the human when faced with the gaze from the animal. In the first elegy he writes that animals notice that we are not at home in the world: "und die findigen Tiere merken es schon, / daß wir nicht sehr verläßlich zu Haus sind / in der gedeuteten Welt" (*Werke* 441). [The knowing animals know / we are not very securely at home / in our interpreted world (5).] The phrase *gedeutete Welt* refers to a world signified through language, the act of interpretation that, say, Derrida's cat or Hockney's dogs, with their stillness and centeredness, have no need to command. But it is the eighth elegy that most famously juxtaposes human and animal gazes. It begins:

Mit allen Augen sieht die Kreatur
das Offene. Nur unsre Augen sind
wie umgekehrt und ganz um sie gestellt
als Fallen, rings um ihren freien Ausgang.
Was draußen *ist*, wir wissens aus des Tiers
Antlitz allein. (470)

With every eye the creature sees the open.
Our human eyes alone are inward-looking
and stationed there for all the world like traps
around the exit which they interdict.
The world outside of mind we only know
from the beast's face. (57)

For Rilke, the human is always a mere observer (*Zuschauer* [472]), never a participant in the immediacy and unboundedness of life. The animal's seeing is a full immersion in this openness. Our eyes, by contrast, are not focused on what should be manifest and clear; they are "turned around" or away (*wie umgekehrt*), in a sense blinded, so that they perceive what *is* only indirectly, via the face of the animal in which is embedded "the open" (*das Offne, das / im Tiergesicht so tief ist* [470]).

In a line that speaks to the gaze of Hockney's dog, Rilke furthermore writes, "daß ein Tier, / ein stummes, aufschaut, ruhig durch uns durch" (471). [A dumb brute, / in looking up, serenely looks straight through us (57).] The phrase *durch uns durch* suggests simultaneously both a penetrating look that sees through human dissimulation and a disinterested gaze that goes through us, as if we didn't exist at all. Either way, this gaze positions the human as always standing outside, in opposition to life (*gegenüber sein / und nichts als das und immer gegenüber* [471]), in contrast to the animal's state of grace in oneness with life. The animal perceives a world that is intact (*geheilt für immer*) and sees itself not just as part of a whole but itself in the whole (*sich in Allem* [471]). Whereas the first elegy suggested that man was not at home in this world because he interpreted it, here the key to the animal being able to see such wholeness, oneness, and openness is that it is *stumm*.

And yet (*Und doch*), Rilke cannot help but register that a certain melancholy with its weightiness and care (*Gewicht und Sorge einer großen Schwermut* [471]) also clings to the warm-blooded animal, that it is often overwhelmed by memory of a happier past. Again, then, we come back to the question, Whose melancholy? Are Hockney's sleeping dogs reminiscent of the tired hound curled up in Dürer's engraving and thus related to the iconography of melancholia? Although the eye is open in expectancy, is it about to close again out of the boredom and listlessness that characterize the melancholic temperament? Because the dogs cannot tell us how they feel, ultimately we cannot interpret their pose, and it is this uncertainty and unbridgeable distance from the pet that is otherwise so close—and our resignation to the fact of this separation—that renders us bereft. However long we immerse ourselves in gazing at Hockney's dogs, we cannot reach into the painting and stroke them.

Yet it is also our melancholic longing for the grace and redemption though the animal, for this closeness to it, that creates the loveliness of Hockney's art. Beauty resides, too, in seeing the perfection of the animal Other, in the idealization of the beloved object with which, though, the melancholic can never be intimate enough. This idealization and yearning also inform the labor of artists to be discussed in the next chapters— among them Michael Field, Marie Bonaparte, Elizabeth von Arnim, Rhoda Lerman, and Sally Mann, who in their works, in the last words of Rilke's eighth *Duino Elegy*, are constantly taking leave of their beloved pets: "so leben wir und nehmen immer Abschied" (472). [Thus, do we live, forever taking leave (61).] Thus art tries to articulate loss and silence and, in some measure, to compensate for them, yet art is also consciously marked by its deviation from its original model in the living animal. As Kristeva points out, the melancholic is deeply familiar with the arbitrariness of the signified. As I have attempted to show, all the artists discussed in this chapter grapple with and reflect on the limits of representation. They do so in mute sympathy with what the animal itself cannot utter.

TWO

Shame

Under the knife of his murderers, Josef K. dies in Kafka's novel *The Trial* (1925) comparing himself to a dog: "'Like a dog,' he said, it were, as if shame [*die Scham*] should survive him" (*Der Prozeß* 165). A sense of shame, both Freud and Lacan intimated, is what sets the human apart from animal. Lacan noted that the animal became human the moment it confronted the problem of what to do with its excrement. And in *Civilization and Its Discontents* (1930) Freud remarked that the two traits of the dog that make it repugnant to man are its lack of shame about its excrement and its sexual functions (14:459). If Josef K. dies in disgrace, is he paradoxically more human than dog for his sense of ongoing shame? In the vivid experience of shame, our entire being feels engulfed and overcome. It leaves us grappling and hopeless. Thus Josef K. muses in his abrupt last thought that it seems shame would outlast him. Shame indeed can be so powerful that it possesses the whole self to the point that it becomes synonymous with a painful self-consciousness. Western philosophy, of course, has denied animals this capacity for self-consciousness—the reflection on one's present state of being—in order to reserve it as the preeminent characteristic of the human. Dogs are said to lack shame because they apparently cannot internally observe, monitor, and castigate themselves. Why then does Josef K. compare himself to a dog in terms of shame? Is it because he feels, due to a sense of shame, less than human? In this case, since degradation is shameful, it turns one into a subhuman creature, "like a dog." The reader thus confronts the dilemma: Is Josef K. in his shame like a dog or like a human? If the definition of what it means to be human is bound up with policing the borders between human and animal, it would be fascinating to examine, as Kafka does, how shame blurs the divide in the very act of constructing it.

Let us explore another moment in Kafka rife with paradox that similarly links shame to the difference between humans and dogs. In "The Researches of a Dog" the canine narrator comes across dogs dancing on their hind legs (the reader understands that these must be circus dogs):

They had truly cast off all shame [*Scham*], these miserable creatures were doing something that was at once most ridiculous and most obscene—they were walking upright on their hind legs. Ugh! They were exposing themselves and openly flaunting their nakedness [*Blöße*]; they prided themselves on it, and whenever they obeyed their better instincts for a moment and lowered their front legs, they were literally horrified, as if it were a mistake, as if nature were a mistake, and once again rapidly raised their legs, and their eyes seemed to be asking forgiveness that they had to desist a little from their sinfulness [*Sündhaftigkeit*]. (328)

Not only is it unnatural for the dogs to be walking on their hind legs, they thereby appear to be exposing themselves and revealing their nakedness and weakness (meanings resonant in the word *Blöße*). The narrator calls this indiscretion sinful (*Versündigung*). He then feminizes and sexualizes the disgrace: the dogs are "spreading their legs" (329) in order to keep their balance. They thereby cast their shame aside, *Scham* here being understood as modesty or *la pudeur*. The only time the circus dogs seem embarrassed is when they intermittently fall to all fours. Their eyes then seem to ask for forgiveness as if nature had made a mistake in reverting them to their normal posture. Is to experience shame, then, to feel improper or unnatural at doing something natural?

Since the narrator will not admit that any species exists apart from dogs, it remains unstated that the dogs stand upright like human beings, suggesting that shame (meaning disgrace, *Schande*, or *la honte*) arises once one crosses the species boundary. The question comes to mind that if dogs should not act like humans, can it be that humans are somehow impure and shameless, not possessing the naturalness of animals? Other questions arise from the implicit comparison. If to sense shame, according to Freud and Lacan, is to be human, is Kafka's narrator paradoxically more humanlike than the dogs mimicking humans? And how does performance play a role? The dogs are masking as humans but they lack the self-consciousness of doing so: if shame arises with an inadvertent unmasking, here the dogs are incapable of shame for they are not even aware of the pretense. Kafka further complicates this triangle between self-consciousness, shame, and the species divide by casting his narrator as a dog: like a human he is painfully self-reflexive, yet he is so obtuse as to be incapable of acknowledging the difference between the species. Finally, why does the reader feel shame and discomfort for the narrator who is unable to comprehend the situation and see that these mysterious creatures are in reality circus dogs? Observing the disgrace of another can cause shame in oneself: hence the narrator's bodily affect of shame when confronted with the dancing dogs is to make himself smaller and to whine. This moment of identification with another, as we shall see, plays a crucial role in the workings of shame.

My point is not to disentangle the complexities in Kafka but to illustrate how elaborate the nexus of shame can be. It becomes intricate precisely because the demarcations between animal and human worlds are unclear, although shame, as with Freud and Lacan, is generally invoked as a term of separation. These are precisely the perplexities that Jacques Derrida confronts when he contemplates what it means to be seen nude by his cat. Derrida begins the essay "L'animal que donc je suis" by reflecting on the unexpected shame that arises in him when he catches the glance of his pet cat seeing him naked. He says that he cannot repress a moment of *pudeur* (modesty) and *gêne* (embarrassment [253]).[1] In fact, he is ashamed of being ashamed, the affect being unjustifiable before this unsuspecting creature. I should like to highlight three crucial ways of how, in his reflections on this scenario, Derrida undoes the binaries between beast and human, between ignorance and rationality, and, hence, between those deemed shameful and those imputed to be capable of the awareness of shame. In addition, I want to indicate the course I shall follow in tracking down a similar deconstruction of binaries in various literary and visual texts that strikingly juxtapose human and canine in terms of shame.

First, it is significant that the human being feels ashamed before the gaze of the animal. Derrida relinquishes control of the gaze, an unusual move in that humans usually voraciously direct their gazes toward animals, be they in pet stores, at dog shows, at zoos, or on television. Here, though, the cat is the bearer of the gaze. It is, moreover, a direct, frontal gaze ("*de face*, en face à face" [254]). Derrida calls it "the gaze of a seer, visionary, or extra-lucid blind person" (372). What is it, then, that these visionary yet enigmatic feline eyes perceive? They possess ultra-clarity yet seem to be blind because they are unreadable. Conceivably, Derrida's very inability to decipher the cat's intent results in his shame. According to Sartre, Lacan, and the psychologist Léon Wurmser, it is the gaze of the other that provokes shame. Sartre writes, "Shame is by nature recognition. I recognize that I am as the Other sees me" (221–22). In Sartre, as later in Lacan in *The Four Fundamental Concepts of Psycho-Analysis*, the dilemma is that I cannot see myself as the Other apprehends me. Similarly, if I cannot know how the animal perceives me, my sense of mastery over it is chastened. Thus, it is not only we who can regard the animal and tame it through our gaze, but also the animal who can shame us.

In what follows, I do not consider solely how dogs are denigrated in literature and art as shameful but how their own look is represented and whether this look can rebuke the human. I shall examine works by the photographers William Wegman and Walter Schels whose animal portraits capture this blank yet profound gaze of the dog: What is it that the dog sees and what are its eyes communicating? And what would it mean if the dog were deliberately avoiding the gaze of the camera? Do we in turn sense a feeling of modesty or unease (*pudeur*) about what is or is not being revealed to us? Which viewer is blind—the human or the animal?

The second point I should like to underscore in Derrida is that he questions whether in his nakedness he resembles more the human or the animal. The animal, of course, wears no clothing and can thus be said to be the naked beast. Yet only with the sentiment of being revealed as nude is one truly naked, that is to say, shamed, which is why the animal can be said to be neither naked nor to possess shame. But in asking whether, in his nakedness, he is animal or human, Derrida performs a leap of identification across the species gulf. Echoing the title of his talk, he muses: "Qui suis-je alors? Qui est-ce que je suis?" (255). [Who am I therefore (pursuing)? Who is it that I am (following)? (374).] Moreover, clearly mindful of Sartre and Lacan, he wonders whether it could be the Other, in this case the animal itself, to whom he must address the question of his identity.

In the chapter that ensues, I want to examine figures in literary fiction and art who could ask "qui suis-je?," for they do not know if they are human or canine. Hybrid, mutant, contaminated beings, they unsettle the neat distinctions between species. Such imaginative creatures—in some instances, literal cyborg-crosses between humans and dogs—particularly give rise to shame. One example are the dog-women of the contemporary Portuguese-British painter Paula Rego. Here Derrida's trope of nakedness can be taken figuratively as the revelation of one's poverty and gender. This chapter shall investigate how women and the lower class are portrayed "like animals" or "naked" before the chastising gaze of the other. Complicating this representation is whether those regarded to be socially inferior feel shame or are immune to it. Do they act out shamelessness before a hostile gaze or do they chose to ignore it? More important, do they disavow the feeling of exposure and displace the shame onto the lowly dog, thereby dis-identifying with the animal?

Third, I wish to emphasize the reflexivity of shame for Derrida. His embarrassment is intensified or compounded, for he is ashamed of being ashamed. Alluding to the biblical story, Derrida speaks of this self-consciousness as the knowledge of good and evil, that is to say, of human nakedness. It is said of animals, Derrida recalls, that they totally lack self-consciousness and hence shame, "naked as they are, or so it is thought, without the slightest inkling of being so" (373). At the core of theories on shame—from Hegel to Sartre, and from Freud to Silvan Tomkins—lies this notion of self-consciousness; shame is such an important affect for it is constitutive of the subjective experience of selfhood. Sartre writes: "Now shame . . . is shame of self; it is the *recognition* of the fact that I *am* indeed that object which the other is looking at and judging" (350). A major psychologist on shame, Helen B. Lewis similarly observes: "Because the self is the focus of awareness in shame, 'identity' imagery is usually evoked. . . . There is also vivid imagery of the self in the other's eyes. This creates a 'doubleness of experience,' which is characteristic of shame. . . . Shame is the vicarious experience of the other's negative evaluation" (107). Because shame separates one from others and endows one with a vulnerable self-image, it closes one off, so that one is left feeling alone with a wounded self-esteem. When the self feels violated, it internalizes the shame and hides it from public scrutiny. Thus shame lies at the basis of the disorders of narcissism, where defenses are erected to protect the self against future pain of violation.[2] But this emphasis on *self*-consciousness or, as Lewis says, "identity imagery" should not obscure the fact that, for Sartre, Lewis, and more recent theorists, shame is truly the most interpersonal of affects. If animals, and dogs in particular, are denied the capacity to feel shame on the belief that they lack self-consciousness, it could be argued, with the reverse emphasis on the interrelationality of shame, that they are not immune to belittlement and—due to their refined sense of the pack—have keen sentiments of propriety and intimacy, the latter of which involves the sharing of affect.

It is this avenue of the interpersonal dimensions to shame that I want to pursue more thoroughly.[3] Although Derrida is clearly aware of the active dynamics between himself and the cat, his emphasis on self-consciousness and his own feelings of shame prevent him from tracking this route further. It is my own belief, though my reasons for it are merely based on living attentively with female whippets, that isolation from community, which is what shame is about, is much feared by dogs. I am not an animal behaviorist, but it does seem to me that dogs can look hurt and reproachful when made fun of; they are extraordinarily sensitive to humiliation; and they have a developed sense of etiquette and cleanliness that, if transgressed, can lead to great shame, for instance, if they involuntarily defecate or vomit in the house. My older whippet has even covered up the vomit of the younger one in the car and not out of fear, for I, of course, have never scolded her for retching.

Human psychologist Tomkins has stressed the bodily signs of shame—the dropping of the eyes and head—affect that the dog shares with the human, although dogs tend to look away instead of down. They can even display other external signs of inner cringing, such as when they pin their ears back or put their tails between their legs.[4] Whether these signs betoken a self-consciousness of inferiority or are purely due to fear of punishment, I cannot say. I cannot know if they internalize being watched. But then Wittgenstein said of humans: "The essential thing about private experience is really not that each person possesses his own exemplar, but that nobody knows whether other people also have *this* or something else. The assumption would thus be possible—though unverifiable—that one section of mankind had one sensation of red and another section another" (*Philosophical Investigations* 95, no. 272). As shame is such a private experience, one that I have no access to in others and barely admit to myself, I do not want to exclude dogs, with their strong desire to uphold pack etiquette, from the possibility of experiencing shame when they are reminded that protocol has been breached. At the very least, I should want to spare them the feeling of humiliation.

But it is not only that shame inherently operates intersubjectively and hence is possibly active in the canine sensibility. What interests me even more is that, according to various psychologists, shame is also interrelational in the sense that it evokes feelings of empathy and compassion. As a domestic pet, the dog is an animal extremely reliant on human care. If one takes this responsibility for the vulnerability of the pet seriously, to see it humiliated, treated without dignity and respect, or merely reminded of its subservient position may evoke what Silvan Tomkins called "the vicarious experience of shame" (Sedgwick and Frank 159). Tomkins explains: "The human being is capable through empathy and identification of living through others and therefore of being shamed by what happens to others. To the extent to which the individual invests his affect in other human beings, in institutions, and in the world around him, he is vulnerable to the vicarious experience of shame" (159). In fact, among his examples Tomkins includes feeling "shame at the indignity or suffering of any human being or animal to the extent to which I feel myself identified with the human race or the animal kingdom, and have reverence for life as such" (160).

Because shame tends to be a feeling that is internalized and protected from public scrutiny, one does not want to see either oneself or others openly embarrassed. One wants to shield others from shame. Nietzsche therefore wrote in *The Gay Science*: "Was ist dir das Menschlichste?—Jemandem Scham ersparen" (5:177, no. 274). [What do you consider the most human?—To spare someone shame.] Tomkins similarly takes this reverence for the other as the aspect of shame that is most crucial for defining what is quintessentially human: "The vicarious experience of shame, together with the vicarious experience of distress, is at once a measure of civilization and a condition of civilization. Shame enlarges the spectrum of objects outside of himself that can engage man and concern him" (Sedgwick and Frank 162). Consequently, even were one inclined to deny the dog the empirical faculty of shame, one can nonetheless vicariously feel for its mortification. This substitutive move thus further resists the neat separation of animal from human that Derrida is at pains to interrogate.

One could argue that empathetic shame can be all the more powerful because we are otherwise loath to reveal embarrassment. Vicariousness serves as a means to release, identify, and represent the affect of shame that we are trained to avoid showing. In other words, we might more readily recognize an animal's distress than acknowledge our sense of inadequacy. Such empathy is facilitated because to us the dog seems unable to conceal its apprehensiveness or humiliation and thus it palpably embodies its creatureliness. For this reason Thomas Mann notes that animals are more human than humans: "Animals are more unrestrained and natural than we are, therefore to a certain extent more human in the bodily expression of their feelings [*Gemütszustände*]" ("Herr und Hund" 2:457). This apparent candor is important because in shame "what is revealed is the existence of abiding mystery, a personally resonant something-that-has-been-kept-hidden" (Katz 235). To keep face is precisely not to reveal distress at shame: the canid's open display of affect may thus serve as a therapeutic release for emotions humans otherwise keep under taps—to wit, why one readily experiences vicarious shame vis-à-vis the dog. The sight of unfettered dejection, moreover, can arouse the immediate response of wanting to alleviate it.

This identification, however, is clearly not universal: the weakness of shame can be disavowed by people who mistreat animals. Child abusers may deny that they are causing pain, because the way they administer discipline, they tell themselves, must result in a punishment different from what they experienced as children. In other words, they deny the shame of once having been abused. Along similar lines, if they can assert strength and power, it denies that they were ever wounded. Abuse, because linked to this secrecy, creates a shame that has to be denied even once the harmed child becomes the shameless adult. Clearly, the disavowal of identification can be even more intense across the species boundary. In light of these considerations I wish to examine the dynamics linking the disavowal of the other's gaze and acts of shameless cruelty toward dogs in works ranging from Thomas Mann's story "Tobias Mindernickel" to Ulrich Seidel's film *Tierische Liebe* and Sue Coe's illustrated book *Pit's Letter*. As Léon Wurmser notes, shamelessness is a "reaction-formation against shame" (264).

In sum, in this chapter I present how artists and writers imagine blurring the distinction between human and canine. Identification with the dog proves unsettling and can lead to shame or convert into its disavowal. In each case I put the mechanisms of shame under the microscope. I start with a number of works that hypothesize a human-canine hybrid. Crossing the species divide invariably results in a contaminated, impure being. In the case of the painter Paula Rego identification with the dog embodies a woman's sense of shame. Next I look not at how the human poses like a dog (as in Rego) but at how the dog poses as human in the photography of William Wegman and Walter Schels. Here, theories on the role of the face and gaze in shame become instrumental in answering what causes the viewer's unease before these portraits. Can it be that these dogs are expressing shame before the intrusive camera? As if one were prying, one wants to look away from the undissimulating canine faces that Wegman and Schel capture on film. I progress to the disavowal of identification with the dog in representations of poverty and cruelty in disparate but powerful texts by Mann, Seidel, and Coe. Here, too, I study the dynamics of the gaze, for the disavowal results in shamelessness—namely, the refusal to admit that one's abjectness can be detected by others. Instead, misery is projected onto the dog.

Given the taboo on shame in contemporary culture, the courage of these artists and writers is laudable: they explore the intricacies of the most secretive of affects. As Joseph Adamson and Hilary Clark observe in their collection *Scenes of Shame: Psychoanalysis, Shame, and Writing*: "If severe feelings of shame compel us to hide and conceal inner reality from others and from ourselves, it is often countered in the writer by a creative ideal, a defiant and even ruthless decision not to turn away or to lie, a courageous and almost *shameless* will to see and to know that which internal and external sanctions conspire to keep us from looking at and exploring" (29). It is all the more inspiring that artists as diverse as Coe and Rego search out the dog at the nadir of its oppression—in its rejection from human companionship—as the moment with which to identify with it and thereby to explore empathetically the depths of shame.

Paula Rego

The inspiration for her pastel series *Dog Women* (1994) came to artist Paula Rego (1935–) from a Portuguese friend who had written her a fairy tale.[5] In it an old woman who lives alone with her pets hears the voice of a wailing child as the wind sweeps down the chimney. It commands her to devour her pets, which she dutifully does, one by one. This suggestive tale evokes the struggle between love and dominance, a theme that appears regularly in Rego's oeuvre: one desires to destroy what one is close to. Correlatively, love can demand subservience and lead to shame: iconographically the dog represents such servility, which is why it can be linked to the traditionally dependent status of women. For this tale to have inspired Rego to portray women as dogs, it must also have suggested to her that the old woman becomes the animal she devours: she is transformed into the beast of prey. She can be compared to Heinrich von Kleist's Penthesilea, who, in the 1808 play of the same name, calls on her hunting dogs to join her in the killing of her beloved Achilles. Penthesilea then, as if she were a dog herself, devours him. Thus, in *A Thousand Plateaus* Deleuze and Guattari speak of "the becoming-dog of Penthesilea" (268). In Kleist's play, the heroine, breaking the Amazon rule of not going into battle to kill, ostracizes herself from the matriarchal society. The old woman, too, is alone and even destroys the few who share her abode. Rego casts her dog-women as solitary, wild beasts, who have renounced social customs and the shame that arises from internalizing normative strictures. Such shame, Rego realizes, otherwise haunts women.

With this tale in mind, Paula Rego asked her model Lila Nunes "to crouch down and be a woman with her mouth open as if she's about to swallow something" (quoted in McEwen 212). The result was a five-minute sketch that became the basis for "Dog Woman," the first in the series. In this powerful work, a woman squats down on all fours, lowers her head, and bares her teeth (fig. 7). The earth on which this dark-skinned, squalidly

7   Paula Rego, *Dog Woman*, 1994. Pastel on canvas. 120 × 160 cm. Copyright Paula Rego.
     Courtesy the Saatchi Gallery, London.

clad woman crouches is blackened, the sky gray above her. The brightest spots on the dark canvas are the whites of her glistening eyes.
Sketched from a low angle, she takes up most of the frame. As in the
other works in the series—*Baying, Grooming, Waiting for Food*, and *Scavengers*—Nunes bares her legs and arms to reveal a muscular, strong body,
whose appendages Rego has foreshortened to make her look especially
squatty. Her bare feet and hands, together with her ungroomed head,
are painted large, further giving the impression of brute physicality. The
lips are parted wide but not to speak. Throughout the series, the dog-
women open their mouths to eat, lick, howl, or bare their teeth against
predators, but whatever sounds might arise are bound to be inarticulate.
Thus, although Rego's creatures are still women (not literally hybrid- or
cyborg-crosses as in Lynn M. Randolph's painting *Cyborg* [1989]), their
gestures are unmistakably canine.[6] Their sheer physicality and animality endow this series with its energy. The pastel medium further
enhances such immediacy, for it lends itself to quick work and the
imprint of the artist's hand.[7]

Rego clarified her intent:

To be a dog woman is not necessarily to be downtrodden, that has very little to do with it. In these pictures every woman's a dog woman, not downtrodden but powerful. To be bestial is good. It's physical. Eating, snarling, all activities to do with sensation are positive. To picture a woman as dog is utterly believable. It emphasizes this physical side of her being. What is important is that the dog is the animal most like a human. A dog learns people's ways and behaves like a person; just as people do. Women learn from those they are with; they are trained to do certain things, but they are also part animal. They have independence of body, independence of spirit and their tastes can be quite gross. (Quoted in McEwen 216)

Despite and perhaps because of their feral behavior, Rego's women look extraordinarily natural. Germaine Greer has written of her: "It is not often given to women to recognize themselves in painting, still less to see their private world, their dreams, the insides of their heads, projected on such a scale and so immediately, with such depth and colour" (34). Perhaps it is the way in which the dog-women rest so strongly and flexibly in their bodies that, despite their wild state, women viewers can identify with them, which is to say can identify with dogs.

What underlies, though, this self-recognition in canine behavior? Although Rego stresses that these women are "not downtrodden but powerful," she also intimates that like dogs women have been "trained." Central to this human domestication is a constant auto-surveillance to insure that one is following proper bodily hygiene, dress, and other societal norms that are thoroughly gender linked. Jack Katz has observed that shame "is generated by the virtually constant monitoring of the self in relation to others. Such monitoring . . . is not rare but almost continuous in social interaction and, more covertly, in solitary thought." He goes on to say that *"if this line of thought is correct, shame is the most frequent, and possibly the most important of emotions, even though it is usually invisible"* (210). Shame is all the more oppressive for being largely unvoiced. Rego's work is so explosive because it intimates silent oppression via the will to break free from it. One would like to be an animal in order not to have the self-consciousness that constantly monitors one's behavior. Among the pastels that immediately followed the *Dog Women* series, *Moth* and *Sit* each depict a woman pinned uncomfortably to a chair. In *Moth* the woman presses her arms back, holds her eyes wide open, and cocks her head to the side in a stilting pose. In *Sit*, a title that evokes the obedience command, she holds her arms behind her back with her ankles crossed tightly. Both works depict the constriction of feminine existence, where any involuntary movement would be the cause of shame.

The dog-women, by contrast, break loose from gender constraints in becoming animalistic, and they do so with an uninhibitedness that belies their desperation.[8] They revert to being unkempt and howl their frustrations. Moreover, *Dog Woman*, *Baying*, and *Scavengers* depict wild, stray dogs rather than the abandoned household pet. Their dark, empty backgrounds suggest an inchoate, lonely dread. Model Lila Nunes throws herself into her body, wantonly assuming her poses; her uncovered, muscular limbs signify that this body would be too large to hide in shame. But such liberation comes at a price, for it threatens the return of the very shame one is trying to escape: one is regarded as nothing more than a coarse, shameless dog. Liberation is also never complete abandon for the dog-woman in the sense that she is still tethered to her body: she is a heavy-set creature, earth-bound on all fours. *Bad Dog*, in particular, depicts the woman as an object of contempt and derision, as a dog who has just been thrown out of a bed, presumably by a man.[9] In an alternate reading, one could interpret the leg raised against the bed as marking it with urine. This pastel is the only one in which the woman's head is turned from the viewer, as if to betoken shame. However, even here she is not cringing, suggesting that she is not abashed and has not interiorized the humiliation of being treated as a "bad dog."

A 1986 series of paintings by Rego features girls and dogs, and here, too, repressed aggression is enacted. In each work a girl holds a large dog like a baby, spoon-feeding it, pouring liquid into its mouth, and even shaving its neck. The muzzle is drawn large as if to suggest a Staffordshire terrier, which is to say, a potentially menacing dog, who has become subservient to the ministrations, which are executed not without force and a desire for dominance. The young girls practice exercising control in the domestic sphere. The serious look on their faces makes them appear older and they could be mistaken for women, suggesting that already as girls they realize the constraint that accompanies caregiving and erotic role-playing: they are trying to take command by acting out such roles. Thus, rather than express unalloyed tenderness toward their pets, these girls play sinister juvenile games, as is even more evident in the acrylics that followed the *Girl and Dog* series.

In *Girl Lifting up Her Skirt to a Dog*, the child looks her pet provocatively straight in the eyes as she invites him to investigate under her dress. In *Snare* (fig. 8) a girl has grabbed her dog by the forepaws and looms over his prone body with her voluminous dress, while a surreal-

8 Paula Rego, *Snare*, 1987. Acrylic on paper on canvas. 50 × 160 cm. Copyright Paula Rego. Courtesy Marlborough Fine Art, London.

istically oversized beetle lies on its back in the foreground. In *Abracadabra* a girl holds her arms up over a dog to cast a spell on it, and in *Two Girls and a Dog*, the children play at dressing another helplessly prone dog.[10] A hammer placed next to a vase suggests the latter is waiting to be smashed. And, as in *Snare*, a cut flower evokes the iconography of lost sexual innocence. Could it be that these girls have or anticipate having their bodies manipulated and are transferring the humiliation onto the dog? A repressed anger lies barely under the surface of their playacting. Yet despite the latent violence, the way the girls clutch their dogs suggests the girls' need for affection and for contact with another physical body. Thus, what these earlier works have in common with the *Dog Women* series is an inner revolt against gender constrictions and their accompanying shame: they express a physicality searching for an outlet.

Walter Schels

Shame is inextricably tied to the exposure of being at a disadvantage—of "losing face." Indeed, this simple colloquialism hints at the significant role "face" plays in the conceptualization of shame. "Why is shame so close to the experienced self?" Silvan Tomkins asks. "It is because the self lives in the face, and within the face the self burns brightest in the eyes. Shame turns the attention of the self and others away from other objects to this most visible residence of self" (Sedgwick and Frank 136). Awareness of one's visibility presupposes the gaze of the judging Other. Discomposure arises with the consciousness of being watched, an awareness that does not even depend on the actual presence of an observer, who can be internalized or imagined: self-consciousness means I am watching or monitoring myself, though ironically the cause of shame is that I cannot see myself as others see me.[11]

What happens, though, when the camera as technical apparatus of the gaze is set before the face of an animal? Does it involve shaming? How would one perceive the animal as registering a sense of unworthiness? Could the sense of shame be read in its face or eyes? And does a queasiness or, very differently, a sense of superiority arise in the spectator who watches the animal presumed to be unaware of its observer? These are the complex questions that I want to address with regard to the animal photography of contemporary artists Walter Schels and William Wegman. They work in the genre of portraiture, which features frontal positioning of the sitter and, as in the case of Schels, facial close-ups. What role, then, does face play in their works? Whereas Paula Rego and novelist Carol Emshwiller embody woman's shame by depicting her as an outcast dog, here the dog takes on human poses. Once again, the crossing of the species boundary, the display of the mis-fit, leads to disquieting issues involving shame.

Perplexed by a photograph to which he is drawn, Roland Barthes writes: "I look at it, I scrutinize it, as if I wanted to know more about the thing, or the person it represents. . . . I want to enlarge this face in order to see it better, to understand it better, to know its truth" (*Camera Lucida* 99). He also notes: "Such is the Photograph: it cannot *say* what it lets us see" (100). The beloved pet dog is like a photograph: we watch it attentively and want it to speak to us, so that we can know the truth of its being. But, as with Barthes's photograph, it cannot speak to us to con-firm that what we see is correct. As to animal photography, it is rare, I think, that it reaches the profundity that Barthes seeks: at best it can capture the beauty of the line, color, or eyes of an animal. Pet photog-raphy, in particular, is often merely satisfied with depicting cuteness and cuddliness. Walter Schels, however, eschews both beauty and approachability in his *Animal Portraits* (2001). His close-ups indicate that he wants to "scrutinize" these animals, as if, by "enlarging the face" he might be able "to see it better, to understand it better, to know its truth." His sitters, however, thwart such attempts and remain resolutely unreadable, lending Schels's photography an aura of sagacity.

Schels's canine snapshots are of repulsive curs, made even less attrac-tive by being photographed close to the muzzle and at low angle.[12] Although the collection begins with a shar-pei—with its disconcertingly strange facial folds—most dogs appear to be of the bulldog and pit bull variety, though without any purebred lines. They have drooping jowls, irregular bites, graying muzzles, and puss collected under their eyes (fig. 9). In some photos, the close-up makes the wet, shiny nostrils or tongue look disturbingly foreign and obscenely large. By sheer virtue of this focus on the ugly face, Schels raises the question of shame. Tomkins writes: "The face is the chief organ of general communication of speech and of affect alike. The self lives where it exposes itself and where it receives similar exposures from others. Both transmission and reception of communicated information take place at the face. The mouth talks, the eyes perceive; and the movements of the facial musculature are uniquely related to one's experienced affects and to the affects trans-mitted to others" (Sedgwick and Frank 137). Behaviorally, humans are trained to read the affect of shame in the face; hence we anticipate that a sitter will express a modicum of embarrassment when his or her uncomely features are revealed in the close-up and he or she is aware of the camera. Yet, as Schels points out in the afterword to *Animal Portraits*, animals "presumably do not worry about their appearance. I found this attitude of self-acceptance most often in the very old—and in babies, who are completely unaware of what they look like" (117). Hence Schels's dogs gaze unwaveringly into the camera.

And yet their look is profoundly sad, as if they knew that they were unwanted dogs. In the next sentence, Schels notes that "animals want to be loved as well. Their well-developed instinct enables them to determine very quickly whether they are liked or not" (117). Are his dogs, then, incapable of expressing shame because they are "completely unaware of what they look like" or, if they can feel rejected, is that experience any

9   Walter Schels, "Dog, English Bulldog," 1992. Copyright Walter Schels, Hamburg.

different from the effects of shame? The creatures' eyes do not reveal the answer to their sadness: as Derrida would say, they have a "bottomless gaze" ("The Animal" 381). Because of this pure, unreadable gaze, I believe that the animal psychologist Dennis C. Turner in his introduction to Schels's collection is off the mark when he speaks of the anthropomorphism of these works, maintaining that "we can assess the mood, the emotions, of an animal reliably and consistently just by seeing its facial expression" (6). One does not expect animal behaviorists, with their desire for empirical verification, to articulate the mystery of photography à la Roland Barthes, for art, like the animal, is marked by obliquity. Schels thus demonstrates how we cannot see the animal straight on, however frontally and close to the dog he positions his camera.

The spectator, as a result of this interpretive failure, may avert his or her gaze in shame: the unknowability of the other renders its observer inferior. The dog exists in its thereness, in the excess of its deformities, in a pure visuality heightened by the close-up that cannot be made to signify. Thus, even though in one photo the dog opens its jaws wide, the gaping black hole cannot be made to speak. Abjection, Kristeva writes, is "the place where meaning collapses" (*Powers of Horror* 2). Shame surfaces in another way as well. The spectator may be fascinated by the inaccessible creatureliness but, all too aware of his or her curiosity, may feel that he or she is participating in the dogs' humiliation. The ugliness of the dogs makes looking at the portraits seem invasive, especially because of the proximity of the camera and its unflattering angle. Tomkins writes of the "taboo on looking" (Sedgwick and Frank 144), because one's gaze can arouse shame in the other. In this example of vicarious shame, the spectator, by examining the dogs closely, could feel guilty because he or she imagines doing something that would discomfort the dogs, were they to be conscious of being the object of critical evaluation, for dogs have a strong gaze aversion that signals their self-awareness of being inferior. Thus, on various levels, the gaze in Schels's artwork is oblique: first, the canine eyes cannot represent the interior of their thought and, second, the human eyes, meeting theirs, must turn away downcast, either resigned to this defeat or ashamed by their inquisitive, invasive probing.

William Wegman

The canine portraiture of William Wegman raises similar questions of empathetic shame, but instead of the viewer feeling unsettled because confronted with the ugliness of the animal, here uneasiness arises not only from the odd fit of a dog in human dress but also from one's lurking sense that one's curiosity comes at the expense of the dog subjugated to strange poses. Wegman's Weimaraners need no introduction: one, Man Ray, was on the cover of the *Village Voice* in 1983 as the "Man of the Year." His successor, Fay Ray, became even more famous in countless Polaroid shots, "Roller Rover" being among the best known: the image of the sleek dog in roller skates has been for sale on everything from T-Shirts to posters. Wegman has done spots for *Sesame Street* and *Saturday Night Live*, appeared on David Letterman, and has made several children's books starring his pets, including the retelling of *Little Red Riding Hood* and *Cinderella*. Like the costumed Harlequin, the Weimaraners look sad or pensive at being made the object of display. Do we read their compliance before the camera as resignation or even humiliation? As with the soulful, silent clown, one wonders what thoughts go through their heads and what lies in their souls. Art critic Ben Marks notes the "palpable melancholia to Wegman's art . . . The look of resignation that crosses the incredibly expressive face of Ray is surprisingly profound, even poignant" (56). In the discussion that follows, I want to locate more precisely how this melancholic poignancy arises and where its implications lie.

Whether it be *Turner and Hooch* or *Beethoven*, Hollywood depends on the hilarious situation of the dog being oblivious to how it is perceived: its inadvertent antics make one laugh. Some of this enjoyment undoubtedly comes from feeling superior to the dumb, clumsy dog, from, as it were, the spectator's ability to see the effects of its actions, to which the dog—and often its equally hapless owner—are guilelessly blind. In contradistinction to this latent feeling of superiority, Wegman's work makes one ill at ease for its blurring of the boundaries between human and animal that occurs once the "naked" animal is dressed. At the heart of this distinction between the species lies the question of whether his dogs are self-conscious before the camera, in other words, are liable to shame, and, if so, whether they can distance themselves from it. What bodily affect, at least in terms of how we are trained to read such affect, would betray such self-consciousness?

The breed that Wegman has selected as his signature is not incidental: the short-haired, sleek, muscular, and uniform-colored Weimaraners have a naked look to them. The fact that they are shot partially clothed or disguised likewise evokes the revelation of skin, as is especially evident in the photographs assembled for *Fashion Portraits*. In "Summer Cottage" (1999), for instance, all that can be seen of the dog is a soft gray ear that dangles over a powdery blue cotton dress, illustrating how parts of the body can be fetishistically highlighted. In "Feathered Foot" (1999) and "Walk-a-Thon" (1999) their long legs are made to look glamorous in high heels. Often the discrepancy of the canine body peeking out from under human dress makes this body appear all too visible, as if they were trying to hide behind their costuming, despite the pose that attracts the gaze. Wegman plays on this

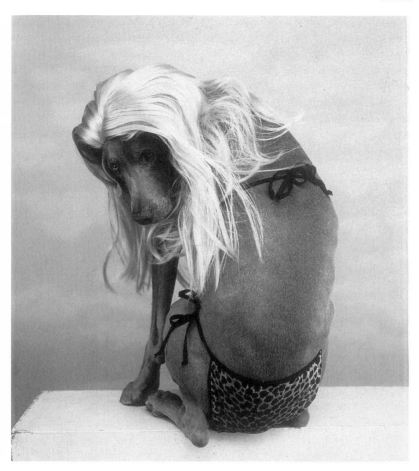

10 William Wegman, "Bikini," 1999. Color Polaroid. 24 × 20 inches. Copyright William Wegman.

nakedness in "Bikini" (1999), where the dog looks uncomfortably out-fitted in a blond wig and bathing suit (fig. 10). Particularly disconcert-ing are the shots where human hands appear from out of the dress, emphasizing the oddity of the dog's face. Yet even more estranging is the paradox that the dogs' expressive, soulful look makes their human drag seem oddly apt.

Kafka's dancing dogs similarly imitated human behavior and were propped up on their hind legs, revealing what the narrator called their "nakedness" (*ihre Blöße*). In fact, the English word "shame" and the

German word *Scham* are derived from an Indo-European root (*skam* or *skem*) that means "to hide" and that is related to the word "skin." By revealing the skin on their stomachs, Kafka's canine dancers make it seem as if they had "alle Scham von sich geworfen" (thrown all shame away). Can one not see Wegman's dogs, too, as compromising themselves in the confusion they create between canine and human—between nature and mimicry?[13] Like Kafka's dogs they seem coerced into an awkward situation. They, too, look as if they would be ashamed were they to break the pose they are commanded to hold. But whose awkwardness is at stake in Wegman's work? Clearly, the artist does not force his dogs to perform and he would desist from photographing them were they actually to feel humiliated. He himself regards them as evolving into mythological beings who are half-human and half-animal, and he literally places Fay on a pedestal where she can feel superior. The awkwardness instead belongs to the viewer who experiences vicarious shame when imagining what it is like to be exposed before a camera. The viewer can also self-consciously feel being toyed with by Wegman who ironically destabilizes species distinctions.

Dress, of course, camouflages the body and deflects the gaze away from it. In photos such as "Duct" (1994), "Cockleshell" (1994), and the series "Evolution of a Bottle in Space" (1999), the dog is almost entirely hid behind massive folds of scintillating, metallic material. In "Scotty" (1999), it is covered in layers of black lace in order to resemble the Scottish terrier. Fashion, however, functions not merely to deflect the gaze; paradoxically, it can also highlight the body all the more. This toying with the gaze can be precarious: the exhibitionism of fashion needs to be faultlessly stylish or it will appear shameful. Wegman has testified that he has "a very awkward relationship with fashion" and, in the introductory remarks to *Fashion Portraits*, Ingrid Sischy writes that it is "full of moments in which we can sense vulnerability, helping provide plenty of chances for the audience to identify" (n.p.). It is clear, then, that even in the elegant *Fashion Portraits*, vulnerability and awkwardness can evoke the workings of shame. Is this the case in Wegman's other works?

In 1996 Wegman created a thirty-minute film starring his two young bitches, Batty and Crooky, as the "Hardly Boys" in *Hardly Gold*, a spoof on the juvenile mystery novel series, *The Hardy Boys*. The adventure story is intriguing for the way in which the artist converts his unique style of photographing dogs into the temporal cinematic medium. The dogs are again dressed as humans, but Wegman faces the additional challenge of how to endow them with voice and movement. In other words, the viewer's sense of shame is enhanced when the dogs' inability to speak and to walk upright are awkwardly camouflaged. Wegman narrates the story in third-person and, for the dialog, in a flat voice "imitates" the characters for the dialogue. Thus the film juxtaposes human voice-over with canine muteness, as well as clothing with nakedness (on one occasion Batty and Crooky are depicted running through the woods without their cumbersome dress). At times Wegman seats the dogs in a floating canoe to give them the illusion of moving from one place to another. At others, he uses a dolly to transport them. The dogs' actual lack of mobility makes them appear like automatons, obediently restrained in their movement as well as by their costumes. Their lack of hands similarly makes them appear like props. And when they turn their heads (the only part of their body that is allowed to break the stay command), they have the look of a bad, distracted actor. This constraint imbues the film with a strange, alienating effect, at the basis of which lies the viewer's discomfort with what appears to be the mortification of the animal body.

Given the above, it is not unsurprising that one of Wegman's children's books, *My Town*, takes humiliation as its major theme. Young Chip has to find a suitable topic for his homework assignment but lacks inspiration. He is under time pressure as it is due the next day, but other kids "have turned in their reports already: nuclear disarmament, global warming, chemistry on parade, etc." With his woeful face, Chip looks like he's a loser. The narrator comments: "Chip should get zipping on that report, or he'll never deliver it" and "the situation is really quite alarming. Chip's homework is due *tomorrow*." Chip meets various schoolteachers and the folk around town in order to enlist their help, but their advice and exhortations seem to cast doubt on Chip's ability and creativity. Town gossip Gladiola Battie even mutters to herself "That boy better buckle down . . . Kids today," while the town doctor pronounces on Chip's depression that once he finishes his report, he'll feel a lot better. Chip eventually completes his report and overcomes his worry and pending disgrace by assembling the photos he has taken on his visits through town. Although the words shame, embarrassment, and humiliation are never mentioned, they form the subtext to this tale.

Throughout *My Town*, as in *Hardly Gold*, the canine-child hero is engaged in a serious investigation and adopts a befittingly solemn mien. That is, Wegman takes advantage of the fact that dogs cannot smile. Europeans are wont to say of Americans' tendency to smile at strangers that they are hiding their embarrassment. Tellingly, one of Wegman's early video shorts, *Rage and Depression*, depicts him grinning before the camera and telling how the muscles in his face froze permanently into a smile while getting electroshock therapy for depression. Here the smile hides his inner pain. The lack of the smile in the animal portraiture, by contrast, underscores that dogs cannot dissimulate before the camera, who thus appear all the more exposed and vulnerable to shame. Given that the genre of photographic portraiture customarily requires a smile, its absence becomes even more disconcerting.

One could argue that the object of Wegman's gentle mockery is not the dogs but the banality and triviality of the genres he copies—the juvenile adventure story, fairy tales, and fashion photography. In *My Town* Wegman recreates the mundaneness and predictability of American small town life. It is uncannily easy to dress dogs up in a mechanic's, fire chief's, or doctor's uniform to make them look like convincing, ordinary human beings. Wegman's deadpan humor could be seen to caricature the platitudes of human speech and behavior, were it not that so much of his recent work is for children. The dogs appear cute rather than ironic. This attenuation of mockery contrasts with the grotesque impersonations in Wegman's early video work (1970–77). What is fascinating is that here it is not the canine but the human body that is on display, inviting a comparison of his earlier and later work in terms of shame. In *Stomach Song*, for instance, the camera focuses on Wegman's fleshy stomach as it moves in synch with the soundtrack, miming a face uttering sounds. In *Deodorant*, he sprays excessive amounts of deodorant on his armpit, spoofing commercials that promise to keep you "feeling good and fresh." In *Horseshoes* he wears painted eyeglasses that make him look as inane as the monologue he holds on how baseball, a team sport, has "more pizzazz" than the game of horseshoes. Wegman's awkward persona in these videos acts as an antidote to shame, insofar as he seems immune to self-consciousness about his homely body and its shameless display of banality.

When Man Ray appears in these videos he may simply wander in and out of the set and is never costumed. His natural behavior is rendered strange via the alienation effects of the medium—either through close-up or the microphone—which is to say it is amplified. For instance, in *Drinking Milk* the Weimaraner laps milk from a glass with the camera and mike at close range. In *Milk/Floor* Wegman juxtaposes bizarre human corporeality with a normal canine response: in the first half of the video he drools a line of milk on the floor from his mouth, while in the second half the dog licks it up. Julia Kristeva's first example of the abject in *Powers of Horror* is milk cream: "that skin on the surface of milk" causes a "gagging sensation," provokes "tears and bile . . . sight-clouding dizziness, *nausea*" (2–3). Wegman literally rejects the milk in a kind of ritualistic performance that is intended to exorcise defilement. He deploys his body in a gross act at the same time that he lets the dog behave instinctively, literally devouring the shame that he has expelled. To put it another way, the human longs for the naturalness that commands the canine, and Wegman's display of his own unclothed flesh signifies a melancholic desire to reclaim his body despite its ungainliness.

My thesis is that once Wegman begins to dress up his dogs and move to the Polaroid medium, the animal is co-opted into the scenario of shame that haunts Wegman's presentation of his own body in his early videos. Once the dogs are dressed up to resemble a person, the unnaturalness and misfit of the canine-human alignment are persistently highlighted. In the videos, by contrast, the dog's appearance serves as a natural foil to the human performance of the abject. Shame, in other words, transmogrifies as Wegman's career progresses, and the question arises whether the dog appears tainted by humiliation in the process. The pressing issue is whether Wegman's more renowned work still offers an antidote to shame or is shame displaced onto the dogs and thereby disavowed?

Wegman forbade laughter on the set, for it could "confuse [the dogs] or hurt their feelings. They *will* get embarrassed. Studio manners were something I became very conscious of while working with Fay due to her fragile and sensitive nature" (*Fay* 64). Wegman's comment is telling for it indicates that he does need to protect his dogs from feeling shame, an emotion of which they were totally capable. I do not want in any way to suggest that Wegman intentionally embarrassed his models, for the cause and concealment of shame are much more subtly operative in his work. Nor do I want to contradict him when he says that his dogs thrived at their work. One can well imagine that they loved to be the center of attention and enjoyed performing. Wegman called Fay the "consummate professional" (*Fay* 102), who even was sensitive to the various styles wigs would lend her (*Fay* 113). She gracefully and elegantly assumes her poses. It is not a stretch of the imagination to then conclude that her awareness of performance also involved a complex relation to the gaze watching her. My older whippet, like Fay, became aware of being photographed and in her advanced years would assume a distanced, refined, even diffident look in her eyes before the camera. It was so aloof that I wondered if it served as a mechanism to deflect the gaze, as if she were thinking: I am aware of being looked at, so I will pose obligingly, but I know it's only a pose.

The Weimaraners' eyes are paradoxically both disarmingly simple yet also, with their unique yellow coloring, the most expressive, enigmatic feature in the photos. Despite the elaborate costuming, we are drawn straight to the eyes. How does one interpret what they want to say? Steve Baker has written that "the *look* of the postmodern animal . . . seems . . . to be that of a fractured, awkward, 'wrong' or wronged thing" (*The Postmodern Animal* 54). Before the camera Wegman's dogs turn their heads distractedly or lift their gazes wistfully upward, as if trapped in their pose yet wanting to be obedient and accommodating. In an optic shyness common to both canines and humans, they glance away, suggesting that they do not wish to acknowledge that they are being looked at and decide not to challenge the gaze on them. Thus, if the dogs do not meet another's gaze, it can signify that they do not want to participate in their humiliation. Particularly disturbing are the fashion photographs where the dogs' entire heads are covered up, as in "Pantyasaurus" (1999), "Pluto" (1999), "Dessert" (1999), "Cream Puff" (1999), and "House of Miyake" (1999). In the series of "Calla Lily" (1999), "Eye of the Dog" (1999), "Hatter" (1999), and "Ben Day" (1999), fashionable hats cover their eyes. Regardless of what the dogs' own feelings are, because these photos evoke the phrase "to cover one's face in shame," the viewer may impute a sense of shame to them. In other words, what makes either the wistful gaze or the very absence of the animal's eyes unsettling for the viewer is that he or she becomes susceptible to empathetic, vicarious shame.

In sum, as with Walter Schels's dogs, Wegman's can arouse empathy in the viewer because of anxieties about the invasiveness of the camera. But is it so invasive? Nothing is ultimately revealed about the psyche of the dogs photographed: they remain unfathomable creatures. Hence the dual cause of the spectator's unease is paradoxical: the camera is both intrusive but not disclosing enough. I want to distinguish, however, between Schels and Wegman in terms of the enigma present in their work.

In 1983 Craig Owens, in an article entitled "William Wegman's Psychoanalytic Vaudeville," addressed the opposition between narcissistic identification and the representation of otherness. He observed: "[Man Ray] represents that measure of alterity that can never be fully assimilated or mastered" (108). He goes on to discuss how, in the video work, the artist attempts to teach Man Ray to spell, smoke cigarettes, and sit still on his lap—all unsuccessfully. Owens concludes: "When we laugh at Man Ray's foiling of Wegman's designs we are also acknowledging the possibility, indeed the necessity, of another non-narcissistic mode of relating to the Other—one based not on the denial of difference, but upon its recognition" (108). Following Owens, Steve Baker concludes: "Man Ray is not seen . . . as a pet. He is not placed in a hierarchical relationship with the artist. Anthropomorphic as the observation may be, the dog's role seems often to be (at the very least) that of co-conspirator. His identity, his status, refuses to settle" (*The Postmodern Animal* 183). According to Baker, Wegman does away with fixed identities in the alliance between animal and human. My suspicion is that, although these observations may be true for Man Ray, more recently Fay and her offspring do not represent an unmasterable alterity, nor are they full co-conspirators. Granted, their cross-species dress exemplifies the undoing of fixed identities, but their costuming and posing can signify constraint rather than the independence Owens and Baker detected earlier.

Moreover, the slickness and high gloss of the fashion photography (it went on international tour beginning in 1999) are evidence of how Wegman's art has become commodified, even a small industry, as any peek into an art museum gift shop reveals. In short, the question of alterity fades before the simulacrum that these photographs have become. Images of the dressed and posing Weimaraner have become so reproduced and familiar with each new children's book that the problem of shame, although a disturbing undercurrent, eventually becomes dulled and disavowed.

Walter Schels, despite mimicking the genre of human facial portraiture, today offers the alterity that Owens located in the early Wegman. Schels and Wegman are similar in that they both impede access to the dog, but Schels because of the inaccessibility of its face and Wegman because of the flatness of the recycled image. Roland Barthes cites Maurice Blanchot's words, which seem to characterize accurately Schels's accomplishment: "The essence of the image is to be altogether outside, without intimacy, and yet more inaccessible and mysterious than the thought of the innermost being: without signification, yet summoning up the depth of any possible meaning; unrevealed yet manifest" (106). But Barthes also noted in his unequaled study of photography in *Camera Lucida* that "photography cannot signify . . . except by assuming a mask . . . the mask is the meaning" (34). Could it be that the garments and fabrics that Wegman drapes over his Weimaraner serve this metaphotographic function of the mask? They externalize that which blocks approach to the animal psyche and reflect the impossibility of photography to access that which—even in the age of postmodernity—we long for it to reveal. Or, as Wegman himself has said, the Weimaraner is aptly called the grey ghost and to photograph it is to work with weaving and darting shadows.[14]

Thomas Mann

Among what Donald Nathanson calls "the many faces of shame" is one that seems, at least initially, counterintuitive. Anger and an over-whelming grandiosity at first appear to be opposites of shame, but only because they serve to camouflage it. Fragile self-respect can be disguised, even to oneself, by a swaggering display of superiority and power. In fact, people who hold contempt or hostility toward others can be particularly vulnerable to any damage to their self-esteem. This denial of shame acts as a defense against it. Just as self-effacement can serve as a protective facade against others' disregard or scorn, so too can self-inflation forestall and avert attack. The disavowal of shame allows one to disassociate from the hurt self—to say "this is not me."

It also leads one to search out an external victim who can represent this "not-me" to oneself and thereby displace the shame. Joseph H. Berke observes the strategy of avoiding "shame by becoming the shamer and making others look bad. In this way, shame and envy act in tandem" (332). To be shamed does not automatically mean one wants to sink into the ground and disappear from the gaze of the Other; on the contrary, when humiliation strikes deeper, it can provoke retaliation. In the concluding sections, I want to examine how the easy target of such retaliation can be the dog. The lowly, servile creature can all too readily be at hand to serve as the object of contempt. "Contempt is closely related to shame and humiliation. . . . Contempt represents one way of handling the buildup of shame beyond a level tolerable to the maintenance of self-esteem. It is . . . the process by which shame may be disavowed as a self-affect, projected into a willing external object (the scapegoat), who then *contains* the subject's shame while allowing him to maintain contact with it" (Morrison 286). The close, familiar contact with the household dog thus permits its owner to preserve externalized this object that represents everything shameful that he denies in himself.

Even more heinous is that the abuse of dogs is never recognized as ignominious by the victimizer. It is precisely because the subject from the outset is covering up and projecting his shame onto the dog that ever more shameful behavior—wanton acts of cruelty—are even less likely to be acknowledged. Moreover, Berke observes that "these people find shameful any indication that they are not bad . . . any weakening of their criminality as extremely shameful, aside from being an insufferable affront to their sense of superiority" (333). If vicarious shame offers the potential for productive social interaction, empathetic failure can be the result of the denial of shame. In the first case identification with the dog is welcomed, while in the second it is shunned and cruelty justified in the mind of the victimizer. In discussing Thomas Mann's story "Tobias Mindernickel," Ulrich Seidel's film *Tierische Liebe*, and Sue Coe's illustrated book *Pit's Letter*, I want to demonstrate how precisely a disavowal of shame, its displacement onto the animal, and cruelty toward it are all linked to a dis-identification.

One of the most renowned dogs in literature is Bauschan, Thomas Mann's hunting dog in "Herr und Hund" ("Bashan and I" [1923]). Less known is a short story by Mann about a painfully shy character who turns out to be hideously cruel to his canine pet. Tobias Mindernickel, perhaps not incidentally, shares initials with his author; indeed the autobiographical account reveals a sinister side to Mann's personality that points in the direction of the fictitious tale. "Herr und Hund" is subtitled "Ein Idyll" and, for its lavish praise of the dog, is frequently excerpted in coffee table collections of sayings about the dog. Far from idyllic, however, are the numerous occasions in which Mann exercises his superiority, both verbal and physical, over the dumb animal.

On one expedition, for instance, Mann teases Bauschan for not catching a rabbit, causing his companion to wag his tail apologetically and ashamedly (*verlegen* [2:461]). But Mann adds that his sarcasm actually veils his own "stirrings of shame [*Scham*] and bad conscience" (2:461), for he helped the rabbit escape. The guileless and, Mann implies, hence rather stupid Bauschan fails to notice the dissimulation. Later in the story, when Mann's amour propre is stung by the dog's admiration for a real huntsman, he locks it out of the house, shrugging his shoulders and scorning the dog, who whimpers for his attention. Like the previous unaccountable, manipulative behavior, the disclosure of this act is narrated without any overt contrition and is doubly shameful for the fact that Mann apparently wants to display his cravenness before the reader, bringing it to light exhibitionistically. One therefore doubts that Mann, at another juncture in the story, sincerely repents in confessing to have whipped his dogs. Some remorse can be detected in the need he has to excuse himself. But the apology he offers is slight: he says he was younger and hot-headed at the time and, besides, the dog's wantonness incited and justified the beating. Mann disavows his cruelty even further by belittling the dog instead of himself: he complains that Bauschan showed no honor and no self-discipline (*keine Ehre, keine Strenge gegen sich selbst* [2:421]) when it squealed at the mere sight of him taking out the leather whip.

If Thomas Mann in the same breath confesses and excuses the shamelessness of his acting out before his dog, he does portray the affect of shame unambiguously in "Tobias Mindernickel" (1898). In fact, this story serves as a perfect illustration of how excruciating shame can lead to its denial through displacement onto the abject dog. It concerns a man so burdened by shame that his eyes "crawl on the ground" before both man and objects (1:106). When he goes out into the streets the children make fun of his old-fashioned black dress and odd physiognomy. On his walks he constantly glances around fearfully, as if a thousand scornful eyes were on him.[15] When indoors his demeanor does not change, leading the reader to surmise that Mindernickel's shame has become so ingrained that he continues to censor his behavior even in the absence of others. It was as if, even after fleeing into the refuge of his flat, Tobias's thoughts were still preoccupied with shame. The only occasion in which the protagonist seems to be transformed is when one of the children taunting him falls down and scrapes himself. Tobias immediately effuses with compassion and binds the child's injured head. His magnanimity lends him confidence but, ominously, a trace of "painful happiness" (1:107) can be detected around his mouth, as if he secretively triumphed at the child's misery.

Since shame is where the inner, personal and the outer, social worlds meet, Thomas Mann begins his story by walking the reader through the city streets, up "The Gray Way" to where Mindernickel lives, onto the apartment landing, and into his quarters. Indeed, during the entire story, private and public places are juxtaposed. Interior and exterior operate metatextually as well: although shame can be read in Tobias's face and gestures, the narrator cannot reveal his thoughts. Because shame is an interiorized and silenced emotion, Mann can only describe his character's actions, which are "enigmatic and beyond all comprehension scandalous [*schändlich*]"(1:105). He then narrates the following developments.

One day while out on a walk Tobias Mindernickel espies a man selling a delicate young hound on a leash. He carefully circles and approaches the hawker and hurries home with his new acquisition, past the laughter of onlookers amused at the sight of him struggling with the recalcitrant puppy. Once in the safety of his apartment, Tobias condescendingly comforts the anxious pet. Afraid of further public derision, he rarely goes outdoors with the dog he names Esau. When resigned to its confined quarters, the creature lies sadly and meekly on the sofa, a behavior that elicits such phrases from its master as "yes, yes, the world is sorrowful, as you are experiencing, however young you are" (1:110). Tobias thus finds satisfaction in projecting his own melancholia onto the dog. When the youngster, though, becomes independent and rambunctious and starts leaping about joyfully, Mindernickel severely beats it into submission, a state of subordination that mirrors his own in the outside world. In another about-face, he then expresses loving, attentive compassion toward the injured dog. In short, this pattern of schizophrenic behavior escalates to the point where Mindernickel stabs the dog to death, as it lifts its "troubled and questioning eyes" on its master, full of "incomprehension, innocence, and lament" (1:112). Mann calls this final deed incomprehensible and infamous, but it is explicable according to the psychology of shame.

Mann describes Tobias's clothing as freshly cleaned and ironed, his face shaven, and hair neatly combed, indicating that the fellow wished to bring his appearance and hence cause of shame under control. Likewise he manically disciplines Esau, as if to insist that he is mastering the situation and conquering disrespect and defeat. On the day, for instance, that Esau escapes into the street and Tobias is especially made the neighborhood laughing stock, the poor animal is mercilessly beaten once indoors. Clearly, Tobias's feeling of inferiority is disavowed by creating a submissive being who can externally embody his wretchedness. Moreover, aggression here serves as a defense against the breakthrough of his own feelings of helplessness. The more shamed Tobias is, the more he needs to deny that shame and transfer it elsewhere.

Given the complexity of shame, this embodiment is split and paradoxical. On the one hand, the dog is both the subdued, harmed creature with which Tobias can empathize and have compassion. Tobias's tidy outward appearance suggests he is unable to acknowledge his feelings of helplessness and loneliness, feelings that he then delegates to the dog and can experience vicariously through it. On the other hand, Esau can also represent the despised Other, someone who is more inferior than he himself is made to feel. Tobias may also be envious (*neidisch* [1:111]) that the dog can express the joy of playful abandon. Shame and envy, as Joseph Berke remarked, "act in tandem" (332). In either scenario—whether Tobias sees himself as empowered to alleviate the hurt or to provoke it—he is no longer the passive victim. Furthermore, he has no apparent remorse about his actions (apart from "weeping bitterly" [1:112] at the end), precisely because he has disconnected himself from the emotion of shame. When the dog is sad, he can identify with him, but he refuses to implicate himself as the cause of that sadness.

Ulrich Seidel

As shame arises when an intimate revelation becomes embarrassing, such intimacy is usually kept under close taps. One example of when disgust can be aroused is when one witnesses others demonstrate immoderate, physical affection for their pets. The display of rubbing, kissing, and cooing is unnerving, especially if, on the cinematic screen, it occurs in the home generally off limits to public spectacle. In a highly problematic flaunting of shamelessness, Ulrich Seidel crosses normal boundaries of social decency in his 1995 feature-length documentary *Tierische Liebe*, entitled *Animal Love* in English but more properly translated as *Animalistic Love*. In a kind of reality TV *avant la lettre*, Seidel stations video cameras in the living quarters of primarily lower-working-class Viennese, although he also shoots inside the luxurious boudoir of an actress, in the bourgeois home of an average middle-class couple, and, at the other end of the social spectrum, in the makeshift trailer of two panhandlers. In tight quarters of either appalling taste (a living-room wall papered with a huge mountain scene) or depressing squalor (paint peeling off the walls in tenement after tenement), he shows paunchy individuals past the prime of life. Often they are clad solely in their underwear as they cuddle their equally homely, overweight dogs: rotund, naked tummies of both human and canine emerge in the same frame. The camera, moreover, is stationary for lengthy shots, entrapping both its object of focus and the uncomfortable spectator. When Seidel's subjects do speak, typically they rant at each other in a near incomprehensible Viennese dialect, engage in phone sex, or read haltingly from sex or dog-training how-to manuals. Seidel makes them appear even more appallingly antisocial by having them interact primarily with their pets and not other humans. The language they do command is that of *Fuß*, *Sitz*, and *Platz*. One dog is instructed to sit and stay on the exit ramp to a highway. Another squats either in confusion or stubbornness as an elderly woman drags it along the floor, coaxing it to heel. Finally, toward the close, one couple set themselves before the camera performing sex "doggy style."

As the documentary is composed without voice-over commentary, countershot to the face behind the camera, or introduction to the featured individuals, several questions arise as to the intent of the filmmaker. One of the main perplexities for the educated, art-house cinemagoer is why Seidel's lower-class specimens display absolutely no shame or self-consciousness. Except for a few exceptions, no one can even be said to be recognizably aware of performing before a running camera. One cannot surmise that these individuals are deliberately shameless in their provocation, because they seem innocently heedless of a critical gaze on them. Instead they are literally shameless, or as it were, oblivious to the remote possibility of shame: they would not recognize themselves as objects of derision. Thus it is not only that human and canine bellies expose themselves together in the same frame, nor that the humans engage in sex in the positions of dogs: the humans resemble their canines in the common lack of shame, especially with regards to their bodily functions, including masturbation and relieving themselves on camera. One might suspect Seidel following in the footsteps of John Waters or Christoph Schlingensief were it not that the absence of self-conscious, over-the-top acting excludes his work from the genre of "trash."

This lack of awareness of how they might be perceived by others makes Seidel's subjects appear self-indulgent, especially because the pets are not presented as beneficiaries of affection and care but as servile objects to gratify the need for physical touch or for the exercise of power and prestige. An example of the latter are the Afghans, the proud possession of a solid(ly) middle-class homeowner, who are made to run ten kilometers a day on a treadmill. Furthermore, Seidel has no interest in capturing the subjectivity that presumably some humans might recognize in their pet and that would prompt their affection. Their amorousness thus appears fatuous and due to emotional, educational, or economic deprivation. One exception is the middle-aged woman who has enough money to travel to the island of Corfu, where she has rescued stray dogs: she introduces each pet by name, as if to announce their individuality. But, in general, Seidel makes no attempt to show the uniqueness, intelligence, responsiveness, or beauty of the various dogs. Even the scene at the pet funeral home where the dog Lady lies in state for a lone mourner is appallingly kitschy: soft music and bird song is piped into the room, followed by the funeral director delivering a cookie-cutter eulogy. A few sequences later, there is a cut to Lady being shoved into the crematorium incinerator, an impersonal, routine procedure that belies the glib sentimentality of the undertaker's farewell address.

The ancient Greek Cynics named themselves after dogs (*kynikos*, literally doglike, from *kynos*, dog) so as to underscore how they, like canines, refused to be embarrassed: they were insolently unabashed in their criticism of social convention. Seidel, too, mordantly exposes the lack of self-dignity in his documentary subjects. Without compassion he lays bare their degeneracy. Hence the elderly woman who mourns

Lady appears ridiculous and undeserving of sympathy. Likewise, the woman whose husband deserted her is presented not with kindness or pity but as pathetic, especially as she comforts herself by smooching with her dog. Seidel is cynical about the unredeemable baseness of his subjects. He is a social satirist, not a moralist. Thus, presumably because the depravity of these individuals speaks for itself, in other words, because they condemn themselves, there is no need for documentary commentary or the overt expression of derision or disgust on the part of the filmmaker. Seidel can thereby cover his tracks. In short, he disassociates himself from the objects of his investigation and disavows his own wanton shamelessness in intruding into the privacy of their homes. He avoids shame by making the other look bad.

In his investigation of how Western philosophy has drawn the lines of demarcation between animal and man, Derrida analyzes Lacan's claim that, whereas animals can engage in disguise or stealth, only man can pretend to pretend. "There is, according to Lacan, a clear distinction between what the animal is capable of, namely, strategic pretense (suit, pursuit, or persecution, in war or in seduction), and what it is incapable of and incapable of witnessing to, namely, the deception of speech [*la tromperie de la parole*] within the order of the signifier and of Truth" ("And Say the Animal Responded?" 130). In addition, to cite Lacan, "*Nor does an animal cover up its tracks, which would be tantamount to making itself the subject of the signifier*" (quoted in "And Say the Animal Responded?" 132). Thus, what makes humans unique, according to Lacan, is their ability to master and manipulate representation to the point of being able to disguise their doing so.

Aside from whether this distinction between human and animal is justifiable (as we shall see, Derrida thinks it is not), it can be used heuristically to clarify Seidel's self-positioning. The filmmaker, by adopting aspects of cinema vérité, feigns that he takes an objective, nonjudgmental view. Social critic Karl-Markus Gauß, on seeing Ulrich Seidel in a TV interview, reports how, when asked about goading his subjects on to display utter abasement, Seidel got a self-complacent look on his face and said, the Austrians were simply like that. He claimed that he would never think of the idea of shaping them according to his designs, of not showing them as they actually are. As if to underscore his ingenuousness, Seidel appeared on camera as quite bourgeois and philistine (as, to quote Gauß, a *Biedermann* [89]). The documentary format of *Tierische Liebe* would indeed seem to confirm the absence of irony. In actuality, though, Seidel is acerbically ironic simply by omitting any self-explanatory commentary.

Seidel thus erects a boundary between himself and his subjects: whereas he hides his disgust, they, like their pets, cannot dissimulate. Seemingly oblivious to the camera, they are unable to indulge in self-irony or self-distancing by deliberately acting out or exaggerating their pet passions. They are neither able to manipulate representation nor capable of recognizing, despite Seidel's protest to the contrary, Seidel's manipulation of them ("incapable of and incapable of witnessing to, namely, the deception of speech"). It is the ignoring of the camera and hence the lack of being able to interiorize the shaming eye and recognize their own shamefulness that makes Seidel's subjects *tierisch*. In other words, Seidel deploys the animal as analogy to belittle the persons he films. Their unreflectedness is epitomized in their impulsive stroking and smothering of their pets. Thus, whereas Lacan utilizes this variation on a definition of consciousness (pretense of pretense) to separate human from animal, Seidel takes this distinction a nefarious step further: he reserves the manipulation of the medium and hence awareness of representation or pretense for himself and denies it to those he documents. He alone, in Lacan's words, is "the subject [as master] of the signifier." He thereby aligns his subjects with animals and denies them status as human beings. Can Seidel's distinction, though, be upheld so rigorously?

Derrida criticizes precisely the deployment of the animal as the term against which the properly "human" is defined:

It is less a matter of asking whether one has the right to refuse the animal such and such a power (speech, reason, experience of death, mourning, culture, institution, technics, clothing, lie, pretense of pretense, covering of tracks, gift, laughter, tears, respect, and so on—the list is necessarily without limit, and the most powerful philosophical tradition within which we live has refused the "animal" all those things) than of asking whether what calls itself human has the right to rigorously attribute to man, which means therefore to attribute to himself, what he refuses the animal, and whether he can ever possess the *pure, rigorous, indivisible* concept, as such, of that attribution. Thus, were we even to suppose—something I am not ready to concede— that the "animal" were incapable of covering its tracks, by what right could one concede that power to the human, to the "subject of the signifier"? Especially from a psychoanalytic viewpoint? . . . Is it necessary to recall that every erased trace, in consciousness, can leave a trace of its erasure whose symptom (individual, or social, historical, political, and so on) will always be capable of ensuring its return? ("And Say the Animal Responded?" 137–38)

With Seidel, it is clear that, as much as he wishes to hide behind the documentary camera, he cannot cover his tracks, that is to say, feign innocence of intruding into others' privacy. Hence, however much he disavows his own shamelessness and claims Austrians "are just like that" (*seien eben so* [Gauß 89]), his superciliousness does return and operates as the guiding question that troubles the film, namely, to what purpose does he desire to expose and shame his subjects, to depict them as shameless? Psychoanalysis uncovers the mechanisms of the disavowal of shame: its symptoms can be retraced through displacement and projection.[16] Whereas Lacan displaces the incapacity to manipulate the signified onto the animal, Seidel goes one step further to displace it onto the human subject, who is then compared to the animal. In both cases, one needs to ask "whether what calls itself [superior] has the right . . . to attribute to himself, what he refuses the animal."

If traces of shame can be read in its disavowal, the converse is also true: shame is always disguised. A shamed person can never conceal well enough the source of his or her shame; he or she wants to disguise the traces of the unguarded self that others can observe. In other words, could it be that the pet owners feel shame about their privacy being invaded but are afraid to manifest it? For how can one distinguish between lack of shame and an invisible shame? What, too, is the effect of this lack of empathetic shame on the viewer? Given that most pet owners are physically close to their animals, it would be hypocritical to be disgusted by the overt display of affection. Thus one would suspect that the squeamishness that *Tierische Liebe* arouses in the viewer is due to one's desire to disavow the identification. Moreover, one is probably also denying one's voyeuristic fascination with abjection and shame in order to indulge in Tomkins's "taboo on looking." This prurient eye is undoubtedly trained on the physical appearance of Seidel's lower-class Viennese. In both the effusive fondling of the pet's body and in the human body spilling out of its dirty clothes, the viewer is lured by fascination with an unsubsumable excess and obscene physicality. Seidel thus encourages his audience to be complicit in his shamelessness.

Sue Coe

If Seidel tries to cover up his own shamelessness by degrading the subjects he films and if Tobias Mindernickel acts with similar cruelty toward his pet hound, Sue Coe is at pains to lay bare such concealment and displacement that lead one to abuse others, be they human or animal. Whereas Seidel lacks compassion, Sue Coe's work is all about empathy. Thus, like Paula Rego, she facilitates identification with the humiliated object. In her frankness and refusal to hide vulnerability she further resembles her fellow female artist.

Sue Coe is one of the most salient social artists working in the United States today. Her illustrations have appeared on the cover pages of the *New Yorker* and the *Nation*, and she has tackled, in her hard-hitting activist art, AIDS, the Gulf War, workers' rights, and the first four years of George W. Bush's administration in *Bully: Master of the Global Merry-Go-Round* (2004). Animal rights are among her most pressing concerns, as can be seen in both *Dead Meat* (1996) and *Pit's Letter* (2000). The former, a visual and written account of Sue Coe's infiltration of numerous slaughterhouses, exposes the meat industry's horrific treatment of both animals and workers. The latter is a foray into the art form of the illustrated book that, in size and format, suggests a children's book, devoted, innocently enough, to a dog narrating its story. Soon upon opening the book, however, the reader confronts a harrowing tale about cruelty toward pets and animal testing.

Pit (as her name suggests, a pit bull) begins by writing to her sister, telling her that she, the sister, is now the lone survivor of their litter of six, intimating that Pit is writing from the grave. She narrates what happens after their mother was taken away and they separated. After living on the street as a puppy, she is picked up by a young boy named Pat Watson, who comes from a cruel home, where his father repeatedly calls him a loser. Pat and his playmates get into mischief and the dog, accompanying them, witnesses their cruelty to insects, rape of a mentally handicapped girl, terrorizing of a homeless woman, and pit bull fighting. In school Pat performs best in biology class when students have to cut up frogs, and he has great faith in scientific experiments, the irony of which later proves to be his demise. On an unsuccessful hunting trip, Pat's father, drunk and angry, raises his fist to strike his son, whereupon Pit defends her friend, with the result that she is abandoned by the roadside. Captured by the pound, Pit is then rescued from death row by a worse fate. She is brought to a laboratory called Eden Technologies Ltd., where men perform hideous experiments on animals, trying to isolate, for the defense department, the gene for empathy. Pat suddenly reenters Pit's life as one of the technicians, however he fails to recognize his old pal. Inadvertently scratched by one of the monkeys, Pat falls ill, becomes himself the object of gruesome experiments, and dies. The ghostly Pit watches over his grave.

Sue Coe juxtaposes the most disparate elements to create her striking tale—grim, unrelenting social realism, a nightmarish, surrealistic vision, and the sentimentality of the anthropomorphized story of an orphaned dog. She indicts bioengineering, sexism, war, hunting, animal "shelters," the prison industry (that tests on humans), the meat industry (animals are dumped into a giant meat grinder), and the Bible ("God gave you dominion over all living things"). What makes her art so powerful is not only her plea for activist intervention but also the visceral quality of her illustrations. She confronts the dilemma of how to make the silent animal speak its pain. She does this not only by giving Pit human language but by depicting affect graphically on the body of the animals: monkeys hunch over in grief, and Pit's eyes swell with sadness. The mortification of the animals is unequivocally represented: the stray dogs who scrounge for food are terribly emaciated, and the creatures experimented on are splayed open while still alive. Because of the anthropomorphization, Steve Baker has accused Sue Coe of sentimentality (178–79), which runs counter to the trend of a deep suspicion of it he otherwise discerns in postmodern art and which he perceives as detrimental to her moral and political outrage. The starkness of her drawings and the harshness depicted in them would seem to challenge Baker's charge of an aestheticized sentimentality. Nonetheless, serious questions do arise: Can one express empathy without falling into sentimentality? Is anthropomorphism dangerous for not realizing the otherness of animals? And isn't trying to give voice to animals deeply problematic because one assumes human symbolic language can breach the divide?

Clearly, Sue Coe grasps the implications of disavowing identification with the vulnerability of animals, but that does not mean she falls prey to its opposite and lapses into the ease of a cloying identification. She realizes that the profound loss of animal dignity and life necessitates recourse to an emotive plea for empathy. But she does not desist from physicality and shock either, which is achieved paradoxically less through pictorial realism than through the artifice and exaggeration of an expressionist stylization. The starkness of her drawings, the rounded, hunched figures, as well as the trenchant social commentary, are highly evocative of the Berlin artist Käthe Kollwitz. In addition, some of the illustrations reach the apocalyptic dimensions and detailing of cruelty of Breughel. Coe underscores such artifice by citing the iconography of the Crucifixion and the Last Judgment, though, heretically, it is animals who are on the Cross and writhing in pain from a mass judgment inflicted by devilish humans. She stages an *apokalypsis* in the Greek sense of the term as a laying bare, here of the atrocities committed against animals. As if she were the eye of God, she adopts an all-seeing gaze on their immense suffering.

Although by no means tender or weepy, *Pit's Letter* does impart a melancholic, elegiac tone. This quality has not only to do with the fact that Pit is writing from the grave, nor solely with the black-white-and-gray or sepia tones of the illustrations, but with the detailed, lavish artifice or hypersignification that bespeak the necessity of sublimation in order to cope with the sadness. The artifice is thus both manic spectacle and depressive shield against loss. As Julia Kristeva writes: "Naming suffering, exalting it, dissecting it into its smallest components—that is doubtless a way to curb mourning" (*Black Sun* 97). Coe's ornate canvases and the hyperbole expressed within them, which extends to the anthropomorphism and sentimentalism Baker criticizes, must be seen as her valiant attempt to signify a loss whose proportions are immeasurable. Also indicative of her melancholia is the inability to seal the borders between herself and the object of her representation, to wit, between human and animal—and this despite her desperate recourse to the distance of artifice. According to Freud, the melancholic cannot separate herself from the lost beloved object. With her deliberate underscoring of empathy, however, Sue Coe hints that melancholia is not a sickness to be pathologized but must be identified as a strategy for protest and survival. In contradistinction, then, to Thomas Mann and Ulrich Seidel, Sue Coe refuses to disavow identification in *Pit's Letter*, a work that investigates empathy on many fronts.

The alliteration of their names, Pit and Pat, already points to the common bond between human and animal. Although the humans constantly brush aside any resemblance between their suffering and that of the animals, as if to deny the shame of their own lot, Pit voices full compassion for the plight of humans: even at the end she exhorts her sister not to hate them. Thus, she is not just a symbol of privation but also of dignity. At Eden Technologies she licks the face of a blinded cat and a dog with an exposed spine so as to give them comfort. And in an amazing reversal of the animal/human dichotomy, it is the dog who experiences vicarious shame over the human's shameless behavior. It is thus in Pit that the gene for empathy is isolated, represented visually by Pit's eye reflected in Pat's face (fig. 11). In the mirror held up to the human, the canine offers a version of a truer self. Sue Coe, of course, also encourages her reader to imagine humans exchanging places with the animal, which she facilitates by such disparate techniques as the first-person narration and the representation of animals on Golgotha.

Coe also portrays the psychology behind the lack of empathy. When the father is humiliated by an unsuccessful hunting trip, he compensates by calling Pat a sissy like his mom. In turn, the boys displace their

11 Sue Coe. *Found*, 1998. Graphite and watercolor on tan sketchbook paper mounted on white Strathmore Bristol board. Copyright Sue Coe. Courtesy Galerie St. Etienne, New York.

shame onto the weaker members of society, the homeless and the mentally handicapped, exposing them to ridicule: "Pat got a good feeling by acting strong with his friends, only acting strong meant being a bully, just like his father." Belittled by his parent, Pat lacks secure ego boundaries and, like Tobias Mindernickel, perversely needs to fortify them by displacing inferiority and inflicting pain on others, be they animals or women. As Pit herself notices in simple prose, "the strong ones bully those who are not as strong; the bullied find others with even less power, to bully. It makes the bullies feel strong." Not until the very end, when he himself is made to undergo experimentation does Pat realize how he shares inequality and degradation with the animals.

Whereas shame trades in secrecy and avoidance of public scrutiny, Coe is not afraid to depict the poverty of the human spirit and animal misery. Given the foreclosure of grief that Western society demands vis-à-vis the loss of animal life (and about which I shall have more to say in chap. 4), it is significant that she is intent on signifying the pain of animals and mourning their deaths. In a world where animal death is not grieved, it is up to Pit to keep loyal vigil instead, as she watches over Pat at his gravestone. She herself goes unmourned and lacks a proper burial, which might explain why she returns as undead. She comes back as a specter to write her otherwise silenced story, signing the letter to her sister, "All my ghostly love, Pit." And we, as the ones wanting to disavow animal shame and death, are haunted by her voice, by the return of what we repress.

It goes without saying that to write from beyond the grave is impossible, as is to have a dog tell her story. But these narrative strategies demonstrate to what lengths Sue Coe must go to lend voice to the voiceless and how daunting and, on final account, unachievable her task is. Sequestered away in pounds, abattoirs, or laboratories, the shame and suffering of animals are largely hidden in today's society. Symbolic of such silencing, at Eden Technologies their vocal chords have been cut because neighbors in the residential district had complained about their whines and cries. Given this imposed voicelessness, Coe fashions the counterspectacle, a visceral and visible resistance to oppression that wants, so to speak, to talk back. But how can one have the animals "talk back"? When Coe ventriloquizes for Pit, she has the dog speak unambiguously and lucidly of her bewilderment; Pit is forthright about her feelings in utter contrast to the myriad ways in which humans try to conceal the shame of their misery (as the father does). Aware of how dissimulating human language can be in order to cover up abuse of animals, Coe sees the need to cut through the deception by the starkness of her drawings and with Pit's unrelenting guilelessness.

But, ultimately, Coe melancholically realizes the inevitable failure of symbolic language; it can never meet the pressing need of animals to communicate with us. Her excessive anthropomorphization underscores the actual nonreciprocity between human and animal. Thus Sue Coe represents what must remain unrepresentable: not only would in reality what she depicts be too atrocious for images, but animals, of course, cannot represent, as Pit does, what happens to them. Coe signals toward this inaccessibility. Her subject matter eclipses its own representation, which is paradoxically why she takes recourse to extreme anthropomorphization and to an exaggerated style bordering on caricature. Hers, then, is a drawing about limits—how animal suffering marks the boundary to human comprehension, representation, and capacity for empathy. Her grand accomplishment, however, is to take us to these limits.

THREE

Intimacy

The June 19–26, 2000, issue of the *New Yorker* published a poem by Margaret Kemp Ross entitled "I Married My Dog." It whimsically and briefly recites the incidence of a conventional wedding ("I was simply beautiful / and my dog looked nice, too"), mundane nuptials ("We put on our nightgowns and fell asleep"), and a typical morning after. The bride arises first, so as to greet her "husband" when he comes down. But when she says good morning, "he didn't notice. / He just lay on the floor, eating." She combats her fleeting disappointment by wedding her cat, whose sex remains queerly unspecified as would befit a socially uncustomary alliance. Left implied is what prompted the woman to marry her dog in the first place—a desire for contentment, domesticity, and closeness. In his accompanying illustration William Steig depicts wife and cat curled up together on the couch, smiling.

However humorous and sweet, "I Married My Dog" hints at a profound aspect of human need. Because the speaker of the poem can never have enough physical warmth and comfort, she wants more than one pet, in other words, more than a husband. And what she really wants is acknowledgment from her dog, usually by nature so attentive, in which he suddenly falters. For, in general, the dog promises not just physical intimacy but the sense that one is recognized in one's very being; one becomes close to oneself or collectedly calm in the canine presence. Perhaps this tranquility— this peaceful state of integration and reparation—is what defines intimacy and trust, and perhaps it can be best attained not with another human being but with one's pet.

Rosalyn Drexler paints a much more satirical view of marriage in *The Cosmopolitan Girl*. Published in 1974, this riotous, picaresque novel tells of the narrator's unusual dog Pablo who has the gift of human speech. It begins startlingly: "Pablo has confessed his love for me. I was stunned. I knew that he was fond of me, the way her licked my hand and slept at the foot of the bed barely moving so as not to disturb me. But a declaration of love!" (13) As Pablo never escapes his doggy nature (licking in this example), Drexler can humorously cut from the ridiculous anthropomorphizing of this talking animal to reminders of his instinctive canine habits. For instance, when Pablo and Helen marry and he is instructed to kiss the bride, first he sniffs under her dress and then slobbers over her face. More cynically than Kemp Ross, Drexler parodies the tedium of wedding rituals. For instance, Helen muses: "Instead of going to a pet store for Pablo's wedding gifts I wandered around town picking up things he might never use. I wasn't sure whether or not to satisfy his fantasy that he is a man. For instance, what would he do with a Hermes tie? Drag it across the floor? And that language record for his trip to France . . . he barely speaks his own language" (173). When a female friend tries to warn her of getting hitched to a lazy, unemployed slob and that they will have battles over such trivialities as "hair on the floor and in the bath" (177), Helen replies: "I am getting married to Pablo because I truly love him and because we have formed an alliance against those of you who think you know the way things should be." (174) She continues, taking a swipe against the messiness of sex: "Living with Pablo will be the ultimate in gracious sexual living . . . I won't have to use the Pill . . . no diaphragm, gel, foam, or abstinence" (174).

To reframe marriage and sex in terms of one's dog, as Kemp Ross and Drexler do, is to insist on the appropriateness of one's passion for a dog, even to the extent of challenging normative assumptions about the appropriate marital-sexual relationship. They delight in silliness and satire as if to divert attention away from the seriousness of their provocation. Dog and woman indeed form "an alliance against those of you who think you know the way things should be." These two works raise the questions of how intimacy with pets is different and special, and why this desire would be so strong as to carry erotic overtones. If romantic attraction is expressed as fascination with a mysterious someone of the opposite sex, Kemp Ross and Drexler seem to ask, why cannot this someone be of an opposite species? Thus, mimicking conventional romance, Helen proposes that she and Pablo should "know everything about each other. . . . Here we are, just the two of us . . . let's open our hearts to each other" (48). In this passage *The Cosmopolitan Girl* parrots and parodies norms in courtship, sex, and marriage. By contrast, the speaker in "I Married My Dog" truly desires such marital intimacy, but redefines it as bypassing sex for the comforting domesticity of night-gowns and for the other sensuality of lying together with her dog in bed. Whereas Drexler teases the prudish reader with bestiality, Kemp Ross reclaims pet intimacy from the label of perverse sexuality. Not without a certain feminist verve, both pieces reassess where intimacy for women can be found. They define the natural not as something normative, aver-age, and socially prescriptive but as an ideal of harmony.

For many people, desire for closeness to a pet needs to be repudiated because it implies insufficiencies on one's own part, such as a malad-justment to social norms, as if the pet were a second-class replacement for human companionship or kinship and not something wholly dif-ferent. Petting might even vaguely be seen as a meager substitute for more proper physical intimacy (between humans). In either case, one refuses to contemplate that the animal would complete oneself, for to do so would admit to weakness. In the chapter, "Unconditional Lovers" in her book *Dog Love*, Marjorie Garber discusses this gesture of conde-scension or pity with which "compensation" through the dog is regarded. She writes: "The point is perhaps not to argue about whether dog love is a substitute for human love, but rather to detach the notion of 'substitute' from its presumed inferiority to a 'real thing.' Don't all loves function, in a sense, with a chain of substitutions? . . . To distin-guish between primary and substitutive loves is to understand little about the complexity of human emotions" (135).[1]

But could one, in fact, as Rosalyn Drexler and Margaret Kemp Ross do, invert the accepted hierarchy of affections? Dog love has the poten-tial to question the regulating strictures and categories by which we define sexuality, eroticism, and love, though not in the sense that it offers different forms of genital stimulation, indeed quite the opposite.[2] Dog love corroborates Lacan's famous dictum: "Quand on aime, il ne s'agit pas de sexe" (when one loves, it is not a question of sex [27]), whether "sex" be interpreted here as intercourse or as the sex of the per-son one loves. Those who have an ardor for dogs know that such pas-sion is unavailable and inaccessible elsewhere: it opens up the subject in unique ways that, precisely because independent of gender and sexual-ity, are liberating. Moreover the relation to the dog cannot be restricted to the singular role of guardian, lover, companion, or child but incor-porates all of those modalities and shifts among them.

In the course of this chapter I want to discuss several works by women writers who, like Kemp Ross, Drexler, and Garber, broach the complex topic of intimacy with dogs. These are writers who refuse to categorize the female-canine experience conventionally, as being either sentimental or, quite the opposite, sexually illicit.[3] But they do discover a different passion, intensity, and tactile knowledge. Above all, these writers learn that, by virtue of its close companionship, the dog offers nearness to their very selves, a certain calmness or equilibrium, or what Elizabeth von Arnim characterizes with the French word *recueillement*—a kind of gathering together of oneself in a peaceful, contemplative mode. Although many of these works ostensibly recall the life of a dog, they actually recollect the scattered self, a task that is accomplished through the process of writing about daily interactions with the dog. They record a lived togetherness that, although often experienced in solitude, alleviates loneliness. In this relation of trust, acceptance, and calm security, doubt and uncertainties about the self become less pressing. Moreover, by remembering seemingly insignificant moments of tenderness and mutual devotion these women authors engage in the representation of affect, affect being the qualitative expression of emotional energy, the subjective response or translation of experience. It is through the therapeutic rememorizing or revivification of affect—in other words, the exteriorization and embodiment of subjective, lived emotion—that the self becomes signified.

I want to postulate that such *recueillement*, or recovery of a collected self, serves in healing melancholia and shame, both variations of self-deprecation. Combating the threat of depression, the pet helps the female character restore a lost subjectivity and combat a sense of inauthenticity. As the Chinese-American author Betty Lim King muses in *Girl on a Leash: The Healing Power of Dogs: A Memoir* (1998): "Dogs trigger memories whose meanings I could not apprehend at the time. Remembrance of pets past and present brings clarity and wholeness to the bits and pieces that make up the collage of a bewildering life" (3). The peaceful presence of the dog reknits the self that had previously disintegrated in melancholia or, in Lim King's case, through the experience of exile. These authors, then, narrate the ongoing process of coming to oneself, not so much through friendship or chumminess with the dog as through a private, deep-seated familiarity, co-situatedness, or what I like to call intimacy. Synonyms for intimate include not only "close" and "dear" but also "innermost" and "intrinsic."[4] Intimacy allows the bond with the animal to be affirmed and, as such, it rebuilds one's sense of inner strength, as opposed to the melancholic disavowal of the object and shame at feeling this identification. This self-exploration entails the opening up of oneself to life with a wholly different species—hence the object is recognized as separate from oneself. Yet there is also the discovery, through the mutual closeness, that this other, foreign, often abject being can be part of oneself. Instead of this part being suppressed and denied, as in melancholia, it is acknowledged and articulated in writing. The female protagonist or speaker can explore the recesses of a personal longing that somehow resonates with the creaturely needs of her dog. Paradoxically then, the dog—a being often denied its own subjectivity—here grants subjectivity.[5]

In reflecting on the difficulties in divulging his "private life," Roland Barthes juxtaposes two ways in which the term can be misconstrued. For the right (the "bourgeois, petit bourgeois: institutions, laws, press"), "it is the sexual private life which exposes most." Here the assumption is that the word "intimacy" is to be equated with genital acts. But for "the left, the sexual exposition transgresses nothing: here 'private life' is trivial actions. . . . I am less exposed in declaring a perversion than in uttering a taste: passion, friendship, tenderness, sentimentality, delight in writing then become . . . *unspeakable* terms" (*Roland Barthes* 82–83). Here the danger in divulging an intimate life is that it will be associated with feeling and emotion, which contain "the traces of bourgeois ideology confessed by the subject." Yet, Barthes openly admits, this is what "you would like to be able to say *immediately* (without mediation)." He implies that such directness also risks inauthenticity.

These dual dilemmas—either the shame in voicing the inappropriate or the difficulty in making one's language apt—are compounded when the "private life" involves closeness to a pet. The photographer Robert Adams, in the introduction to his beautiful collection of pictures of a West Highland terrier in her backyard, addresses the liability of intimacy: "We want of course to avoid sentimentality. . . . In theory the word refers to unearned emotion, emotion disproportionate to the facts." Yet he also acknowledges that "we need a different measure, one by which even small lives and modest safe havens are recognized as important" (6). Endearment to the pet will perhaps always be susceptible to the charge of sentimentality, but disparagement over this "*unspeakable*" attachment is especially a risk women artists face. Those discussed in the following pages truly seek, in Adams's terms, "a different measure" and are aware of the formidability of the task of redefining intimacy to include the pet.

Such a defense and reclaiming of emotion find precedence in feminist responses to animal rights theory. In the 1990s Josephine Donovan and Carol Adams mounted a challenge to Peter Singer and Tom Regan not only for eliding the differences between animals and humans and hence treating them as equal autonomous agents (instead of seeing animals as in need of protection).[6] Donovan and Adams also charged them of devaluing and denying the role of feelings as central to an ethical theory. They recognized that there is an emotional basis for many human decisions and that sympathy, which plays an important role in recognizing animal suffering, cannot be discounted as being irrational. Donovan urges: "[Sympathy] involves an exercise of the moral imagination, an intense attentiveness to another's reality, which requires strong powers of observation and concentration, as well as faculties of evaluation and judgment. It is a matter of trying to fairly see another's world, to understand what another's experience is. It is a cognitive as well as emotional exercise" (152). These writers also countered that many responses to animal suffering are particularized and situational, not always universalizable, as Regan's and Singer's tenets were. Hence they accepted that the near and local might be privileged over the distant, opening the door to acknowledging the role that pet keeping has in concretizing the animal other.

My attempt to recuperate "intimacy" as a productive category does more than echo the valorization of emotion by feminist animal advocates. The word also resonates with the phrase "attentive love" that Donovan and Linda Vance have borrowed from Simone Weil, Iris Murdoch, and Sara Ruddick. These writers characterize "attentive love" as a way of looking that acknowledges affliction in the individual other and responds to it. Donovan quotes Murdoch: "The direction of attention is . . . outward, away from self which reduces all to a false unity, toward the great surprising variety of the world, and the ability to so direct attention is love" (163). Sara Ruddick, whose *Maternal Thinking: Towards a Politics of Peace* has influenced the feminist animal caring ethics, writes that "attention lets difference emerge without searching for comforting commonalties, dwells upon the *other*, and lets otherness be" (122). The authors and photographers discussed in the following pages are, in all their closeness to dogs, eminently mindful of the distinctiveness of the other species, an alertness, even vigilance, that permits them to avoid the pitfalls of sentimentality.[7] It is paradoxically the foreignness of the dog's being that grants intimacy with them its power.

This respect for the dog in turn gives rise to another reversal, whereby the conventional oppositions and strictly policed boundaries between human/animal, cultivated/ignorant, tame/feral, and self/other are called into question. Writers such as Elizabeth von Arnim, Natalie Kusz, Pamela Stewart, and Rhoda Lerman acknowledge that the dog's own "attentive love" can be exemplarily courteous, accommodating, and gracious. To rephrase, in these authors it is not the human being (traditionally male) who is the paragon of virtue or stable referent against which the animal is measured and deemed, inevitably, to fall short, but the contrary. With the animal now the one bestowing care, the meaning of "animal caring ethics" is given a new twist.

Elizabeth von Arnim

According to Greek mythology, the gods took pity on Orion when they banished him from the earth and exiled him to the skies. Recognizing his need, they gave him the gift of the dog Sirius, who, also a star, follows his master as he moves through the firmament. This narrative of banishment and loneliness is notably different from another narrative of journey and hardship—that of coming of age. Stories and movies that tell the adventure of a young boy and his dog always involve a socialization process for the boy, often signifying the boy's maturation through the perils the dog encounters; the dog thus functions as his surrogate. Such is the case with the famous film classic and model for subsequent remakes, *Lassie Come Home* (1943). Exiled from the boy she loves, Lassie spends much of the movie enduring cold, hunger, and injury in trying to return to him. Lassie finally makes it back to her young master (Roddy McDowall) and, in the reconciliation of class differences, brings him together with the little rich girl (Elizabeth Taylor).[8] In watching the film, the young male spectator can identify with the dog, who serves to initiate him into life's hardships, more so than sole identification with the helpless stay-at-home male protagonist could accomplish.[9]

The narrative of women and dogs differs starkly from this juvenile male narrative of maturation, for it is centered not on trials and tribulations but on a kind of inner seclusion and exile. Retreat from the world, not struggle with it, typifies these stories of *recueillement*. Like Orion, the woman has the company of her dog in solitude. Elizabeth von Arnim (author of several novels, including *Elizabeth and Her German Garden* [1898] and *The Enchanted April* [1922]) narrates her own life of exile in *All the Dogs of My Life* (1936). Significantly, though, she counters geographical displacement with the emotional security offered by her dogs. First, she marries into Pomeranian nobility and lives on her husband's estate in this remote eastern part of Germany. Once widowed, she moves to England and subsequently to Switzerland and Provence. Marking the circumstances in her life are her succession of dogs: indeed, she measures the important stations in her life not by place of residence, marriages, the birth of her children, or political upheavals but by the character of the dogs she owned.

Solitude and retreat figure as important resources for "Elizabeth" as she was known to her reading public: "Moments of wonder and blessing. And I who had been afraid I might be lonely! Lonely? It was here, in the first complete solitude I had ever known, that I began to suspect that what is called loneliness is what I love best" (84). Unaccompanied walks with her dogs provide her with a simple contentment: "These very things, just sun on my face, the feel of spring round the corner, and nobody anywhere in sight except a dog, are still enough to fill me with utter happiness. How convenient. And how cheap" (27). Part of her joy comes from her being utterly alone: "How beautiful this security seemed to me, this enchanting security of knowing oneself unnoticed and unseen!" Solitude—in other words, the quiet composure of oneself in the sole presence of dogs—is thus set in direct opposition with loneliness: "I for one am unable to imagine how anybody who lives with an intelligent and devoted dog can ever be lonely" (81). Conceivably, it is the dog's own sense of place in the world—something that Elizabeth lacked in being so often uprooted—that lends her the sense of rest and belonging.

"I recommend those persons of either sex, but chiefly, it would seem, of mine, whose courage is inclined to fail them if they are long alone, . . . who are full of affection and have nothing to fasten it on to, . . . I would recommend all such to go, say, to Harrods, and buy a dog" (86). Because such a passage would seem to suggest that dogs compensate for the absence of human companionship, it is important to stress that solitude is something the author, with a succession of children, friends, suitors, and spouses in her household, consciously seeks. Although she often fails and, for instance, finds herself remarried and living apart from her dogs, she tries to resist adaptation to early twentieth-century social norms. Solace for her lies outside gender strictures in the enjoyment of her widowhood, solitary walks, and writing, all inseparable from the presence of a dog. She recognizes "that need for something more than human beings can give, that longing through greater loyalty, deeper devotion, which finds its comfort in dogs" (5). Indicating how unconventional this desire for the nonhuman can be, she tells of a misunderstanding between herself and her husband when she voices her sense of amputation and desire to be "complete": "And he was, I am afraid, very much disappointed, in spite of there already being five children, when I explained that all I wanted was a dog" (48). The fact that the relationship with a dog is here juxtaposed with procreation suggests that it is desexualized in the sense that it releases Arnim from the male-female binary. In being with the pet, such divisions dissolve, leaving room for a different kind of tactile and emotional intensity.

The integrity of being for which Elizabeth von Arnim so deeply longs and that she finds beatifically granted in the company of dogs is what she calls *recueillement*: "In this condition, then, of enraptured *recueillement*, of fusion with I don't know what of universal and eternal, I spent each night before going to bed" (85). Such *recueillement* occurs at a time of quietude and meditation: the recentering and yet opening up to the "universal" transpires in the calm and shelter that the canine presence bestows. The dog may not "outweigh the sorrows" but it does encourage the writer "back to something almost like contentment" (147). Lest *recueillement* be conceived as narcissistic self-absorption, Elizabeth herewith indicates that, rather than become preoccupied with worries and grief, she steps outside this solipsism. Her solitude and concentration are only possible with a being that is likewise apart, equally in its own world.

The temporal factor Elizabeth von Arnim here broaches is important: the soothing ritual of being with her dogs "each night" before going to bed evokes the "eternal," aids her in recovering a calm, composed self unafraid of loneliness, and restores a sense of purity. The significance of repetition for the paradisiacal state in which canine and human can inhabit together is heralded in one of the most eloquent tributes to the dog, Milan Kundera's *The Unbearable Lightness of Being* (1982). Significantly, it is the female character, Tereza, to whom it is given to ponder most deeply the relationship to the dog, named Karenin. As the novel depicts her worried but unwavering love for her philandering husband, it comes as a surprise at the end to read: "The love that tied her to Karenin was better than the love between her and Tomas. Better, not bigger. . . . The love of man and woman is a priori inferior to that which can exist (at least in the best instances) in the love between man and dog, that oddity of human history probably unplanned by the Creator" (297). Kundera pursues the allusion to the biblical Creation story: "No one can give anyone else the gift of the idyll; only an animal can do so, because only animals were not expelled from Paradise. The love between dog and man is idyllic. It knows no conflicts, no hair-raising scenes; it knows no development. Karenin surrounded Tereza and Tomas with a life based on repetition, and he expected the same from them. Human time does not turn in a circle; it runs ahead in a straight line. That is why man cannot be happy: happiness is the longing for repetition" (298). It is the same "life based on repetition" that offers

Elizabeth von Arnim a sense of the eternal and guarantees her an idyllic existence in the midst of exile.[10]

The connection between repetition and life with the dog also provides Stephen H. Webb a springboard for his profound, wide-reaching study on animal rights theology, entitled *On God and Dogs*. Webb finds "in the extravagant gesture of petting, of bending down to touch, an act worthy of reflection, repetition, and amplification" (106). "The human-dog relationship," he argues, "always entails a dimension of extravagance and excess on both sides, [which] can empower our lives with an outward emanating care" (101). It is this excess or surplus, best symbolized in the pointless but endlessly repeated act of petting—both simple and lavish—that opens the human mind to liberality and munificence. Playing further on the notion of excess, Webb writes: "The dog is always more than we know, extending beyond our knowledge and calling on us to match his or her excess with acts of generosity of our own" (102). "The anxiety of the question 'What do you mean to me, and I to you?' or 'What can we give to each other?' allows us to see in the other more than what we find in ourselves and to pass on this surplus to others in turn" (101–2). If the dog enables one to gather oneself together in *recueillement*, it also draws one out of oneself to discover a creature who can offer "more than what we find in ourselves."

E. J. Bellocq

Stephen Webb also postulates that "petting can overcome the arrogant eye" (83).[11] Women's literature on dogs frequently juxtaposes the human with the canine gaze. The confirming, benevolent gaze of the dog disempowers the arrogant male eye that traditionally inspects and judges women. Kundera, for instance, writes in reference to Karenin's gaze that "Tereza knew that no one ever again would look at her like that," implying that her husband never would (300). Sharpening her own powers of observation in response to the dog's keenness, Elizabeth von Arnim notices: "Rarely did he take his beautiful, kind eyes off me. When he went to sleep, and was obliged to shut them, he still had the thought of me vivid in his heart, for at my faintest small movement he instantly opened them, and looked at me inquiringly, as if asking whether there was anything I wanted and he could do" (203).

For Elizabeth von Arnim, the dog's "attentive love" constantly notices her presence. To put it another way, it confirms her being in her slightest movement and emotion. Pamela Stewart stresses the significance of such confirmation, especially to counteract the judging, arrogant gaze of others, in her poem "Newfoundland-Praise."[12] It begins: "On days I don't feel pretty I go downstairs / and watch my dog stretch and yawn awake. / Molly doesn't care how my lank, electric hair / sticks to my mouth, how my eyelids swell / from bad dreams." At the start of the poem, then, the speaker is presented as self-deprecatingly interiorizing the critical gaze of others. Perhaps it even haunts her dreams. After innocently describing Molly's daily pastimes, the poem returns at the close to the speaker's sense of vulnerability: "Molly undoes my vanities and fear so I / feel almost safe." The single word "almost" betrays the dimensions of her fear and insecurity. But the final word "safe" emphasizes how effectively the immense dog shelters her from anxiety and bestows her with praise. The speaker can make emotional contact with another being who does not violate or distort her sense of integrity.

Stewart and Kundera implicitly compare the canine with the male gaze. The dog is therewith not a convenient substitute for a male partner but quite the opposite—a compassionate antidote to the shame suffered in a male-dominated world. The turn-of-the-century New Orleans photographer Ernest J. Bellocq demonstrated the ability of the pet dog to counteract the male gaze in three of his amazing photographs of Storyville prostitutes. Nan Goldin wrote that the collection contained "among the most profound and beautiful portraits of prostitutes ever taken" (89). And no less a stellar figure than Susan Sontag has opined that Bellocq's "pictures are unforgettable . . . how touching, good natured, and respectful" (7–8). Conceivably, the woman posing for the pornographic camera would best exemplify the objectification of the female body, for in pornography, she is purchased and owned. Though it is a far cry to compare pets to women in this respect, they too are kept for the purpose of pleasure; moreover, the term "pet" when used for females, suggests a relationship, however affectionate, of dominance and ownership. Bellocq ingeniously reverses these terms by photographing his sitters in relaxed settings with their dogs, offering a different definition of intimacy than one suggesting sexuality. Although none of his thirty-three extent pictures depict women engaged in sexual acts, some do depict them naked or semi-dressed in arousing poses (though both Goldin and Sontag deem none of them salacious). The photos with the dogs are markedly different, however: they impart a sense of the women's everyday lives, the truly intimate side of which involves closeness to their pets. Perhaps the voyeuristic interest in the household lives of prostitutes could have been used to pornographic purpose, but the natural, open affection these women hold for their dogs establishes a different relationship to the viewer.

In one photo, a woman smiles at ease into the camera as she holds a French bulldog on her lap. Her candor suggests one does not have to pose awkwardly if one is close to one's pet. The heat of a Louisiana summer has left her clad for comfort solely in a cotton chemise and bloomers, while she sits outdoors in a cobblestone courtyard. She has neatly placed a white cloth on her lap so that the dog doesn't dirty her clothes. The undergarments and the small detail of the cloth are thus used not to erotic purpose but to show particularities from her daily life. How quickly this scenario can change is illustrated in another photo of the same woman: although in the same chair, backdrop, and clothing, she is now asked to pose erotically, with the chemise pulled off her shoulders to reveal her cleavage. The camera comes invasively closer to her naked skin. Her arms are tightly pressed to her body and she looks aside unsmilingly. The difference betrays her reluctance and shame at being so used, and even suggests that this photo was taken after the one with her dog, suddenly breaking the rapport Bellocq was first able to establish with her.

When the woman poses with her dog, one senses that her companion, positioned as it is between herself and Bellocq / the viewer, offers protection and deflects the intrusive gaze. A portrait of another prostitute is similarly composed: it too shows the woman clad in lace undergarments and clutching a dog in her lap.[13] This time, though, the terrier half covers her face, literally blocking the gaze (fig. 12). As the woman sits diagonally with her leg crossed and her bare arm covering her chest in order to hold the dog, she seems further to restrict the viewer's access to her body. As a result, she and the dog form a closely knit group. Mary Elizabeth Howie comments insightfully: "While this image clearly does not traffic in pornographic eroticism, it is imbued with an eroticism all its own. Physical intimacy is expressed in the tactile communication between the woman and the dog, as well as in the way that she hides behind him, while he simultaneously seems to gain courage from his position on her lap. Their behavior toward each other in the photograph suggests a much more truly intimate relationship than the uncomfortably faked sexuality in the explicit stereoscopic images" (36).[14]

In contrast to the portraits with dogs, when Bellocq requests the women pose erotically, they assume a cool distance from their artificial stance: they resist the prying gaze that would demand intimate revela-

12 E. J. Bellocq, "Storyville Portrait," circa 1912. Copyright Lee Friedlander. Courtesy
Fraenkel Gallery, San Francisco.

tion from them, using their very bodies as shields from their inner
nakedness.[15] Could it possibly be that these women asked Bellocq for
portraits with their pets in return for the erotic ones? Even if this were
not the case, the presence of the dog immediately changes the
demeanor of the women and reveals their domestic joys and intimate

source of strength. The dog allows its owner to reverse the dynamics of the voyeuristic, shaming gaze.

Virginia Woolf

To remain within the theoretically rich framework of the visual field but to complicate the terms of debate, a number of questions remain to be posed: When the canine gaze is a confirming one, does not a danger lie in that it can serve to mirror one's own desires? If it authenticates one's being, is one not indulging in egocentric specularity? Most often the trope of the mirror betrays a narcissistic seeing oneself in an idealized other; this other serves solely as a mirror of whom one longs to be. When applied to canine-human interaction, specularity raises the question as to whether all one's interactions with the speechless pet involve mirroring. Could the dog not represent the holistic, natural, and integrated other, qualities with which one wants to identify? Does not one always project desires onto it, given that it cannot respond back? This projection can run the gamut from imagining that one knows what a dog is thinking to bolstering one's self-image as one walks down the street with an accessory (whether it be a macho pit bull or elegant saluki).[16] The dog becomes a prosthesis or prop to the amputated self. The question of whether and how one can escape specularity is of particular import for women, given their conventional association with narcissism. Where, then, do the distinctions lie between a bad narcissistic self-absorption in relation to a pet and a healthy attempt to collect one's scattered self in its presence? And in the latter case, is the dog merely instrumentalized as a therapeutic aide, its own needs and separateness not acknowledged?

Natalie Kusz is one writer who complicates the mechanisms of specularity, at the same time that she uses the dog as intimate mirror to her self.[17] "Retired Greyhound, II" appeared in *Unleashed: Poems by Writers' Dogs*, a collection that takes as its conceit what the dog would say if gifted with speech. Although, as earlier intimated, the assumption that one can know the other's mind is a hazardous one (making a number of the poems in this collection trite), Kusz realizes the delicacy of her task. The poem is divided into two stanzas that recollect past trauma, first for the greyhound and then for its owner. It begins "Leaning into you now, my dark head / seeking your hand" (100). Touch (the leaning, the hand) plays an important role, substituting for vision, for the *gaze*hound's natural instinct to hunt by sight had been earlier abused for racetrack profit. Its current owner has actual scars around her eyes from a dog-mauling as a child. Perception must therefore come not from empirical vision but through memory and physical contact. Touching allows the subject to extend her body into the dog's fur, causing a feeling of expansion of the self. The warm contact, the gentle flow between bodies that occurs in petting helps to explain the comfort and reinforcing of self that the dog brings—and that the human bestows in return. Kusz's poem concludes: "we can lean / in and perceive ourselves, you and I: the astonishing exceptions among our kinds" (100). Significantly, this recognition that comes from the intimacy of physical closeness bypasses the scopic regime, so often associated with narcissistic self-absorption and self-projection.

In the canon of literature on dogs and women no piece is as famous as Virginia Woolf's *Flush*, a re-creation of the life of Elizabeth Barrett Browning through the eyes of her King Charles Spaniel. Although mirroring is an important conceit in this novel, Woolf uses it to raise questions regarding the sentimentality latent in identification. Coyly, she toys with mirroring for humorous effect: "Heavy curls hung down on either side of Miss Barrett's face; large bright eyes shone out; a large mouth smiled. Heavy ears hung down on either side of Flush's face; his eyes, too, were large and bright his mouth was wide. There was a likeness between them" (22–23). However paradoxically, at the same time that Woolf ironizes the mirroring, she expresses great sympathy for the desire between woman and dog for a symbiotic relation. Over the weeks Flush becomes compliant out of the "bond, an uncomfortable yet thrilling tightness" (35) that joins him to Miss Barrett. In words repeated both at the start and finish of the novel, the two are: "Broken asunder, yet made in the same mould, . . . each completed what was dormant in the other" (23, 161). One of the great accomplishments of this novel is that it sensitively balances pet affection with a subtle ironization of it.

The likeness between Flush and her owner bespeaks their affinity for each other and comes to represent their closeness, but, as if to avoid any Victorian sentimentality that such an attachment might evoke, Woolf also "breaks them asunder": "As they gazed at each other each felt: Here am I—and then each felt: But how different! . . . Between them lay the widest gulf that can separate one being from another" (23). Even the hyperbole that Woolf uses ("the widest gulf") delicately makes fun of the intensity of the relationship between woman and dog. Woolf disturbs any cloying projection onto the beast by having Miss Barrett be aware of its potential error: moreover, not only does the owner doubt specularity, the dog does as well! In fact, Woolf's humorous insight into Flush's mind demonstrates that she self-reflexively mocks her own attempts at projection into canine consciousness. Furthermore, she ridicules the seriousness of the biographical genre by dedicating it to a dog.[18]

As the above passage suggests, Woolf balances her irony with an appreciation for the sincere longing to bridge the gulf that exists between species. Underscoring the impossibility of perfect mirroring, Woolf later writes: "There were vast gaps in their understanding. At times they would lie and stare at each other in blank bewilderment" (36) and "the fact was they could not communicate with words, and it was a fact that led undoubtedly to much misunderstanding. Yet did it not lead also to a peculiar intimacy?" (37). Woolf here raises the brilliant paradox that estrangement can also lead to intuitive comprehension—to intimacy. Perhaps intimacy, then, cannot arise in a specular relation (or only deceptively so) but solely once differences are appreciated. Thus, when in *The Unbearable Lightness of Being* Tereza calls the love between her and Karenin "completely selfless," it is precisely because she recognizes their differences and resists projection: "Tereza did not want anything of Karenin; she did not ever ask him to love her back. Nor had she ever asked herself the questions that plague human couples: Does he love me? Does he love anyone more than me? Does he love me more than I love him? Tereza accepted Karenin for what he was; she did not try to make him over in her image" (297).

The symbiotic relationship between Flush and Miss Barrett calls for further nuancing in terms of how women's economic and emotional status are represented via the dog.[19] The pet dog marks the space of interiority, whether this be construed as the sick room to which his invalid owner was confined or Miss Barrett's own emotive realm. Confined within her quarters, he becomes preoccupied with gauging and responding to the slightest shifts in her feelings. As Elizabeth Barrett Browning herself wrote: "This dog watched beside a bed / Day and night unweary, / Watched within a curtained room / Where no sunbeam brake the gloom / Round the sick and dreary" (347). The spaniel "shar[ed] in the shadow" that she inhabited. Flush's monitored life thus symbolizes that of a female shut-in; the dog comes to stand for the realm of the Victorian woman's sheltered introspection.

Cultural histories of the dog link the rise of pet fancy to the development of the bourgeois class and its self-definition. Harriet Ritvo has analyzed, for instance, how Victorian bourgeois class consciousness—its setting itself apart from both decadent aristocracy and the dirty lower classes—informs such phenomena as rabies paranoia and purebred dog shows.[20] Victorian art, moreover, with its renowned animal portraitists, such as Edwin Landseer, Horatio Henry Couldery, and John Sargent Noble, testifies to the sentimentalization and anthropomorphization of the pet. A cultural studies approach, however, that exposes the specular construction and bolstering of bourgeois subjectivity via the pet dog loses sight of what intimacy accomplishes for the invalid Miss Barrett. It may be that she led a sheltered life whose only protest was to develop undiagnosable bodily illness and to cultivate a life of the imagination in her poetry. But to speak solely of societal restrictions on women as the cause of her physical impairment and its various compensations (which include her closeness to her pet) is to ignore Elizabeth Barrett's own agency in combating these restrictions and hence to belittle how she attempts to heal her frail psyche through writing about her pet.

Here Virginia Woolf's half-ironic (though benevolent) portrayal of the poetess is less telling than the latter's own words. In registering Flush's devotion, the nineteenth-century writer is able to give voice to her own suffering and how it is overcome. She recollects and records her own bodily affect—tears and sighs—to which only the dog is privy and which is hidden from the male-dominated household (which Woolf does depict). As hysteric somatic symptom, the tears are not ascribed a cause: they only mark an unretrievable traumatic source. Barrett's poems dedicated to Flush, though, depict how the dog's love conquers these tears: "And if one or two quick tears / Dropped upon his glossy ears / Or a sigh came double, / Up he sprang . . ." (348). "To Flush, My Dog" then closes with the words: "With a love that answers thine, / Loving fellow-creature" (348). Elizabeth Barrett overcomes her sense of isolation in response to Flush's love. One could read this act of reciprocity or mirroring as an instance of anthropomorphism: the dog is granted a Victorian sensibility. But, more appreciatively, one could notice that Barrett, participating in the burgeoning discussions on animal rights and protection, raises the dog to the status of a "fellow-creature."[21] This elevation occurs more in humble recognition than in the sentimentalization of the dog's devotion.

Rhoda Lerman

In a deservedly renowned phrase, Gertrude Stein pithily wrote: "I am I because my little dog knows me" (*What Are Master-pieces* 71).[22] This statement could be taken as an example both of sentimentalization and narcissistic mirroring: because my dog confirms me, I love the little pet.

But such a misreading would ignore the profound yet simple manner in which Stein deconstructs Cartesian self-reflection: the ego is not the source of reflection and reason but is insignificant until it is posited by the other, in this case a mere dog.[23] Moreover, the dog's knowing is somehow more intuitive about myself than I could ever be. I should like to continue to analyze how women writing on dogs take very seriously the charge that, in their intimacy with dogs, they are solely involved in narcissistic self-indulgence and self-mirroring. To be sure, the trope of the mirror, while evoking reciprocity and mutuality, can mean over-identification and self-projection. But, as Stephen H. Webb, would say, the dog represents an excess, or as it were, what lies outside the mirror: "The dog is always more than we know, extending beyond our knowledge and calling on us to match his or her excess with acts of generosity of our own" (102). Indeed, the presence of this other species disrupts solipsism. In other words, the way in which the dog facilitates the regaining of a lost subjectivity lies less in the dog's empathetic qualities that reconfirm or mirror the self. It is more likely the case that the rebuilding of a sense of self-integrity arises with respect for the otherness of the dog—and, as Gertrude Stein intimates, the dog's acknowledgment of our own apartness and uniqueness.

The psychoanalyst Jessica Benjamin explores such paradoxes arising from the workings of intersubjectivity. In response to Lacanian and Kleinian psychoanalytic theories of identification, Benjamin conceptualizes a model for relating to others that is wary of melancholic incorporation and repudiation. She asks whether a subject can "relate to the other without assimilating the other to the self through identification" (94). For this to occur, she maintains, there must be a relationship of two subjectivities. The other is respected as irreducible to one's own ego and recognized, not repudiated, for its difference. Benjamin emphasizes "the intersubjective relationship in which one goes beyond identification to appreciate the other subject as a being outside the self" (xiii). Recognition involves a different kind of identification that "can become not a collapse of differentiation, but a basis for understanding the position of the other" (28). "In the intersubjective conception of recognition, two active subjects may exchange, may alternate in expressing and receiving, cocreating a mutuality that allows for and presumes separateness. The arena for this catching and throwing is the intermediate inbetween space, the dialogue" (29). Clearly, intersubjective communication plays an important role for Benjamin: "Speech no longer figures as the activity of a subject empowered to speak, but as a possibility given by the relationship with a recognizing other" (28). Although she does not address the companion animal, Benjamin's position carries profound implications once applied to it. If the human subject ceases to abrogate to itself the sole empowerment to communicate, then the opening up of a "relationship with a recognizing other" (i.e., the animal) becomes possible.[24] An interpersonal space is created once the animal, acknowledged as a separate subject, looks back and addresses itself to the human subject. Once such overlapping terrain is established, one not only heeds the possibility of error in communication but deferentially accepts it.

The autobiographical novel by contemporary award-winning author Rhoda Lerman, *In the Company of Newfies: A Shared Life* (1996), sensitively explores the creation of Benjaminian intersubjective space between herself and her dogs, whereby the author learns to listen attentively to how her dogs are communicating with her.[25] What is so remarkable about this story is that Lerman is vigilantly aware of the gulf that separates her from the dogs; hence she is resistant to projection and reflects on it. Yet in this recognition and respect for difference she discovers a space for mutuality and shared sensibilities. Thus, rather than seeing the dog as an Other and imposing her language on it, Lerman attempts to understand the language of the dog and to communicate with it in terms of its own language; the Newfoundlands, in turn, accommodate themselves gracefully to human rules of behavior. If Jessica Benjamin stresses how difficult it is to develop and maintain a space for intersubjectivity, then one can better appreciate what a mammoth task Lerman undertakes in articulating a space between species who do not share the same codes of communication.

Reciprocity and hence the potential for intimacy are broached at the opening of *In the Company of Newfies*: "In the company of Newfoundlands, nothing is hidden. I slip the halter of what I've become. They slip the halter of what they've been, and we live together, passionately, changed. . . . This is a book about . . . communion, commitment, and intimacy" (1). Much of the strength and authority of Lerman's writing comes from the intensity of such words as intimacy that rarely are applied to dogs. She addresses the impasse in conveying her fervor to others. For instance, when the vet asks if she would prefer to leave the room during whelping, she reflects: "There was no way to explain to him that we are intimate; that we have done everything together. That we have pierced each other's worlds. That I am—what?—her other half. She is not only dog and I am not only human" (7). The closeness to her dogs means that "nothing is hidden in the company of Newfies. I can have no secrets" (10). Like Derrida (though here figuratively speaking), she stands naked before the attentive gaze of her pets. But, because she explores the intersubjective space of mutuality, unlike for Derrida the gaze of the pet is not completely enigmatic, for Lerman is keenly heedful of what the dogs are attempting to signify to her. Intimacy is not solely the result of standing naked before the pet: it is dependent on reciprocity and a kind of intercorporeality. Thus the fact that she cannot have any secrets from her dogs means that she, in turn, is intimately familiar with their very bodies. As a conformation judge examines one of her bitches, she thinks to herself in words of a true lover: "I know every bone and muscle, every curl of hair, ears, nipples, tail, toes. I have felt, touched, stroked every bit of her" (151).

Paradoxically—and to follow Jessica Benjamin—what allows for such intimacy is the respect Lerman has for the different, "parallel universe of animals" (18). To the dogs, ours is an "alien universe, their unknown" (54). Out of deference Lerman reads them very carefully. Indeed, in her anxiety over the growth of her puppies, she realizes the danger of over-interpreting: "Knowing so little, I watch for too much" (21). The strangeness and fragility of the newborns place them beyond meaning and represent the enigma of their entire race. For Lerman, the intense, maternal love she has for the puppies makes her keenly aware of her lack of comprehension and the futility of being able to assist a dying one.

Yet, ever cognizant of the silence between them, Lerman listens more intently: "It isn't easy to let her lick my face, but it is her language and I must listen or she will stop speaking to me. Because I've learned to listen, my Newfies have continued to speak . . . [and] have patiently insisted that I listen" (7). Lerman realizes that however much she is attentive, they examine her more earnestly than she them. Thus, each time Lerman records her listening, she discovers the dogs' own attempt to heed her needs. An extraordinary record of mutuality and interchange—based on this acknowledgment of separateness—arises as a result. She circumspectly answers Stephen H. Webb's penetrating questions: "Can the closeness of dogs enable us to see their very otherness? Can their similarity shed light on difference? Can dogs be both our 'best friends' and an intrusion of something persistently other, demanding respect and attention on their own terms? Are they more than what we need from them?" (6).

Lerman recognizes the dogs as subjects in and unto themselves. They are "utterly and completely, fastidiously conscious of themselves" (113). Yet they are also that to one another and their humans. One of her bitches is "courteous, considerate, thoughtful, a Ginger Rogers to my Fred Astaire, firmly attached but never in the way, reflecting my steps"

(140). The way the dog tries to advance out of itself and into the human world offers a model for how to create the intermediate space of dialog that Jessica Benjamin articulates. Lerman's dog Molly works "toward becoming a different sort of dog in that endless, uneasy shift and struggle between dog and human" (74). In its adaptability, the dog exemplarily tries to understand the position of the other. Indeed, the Newfoundlands "work to be human, to be other than what they are, something other than dog" (2). For instance, one day Lerman sees her Celeste "pick up a bright pink leash and walk around the driveway with it in her mouth, head held high, making believe she was on lead. And then I understood why she grabs me, grabs the hem of my jacket, the cuff of my sleeve, the string on my boot. She creates a tether between us, holding me so I don't stray from her. Now I put her on lead for no practical reason at all. She holds the leash in her mouth so we are holding each other. . . . The leash is both faith and connection" (130–31). For Lerman to appreciate Celeste's attempt at connection does not mean she collapses the distinctions between human and dog, as so many stories or cartoons do that facilely put words into a dog's mouth; rather, Lerman notices how arduous the dog's efforts are to create and sustain this tie. Correspondingly, her dogs encourage her to "work to be other than what I am. We stretch our limits and change our lives" (2). In this exchange and modest recognition of dependency, the woman is tethered to the dog and not, as customarily, the other way around (140).

This reciprocity allows Lerman to grow emotionally in unexpected ways. She speaks of living passionately and escaping into an animal self (35) as she sits in the whelping box and Molly licks her as if she is one of her puppies. It is a moment full of mutual trust, where Lerman is not afraid of developing identification with her dog's universe. As later the puppies burrow against her own breasts, "for a brief moment I am their animal and nothing, no one, else. It is an ecstasy, a stepping out of my world into theirs" (63). Rather than repudiate these creaturely, abject impulses, Lerman has the faith to explore them. The dogs are responding to something latent and archaic inside of her and unearthing it, although she is at pains to name it: "What instinct, what old connection, exists in us that so responds to them?" (96), she asks. She never presents her interactions as risking the dissolution of the boundaries to her self; instead she stretches these boundaries. It is this very in-between space that marks the true site of intimacy. Such shared emotion and interconnectedness are perhaps best captured when Lerman describes parting from one of her dogs: she weeps for the dog's confusion and loneliness but then realizes that, reciprocally, she is weeping for her own loneliness at leaving him (119). She realizes the fragility of an unenclosed self as well as the impossibility of incorporating otherness.

Karen Duve and Rebecca Brown

Stories of the cohabitation of women and dogs do not have to follow the (auto)biographical, realist genre: they may also explore the realm of the fantastic. Such is the case in Karen Duve's short story "Besuch vom Hund" (Visit from the dog [1999]) and Rebecca Brown's novel *Dogs: A Modern Bestiary* (1998). In both works the dog is not an affectionate, sensitive companion but transmogrifies into a mythical, independently minded beast endowed with human characteristics. These dogs do not guarantee self-identity; they shatter it and, in the process, destroy the casual interhuman relations of the female narrator. In each story, the dog, appearing suddenly, seems to represent the surfacing of unconscious drives and thus announces a special kind of intimacy or avenue of exploring oneself.[26] As animals they embody an enigmatic difference from the rational mind, which could represent the mystery of both the human unconscious and the canine world. Whereas the narratives discussed above establish an egalitarian relationship with the dog, here the works relinquish control to the canines. But they all can be deemed feminist in their critique of the presumption that human beings should exert dominion over the animal kingdom: in these two stories the tables are turned.

In the curious, surrealist "Besuch vom Hund" a stray collie appears on the doorstep of the narrator just as she is preparing to go out to a party with a "nice, very good-looking guy." The dog tries to get her attention with such cocky remarks as "I'm not really a dog. I am an emaciated wolf and howl at night on the city ramparts" (47). Finally, he says to her that he has chosen her because she is a poet, who is "the sound of our silent cries . . . the truth of our worst dreams" (49). When the woman's date for the evening arrives (accompanied by another couple) and comments that she doesn't look properly dressed to go, she retorts that maybe she has something better to do. When he asks her who she thinks she is with such a remark, she answers by echoing the collie: "I am an emaciated wolf . . ." and "I am the sound of your silent cries." Not surprisingly, she finds herself alone with the collie for the evening—and the two go to the corner Esso gas station to buy something to eat. Liberated, the narrator does not have to rely on looking her best for a supposedly "nice man"; nor does she have to stomach his snide comments. Instead, identification with the lone, stinking, and shivering collie empowers her to find her unique voice. Paradoxically, the talking dog endows her, the poet, with language.

The narrator of "Besuch vom Hund" takes this bizarre collie as her mirror; she mimics it. Yet the story complicates specularity precisely by reversing the pattern of mimicry. In the conventional talking-dog story, human speech is given to the dog, but here the human borrows back the words of the dog. Nor does this story illustrate the typical scenario where the author projects thoughts onto the dog and vocalizes them. Confounding the vector of the human projecting itself into the animal's mind, the collie projects himself into another creature, a wolf, and claims he's not a dog. Moreover, his outlandish propositions defy interpretation, so that they seem to represent the very impasse of communication between species, even though he speaks German. When the narrator begins mimicking his language, she in turn becomes incomprehensible to her visitors. In criticizing the banality of everyday language (what is a "nice guy"?), Duve seems to suggest that liberation comes from abandoning conventional human discourse. It is not that humanity defines and confirms itself by setting itself off from the speechless beast; this would be the othering that occurs in specularity. Instead, Duve fantasizes what it would mean to try to appropriate another species' mode of communication and, in so doing, to discover a different voice for oneself.

The remarkable novel *The Dogs: A Modern Bestiary* by American lesbian writer Rebecca Brown begins with a strange, terrifying, black dog appearing one night in her apartment. The commanding creature watches every inch of her, but the first-person narrator doesn't know what the dog wants of her (6, also 139). The dog comes to stay and lead a life so intimately bound with the narrator's that she writes, "She lived inside my life" (7), "I loved the way she looked the way I felt" (11), and "I'd close my eyes and know what she desired" (16). They curl around each other in bed to fit together (144). The narrator adores her animal beauty. As in any love affair, the narrator learns to accept the manners of her companion and adapts herself to them. Household dogs indeed regulate our daily routines, intuit our feelings, anticipate our moves, even take over our furniture, but Brown uses these ordinary occurrences to turn them into a nightmarish relation where the dog disciplines the human, reversing dominant/submissive roles. Miss Dog and her numerous offspring creep not only into the narrator's life but into her very brain: "But I couldn't hide myself when they moved in. They numbered every hair of me, each gasp of fear, each clutch of want, each shrug of hope that ever spasmed through me. They tapped my phone, my brain, my heart. I swear it's true, they monitor my dreams" (66).[27] In this intimate relation, they know more about the narrator than the latter knows about herself (74).

Hence *The Dogs* transforms the daily, near-and-dear closeness we have with pets into their manifesting an inner, untold part of our selves. It is not unusual to confide in our dogs, while knowing that they cannot understand every word we say. So, too, the narrator whispers her secrets to Miss Dog (10), but as the dog must be hidden away from a landlord that prohibits pets, their alliance comes to represent secrecy itself. The narrator in fact lives alone so that no one would embarrassingly see how she truly is (66). Their relationship adopts a queer dimension, insofar as it is closeted and unfit for public view. Apart from the echo of the word in the title, there is no indication of sexual bestiality in the novel. Yet from the start the dog sleeps with the woman, and the bed becomes the site of both closeness and torture. Like Kafka's "The Metamorphosis," where Gregor bestirs to find himself transformed into a giant bug, the bed seems to symbolize the locus where unconscious drives arise. But Brown's tale is, in Kafka's words, "no dream" from which one awakes; that is to say, there is no outside perspective on which to anchor a psychoanalytic "interpretation of dreams." And, as in Kafka, the first-person narrator offers no interpretation of what is occurring. She is as close to the dogs as to the events transpiring, maintaining no analytical distance to them. The problem thus arises as to how to pinpoint the precise nature of the unvoiced suppressed self into which the dogs tap.

As mentioned previously, projection of human emotions onto dogs is an everyday occurrence. But Brown literalizes such projection, insofar as the dogs eventually metamorphose into monsters who dress up, perform, and otherwise act as humans. Dogs can break our hearts, but when Brown writes, "I always feel them tearing out my heart" (62), she is referring to how they lunge and literally rip her open. They even offer the heart to her as a delicacy to eat. Tropes of introjection (as here in food), even more than projection, dominate the narrative. Something has been entombed secretively, which is to say, melancholically within the narrator that the dogs unearth. In the end, they dig up the bones of a child whom the narrator restores to life and to whom she then listens ("She pulled my face toward her face and put her mouth against my ear and told me the unspeakable" [65]). But earlier in the narrative, the mouth tries unsuccessfully to utter something that comes from within: "Something catches in my throat. I try to cough it up. It's stuck" (53).

She arrives home to aid in the whelping of Miss Dog's puppies but then this "something" pushes up out of her mouth—a paw. Elsewhere in the story she tries to speak but her "mouth is dry" (62) or she takes "one huge and final gulp to seal the place down deep inside my throat that keeps me in and keeps the world out" (119). What could she be trying to verbalize?

Medieval bestiaries served as compendia of actual and mythological creatures (making no distinction between them), listing their physiological, medicinal, and symbolic attributes and including didactic fables. Many animals were bizarre or demonstrated unusual behavior chosen to depict a Christian moral allegory. Alluding to such moral instruction the chapter titles of Brown's novel read: "DOG: in which is illustrated Immanence" or "BONE: in which is illustrated Constancy." The allegorization is opaque, however, for how the chapters illustrate the various virtues they announce can only be conjectured. Brown thus works at the margins of representation. Like Dürer and Kafka her story invites an allegorical decoding at the same time it resiliently wards it off. Most perplexing is how to determine what the dogs themselves signify. It would be too simple to postulate that they point to a dark side to the narrator's psyche. Instead of a referential equivalent, their staging of scenarios (dressing up in her clothes to parody her or performing a dominatrix number) suggests a sheer representational quality. They serve as a screen whose function it is precisely not to point at something behind it but to block meaning. If they point to a trauma in the narrator's childhood past (such as her being abused), it is only indirectly by the fact that the narrator is forced into reenacting a sadomasochistic relationship. As mythological creatures who only in name resemble actual dogs, they offer the sheer fantasy of a referent.

Rather than surmising that the dogs represent a buried, inner part of the narrator, one could acknowledge their allegorical indirectness by pointing to their extimacy: they seem to function as an interior exterior, which is embodied precisely in their external, shaming gaze on the narrator, who is the object of stigma. The dogs, in other words, occupy the position of a constitutive outside. From the start the narrator is engaged in deadpan self-deprecation. She is self-mockingly aware of her poor quarters and her dull appearance. She repeatedly experiences mortification from her bungling and is not particularly noticed by others. In her social invisibility she resembles the dogs, whom no one sees except herself, as in the episode, full of black humor, when they enter the supermarket. Maladroit and isolated, the narrator therefore needs the gaze of others and unconsciously desires to provoke it, even if solely in the humiliating scrutinization by the dogs. She calls the dogs "Inquisitors. Their job is to observe and see, to catch one in the act" (74). "They know about me what I don't. They know what I would not and they are merciless" (74). The pack stands around her, inspecting her, as if she were "on show, an auction block" (120). When the narrator brings a girlfriend home, all attempts at lovemaking are thwarted because she sees the dogs snickering at the performance. Paradoxically, so as to retain their gaze, the woman stays with these obnoxious creatures, "because each hate and fear she knows, each longing, every clutch of love, and that which turns desire into need abides in them" (92).

But it is not only the dogs who keenly observe the narrator; she is constantly envisaging herself from the outside, "from somewhere else" (95). In the nightmarish life with the dogs, everything transpires "like it happened to someone else" (51). For example, in the chapter "GLASS" she sees herself as if she were "another person, separate, outside" (91), passing by in the street and looking in through the window on the apparently contented domestic life of a girl with dogs. On different occasions she examines herself in a mirror (2–3, 116, 119) and in the reflection of a river (164). Elsewhere she imagines herself being strung up by a noose, but her identification in her fantasy shifts as she also sees herself as "someone else. I also wear a hangman's mask, a mercy mask, a mask of shame so I can't see my face" (108). Thus, however much this self-splitting is an attempt to reflect on herself, to see herself objectively from a distance, or to assume the active role of spectator (rather than remain the passive object of view), her self-perception is blind. Insofar as the splitting entails that she moves away from herself, a misrecognition is inevitable. As in a dream, she tracks her movements but does not apprehend herself. In similar self-detachment, she describes a repeated scenario where she would be "in a room with someone . . . part of me floated up and far away. I went away from where we were" (116). She claims that she needs the dogs to rescue her from this disembodied situation, but how this kindness is accomplished given their cruelty is consternating.

Conceivably the dogs embody the narrator's internalization of the critical gaze of others, her melancholic self-punishment for being queer and not fitting in with the rest of society. Or one could postulate that this imagined self-externalization is required so that a certain part of the narrator is excised, or—as with the torture practiced by the dogs (they shove rods up her limbs)—so that she can be seen to survive the shattering. I would prefer to argue that, instead of a repressed fear being manifested and represented to the observing self, it is quite the opposite that occurs. That is, when the trope of performance arises in the novel, it is to suggest that something beyond the performance is being evoked. The purpose of a splitting and an externalized gaze would conceivably be to recognize something hidden, except that, since the scenario is repeated, it signals that the subject fails to see. The dogs are the exteriorization of this pure, unapprehending, inscrutable gaze. Again, they do not represent a secret part of the self but something relentlessly foreign to the self that commands it. In the episode entitled "FOOD" the dogs take the heart out of the woman in order to show it to her and get her to eat it. They must, however, slam the tray against her face before she takes it. Something thus resists being recognized, it being in the nature of the Freudian unconscious to remain inaccessible. Symptoms of previous trauma recur insistently, but they do so in the displaced fantasies that block its painful remembering, all while suggesting something behind the screen.

Dogs cannot communicate in human language. Their insistent otherness commands respect and resists co-optation to human demand. As the narrator humbly recognizes, she "can't speak their tongue" (77). Embodying this otherness, Rebecca Brown's cruel dogs cannot recall the narrator's past for her. However much they restage sadomasochistic scenes with her, they cannot tell her where their significance lies. At most, the dogs let her go and signal to her, by their digging, where to search for the lost child in her. In the final chapter, after the dogs unearth the bones of a deceased girl, the narrator shoos them away and resurrects her, that is, the narrator's, own memories: "I saw inside what covers me, I see inside the skin: *I see the child swimming whole*" (166). As even this closure resists naming what the precise nature of the trauma was, the story remains in its abstract mode, hesitant to specify what the allegorical referent is. Throughout, *The Dogs* remains a novel true to the enigma of this other species, embodied above all in its inimitability and supremacy.

What is emotionally unsettling yet beautiful about Rebecca Brown's novel is that, in spite of the sadistic roles the dogs assume, a searing intimacy binds the woman to them. Brown terrifyingly brings shame and intimacy into proximity with each other. The legendary faithfulness of the species here results in the closest of bonds: the dog "never growled about me kicking or sweating up the sheets or the shouts I made when I bolted awake from a nightmare. She remained, despite her constancy, my truest friend. She was my only comfort. She met my every single need that she had made in me" (20). Later the puppies are described as "loyal, patient, prescient . . . sent to teach" (108). However indirect, a link exists between their virtues and the chapter titles that point to the moral element of the story, which is to say, the way in which the chapters illustrate charity, perspicacity, obedience, solace, and so on. Moreover, the appreciation for the dogs is not restricted to such virtues but extends to their physical beauty. Even while an acquiescing victim of the dogs, the narrator cherishes their loveliness, elegance, even stylish glamour. Their intimacy is paradoxically best expressed when, after the narrator strikes out at the unsuspecting puppies with a hammer, bruising but not, as intended, killing them, they look back with "blaming, knowing, begging eyes" (142). Gazing into her, they relentlessly and patiently forgive her. The same puppies then sleep around her "warm as milk" (143). Conceivably, it is forgiveness that allows the narrator to be reconciled with her past in the end. Thus, however cruel the dogs appear, at every stage they are a reminder to the narrator of an intimate warmth, and hence they lead her back to her intrinsic self.

Cultural theorist Yi-Fu Tuan in *Dominance and Affection: The Making of Pets* asserts that affection, whether it be toward pets, children, or women, conceals its true motives—dominance, superiority, condescension, indulgence, patronage, and paternalism. Most cultural theorists and historians on pet keeping come to similar conclusions (for example, Marc Shell, Harriet Ritvo, and Kathleen Kete). Rebecca Brown clearly reverses this position, as well as debunks the commonplace that intimacy with dogs equates with sentimentality. Power and authority here lie with the dogs, and not without a modicum of veracity, for the household dog dictates how our lives are to be regulated around its bodily needs and schedules. It always asserts its own independence and will. Moreover, if for Tuan domination invariably underlies affection, for Brown, despite the domination of one party, a powerful affective, intimate bond ties them together. The other women writers discussed in this chapter also relinquish dominance in order to explore and heal their own weaknesses. In other words, they resist repudiating affection, in a serious indictment of what Steve Baker calls the "fear of the familiar" among (male) postmodern artists and critics.[28] These women writers suggest that it is imperative to think through what is at stake in intimacy, affection, care, and the healing of trauma and, thus, to come to terms with the abjection with which both women and dogs are frequently regarded.[29]

In conclusion, a note on melancholia. Whether it be Brown, Kusz, Stewart, Lim King, Barrett, or Bellocq, the representation of women involves a story not of loss but of recuperation, hence an acknowledgment of previous damage or deprivation. These artists give voice to abjection and, through the aid of intimacy with the dog, come to terms with it. They thus surmount the melancholic repudiation of loss. In this dialog with melancholia, the works discussed in this chapter link up to Dürer's *Melencolia I* and form a tradition together with Lucian Freud's *Double Portrait*, for they are all about being *alone* with one's dog. A colleague of mine told me how his thirteen-year-old daughter will say she needs to be alone and then takes her golden retriever for a walk. Meditation and *recueillement* occur together in the calm intimacy with the dog, a comforting solitude that requires few words if any. And one final element sets these representations of women and dogs apart from the psychoanalytic description of melancholia. In the wake of Freud, melancholia is equated with the refusal to acknowledge otherness, insofar as the lost object is introjected into the self. As Freud says, the shadow of the object falls on the subject (10:435). The remarkable quality of the works discussed here is that they are vigilantly mindful of the problems of projection and incorporation. Because these artists explore the divisions between human and beast, they recognize that they are cause for respect—not for the denigration or shaming of the animal or for the equally disturbing projection of sentimental human emotion onto the pet.

FOUR

Mourning

There are countless sentimental, anecdotal stories about the intersected lives of canine and human beings. Anthologized in popular collections, they stock the shelves of large-scale book distributors, inevitably to end up gathering dust at used book dealers. I came across one such cute but conventional story while perusing the shelves at the American Kennel Club library in New York. Although pretentiously entitled *Read My Autobiography: I Am the Great Pedro, the Wisest Dog in the World* (1930), the tale is not striking—except for an ending that, by the weight of what is left unsaid, takes the reader by surprise. A spoiled French bulldog, who spends his life traveling in New York City taxi cabs, reflects back on his own death: "But my mama has changed our apartment. She would no longer live in the rooms where I fell ill" (63). The grief is briefly, almost nonchalantly mentioned, in stark contrast to its intensity. What was it, I wondered, about a pet's loss that would cause the owner no longer to bear living in the same quarters? Could there be a fundamental difference in the way pets are mourned? Or is there a searing similarity between an animal companion and a parent, child, or spouse? Moreover, since this story ostensibly originated with the death of Pedro, how does the act of writing about him—indeed giving him voice—function in the work of mourning?

A delicately composed eulogy to a departed pet is William Robert Pedrick's *La nécrologie de Joffre* (1922). The author writes:

Those beautiful eyes would never again intently watch me from that chair. It must be moved away. Never again would little Joffre affectionately lick my hand. Never again would I hear the patter of his feet, or his aggressive barking at the garbage man. His playful antics would no more delight me. There lay his rubber ball, the old shoe and the stuffed stocking with which he habitually challenged me to play. They must be dispensed with; the sight of them distresses me. The house seemed strangely and oppressively vacant.

The mundane detail alone with which the narrator recollects Joffre's life demonstrates the ongoing pain of his bereavement, for his itemized grief testifies to how enmeshed their daily lives were. Although the routine interactions had seemed insignificant at the time, their sudden absence leaves "aching voids which are never filled" (12).

Another contemporaneous, autobiographical reflection on the death of dogs is *Inordinate (?) Affection* (1936) by the famous composer and suffragette Ethel Smyth. Smyth isolates what she calls the *cantus firmus* of her tale: "For a woman who lives alone no sorrow can compare with the death of her dog" (33). She decides to get a new puppy, "because I knew that nothing else would check constant brooding over the companion of the last years, whose presence I saw everywhere . . . everywhere, everywhere" (83–84). In order to recapture the habitualness that she lost with her first old English sheep dog, she names all its successors by the same name, Pan. Each new dog thus recapitulates a prior loss, marking a regressive attachment. In Freudian terms, Smyth cannot fully transfer love to another, completely different object and thereby successfully complete mourning. Yet, in this complicated bereavement, each new puppy marks the attempt to do so, as does her affirmation that the happiness she experienced is not lost on the dog's death.

What these tales strongly suggest is that what makes the mourning of pets unique is precisely what Smyth calls the inordinate affection for them, an affection that one resists—hence why she questions it—and yet is unconsciously profound. Pedrick shocks himself and the reader in the first lines by saying that sorrow for pets is "no less than for children" (1). He then later admits that he could better bear the loss of his mother and only son than that of his dog. Indeed, it often seems as if the nature of the attachment to the dog can make its death more unbearable than that of a beloved human.[1] Why would this be so? In differentiating between mourning and melancholia Freud stipulated that, whereas the former moves toward a terminus in the detachment from the lost object, the latter is ongoing because the indistinction between subject and object makes the acknowledgment of loss difficult to articulate. Applied to our relationship to pets, it is clear that the myriad ways in which our daily lives are intertwined with the constant presence and care of the pet cause the attachment to be inadvertently close. As a consequence, the final separation comes as a shock, the acuteness of which we tend to disavow.

Ingrained, unconscious repetition is what leads Pedrick and Smyth to see small reminders of their deceased dog everywhere, yet they struggle to identify why such trivial moments combine into such overwhelming loss. As Freud says, the melancholic knows "whom he has lost but not what it was about him" (wen, *aber nicht,* was *er an ihm verloren hat* [10:431]). During the life of pets the propensity is to deny to some degree the intensity of the bond, leading one on their death to be perplexed at labeling what had absorbed one. Freud writes that the sadness that the melancholic feels is mysterious because he cannot see what had preoccupied him (199–200). Compounding the attachment is that we are forced to project what the pet is thinking, feeling, or suffering, all causing a form of overidentification. The intensity of this specular relation makes its release problematic at the point of the dog's death. Peter M. Sacks identifies "one of the dangers besetting a mourning [to be] the imprisonment of his affective energies, the locking up within himself of impulses previously directed toward or attached to the deceased" (22). Without such severing, however, according to Freud, successful mourning cannot occur. Hence, in a gamble to break loose from such ties ("the imprisonment" or "locking up"), Pedro's owner has to move.

Even before bereavement—and anticipating it—we can feel isolated from our pets. Julia Kristeva wrote about the love relation: "The visible other is beautiful because we project on him all the affection that we feel for him, while he leaves us tragically alone" (*Tales of Love* 349). "Love," she writes, "is edged with emptiness" (381). One could thus surmise that the very fact that animals are mute and that we desire to be close to them renders us melancholic. In other words, even though the pet lives with us, in a sense it is already an absent object. Its true existence lies deep within a physical, emotive attachment—Pedrick would say in the heart, but Nicolas Abraham and Maria Torok, writing on melancholia, would say encrypted within us. The beloved pet becomes the unavowed "kernel" of our internal support. The distant object is magically nurtured within our psychic life, making the realization and acceptance of its death particularly arduous.

Precisely the animal's need for human responsibility and solicitude— even to the point of deciding the moment of their deaths in euthanasia— can enhance the inescapable sense of guilt experienced at their demise.

What is special about the dog is that it needs us, more than any animal in the wild. We cannot feel responsible enough to these creatures who are beholden to us. Part of this obligation comes from the sense that, although we are entrusted with this care, we do not always know what the pet's needs are. A large part of Pedrick's grief comes from having muzzled his Boston terrier at the request and direction of the veterinarians during the splinting of a kneecap injury. The dog suffocated to death at the unwitting hands of its owner. Attributing a deep sense of shame to the melancholic, Freud observes "the belittlement of self-esteem, expressed in self-incriminations and self-aspersions" (10:429). Pedrick's guilt is exacerbated by Joffre having been such a loyal, devoted companion. The dog had mourned his daily departures from the house and now—in the mirroring that so characterizes the melancholic's inability to separate self from the lost love object—it is he, Pedrick, who must mourn his faithful friend. He faces an injunction to find an equivalent, mutual expression of devotion. Tales about the legendary mourning and waiting of dogs—including Homer's Argos, the dog in Wordsworth's poem "Fidelity," and the Greyfriar's Bobby in Edinburgh—are perhaps the inverse expression of self-reproachful guilt vis-à-vis the dog, as well as the displacement of mourning onto it, precisely because such mourning in a human being would be considered excessive.

Societal belief holds that candid expressive grief over a mere dog is improper. There are consequently few public rituals or customs to commemorate the loss. In North America, for instance, neither is it customary to hold funerals or wakes for pets nor is there any commonly held belief in their afterlife, and there is nothing to inherit, to cherish in remembrance. The absence of official mourning, the social foreclosure of grief, then exacerbates the melancholic, that is, unsymbolizable attachment. On the death of Joffre, for instance, Pedrick is far from receiving condolences. He notes how some people are even contemptuous of his sorrow: "'A dog!' they sneer, by glance or manner if not in words,—'a useless dog!'" (14). He then goes so far as to chastise himself for being selfish in indulging in sadness: "'poor Joffre!' really means 'ah, me!'" (15). Not only does the melancholic blame himself and narcissistically feel deserted, but the author here points to the inner censorship that also accompanies the mourning of pets, turning it into a melancholic disavowal and suppression of bereavement.

The intense specular, melancholic identification that occurs across species and that goes beyond empathy for a suffering creature can especially be witnessed in childhood attachment to a pet. The natural affinity, so often noted, that children have for pets conceivably has its roots in a form of narcissistic identification. The sufferings or death of a pet dog could, if not vie with the trauma Freud ascribes to the breaking of the pre-oedipal tie, then at least mirror it in structure, for the separation marks the child's induction into the adult world. For it must not be forgotten that, because dogs' lives are so brief compared to our own, especially if they are suddenly curtailed, the first encounter with death that many children experience is with a pet. The sudden separation can lead either to an acceptance of renunciation (in which case it would parallel a successful oedipalization of the child) or to the ongoing woundedness that signifies melancholia.[2] Starkly realistic and unsentimental in its depiction of the working-class coal-mining England from which he came, D. H. Lawrence's short story "Rex," illustrates the psychological injury that accompanies the death of a family dog for a child. The story shows how the identification between canid and child represents an ongoing melancholic mourning for one's absent childhood, the loss of which is represented in the dog's death.

In Lawrence's tale, a puppy is given to a family to rear by a rough "sooty uncle" (14). Carrying the shivering puppy home tucked under his overcoat, the boy trembles at being caught on the train with it: like the animal he is fearful. The child's own harsh, callous upbringing is epitomized by the puppy's face being rubbed in its excrement to discipline it. As it grows older, the dog becomes scruffy in its self-reliant wanderings, angry tussles with the mother, and mean defense of what he regards to be his property. Yet despite its fierce nature, the dog "had a terrible, terrible necessity to love" (18), through which one can see symbolized the children's neediness, especially when faced, like the dog, with constant parental rebuke. The children champion the dog out of identification with it: when the mother declares that beds are not for dogs, the children cry, injured, "He's as good as we are!" (15).

It is precisely this melancholic collapsing of the boundaries between self and other, canine and human, that Lawrence tries to renounce in the close: "We should not have loved Rex so much, and he should not have loved us. There should have been a measure. We tended, all of us, to overstep the limits of our own natures. He should have stayed outside human limits; we should have stayed outside canine. Nothing is more fatal than the disaster of too much love" (21). This hardened realization occurs once the uncle returns to claim the dog and attaches it (a fox terrier!) to a cart to pull. The children stand in mute despair on seeing the dog beaten and whipped as it frantically fights being tethered to the cart. In the barren aftermath, the children are left with "black tears, and a little wound which is still alive in our hearts" (20). Because of the melancholic identification (according to which the object mourned is oneself), this wound cannot heal. For what is mourned—unendingly— is an equally exposed, unprotected childhood, one so uncomprehending of cruelty that it assumes the burden of remorse: the children feel guilty at having loved the dog so much that it became unfit to become a cart dog, leading the uncle to shoot it. In an earlier episode, when the dog disappears and they search for him, the children "for the first time realized how empty and wide the earth is, when you're looking for something" (20). Indeed, faced with the injustice of adults against which they are powerless, they have lost an irredeemable innocence. They have also forfeited the wild-spirited freedom that the dog once embodied. In the absence of the freedom to roam and explore, the world can only appear desolate in its expanse—an emptiness signified by the death of Rex, who was never replaced with another pet in the household.

What is striking about these autobiographical works, whether it be the story of Pedro, Pan, Joffre, or Rex, is that the impetus behind their writing lies with the death of the dog. Even more surprising is that memoir after memoir follows the same pattern. Although they conventionally begin with the puppy arriving in the new home, the close invariably betrays that the writing originates in mourning. Whether it is Colette Audry's *Behind the Bathtub* (1962), Willie Morris's *My Dog Skip* (1995), George Pitcher's *The Dogs Who Came to Stay* (1995), or Elizabeth Marshall Thomas's *The Social Lives of Dogs* (2000), these novels begin with their end. Rhoda Lerman's beautiful *In the Company of Newfies* (1996) starts with puppies being born at the same time her old Ben approaches death. The novel then ends with his passing, at which Lerman sobs, "It is as if someone had ripped the skin from my body. I have come apart" (157). Elizabeth von Arnim measures her own life in terms of the dogs' lives and passing. Although she does not dwell on grief, Lerman details and highlights each death with a subchapter ("The Death of Coco," "The Death of Pincher," "The Death of Woosie," and "The Death of Winkie"). She then concludes, "This story, like life, as it goes on is becoming dotted with graves. It would seem that the more you care for a dog, . . . the more, as it were, he dies" (204). Among the recent novels told from the dog's perspective, Paul Auster's *Timbuktu* (1999) and Charles Siebert's *Angus* (2000) end with the dog's death, Timbuktu actually being the heaven where dog and master reunite. Finally, perhaps the most lovely tribute to dogs ever composed, Maurice Maeterlinck's "Our Friend, the Dog" (1903), is occasioned by the death of his six-month-old French bulldog. Maeterlinck's grief is sublimated into a vocabulary of transcendence. Whereas it is "the destiny of man" to plunge "on every side into darkness" (43), the dog "is the only living being that has found and recognizes an indubitable, tangible, unexceptionable and definite god. . . . He possesses truth in its fulness. He has a certain and infinite ideal" (41). Maeterlinck transforms the experience of loss into a discourse of fullness and contrasts the onto-theological uncertainty that humans face with the life-affirming faith and trust that dogs have in their immanent deities, their humans.

There is a paradoxical logic driving such tales—two, irreconcilable temporal vectors that govern how the dog is being mourned and yet that are held in equal suspension. According to the first, the narrative occupies the space of the "not yet": in the story itself the dog is not yet deceased. According to the second, however, the narrative transpires in the space of the "no longer": the dog is dead at the time of writing. In Freud's contrasting terms, the first model operates according to the denial of melancholia, whereas the second strives via the work of mourning (*Trauerarbeit*) for the awareness and acceptance of death. The first reconjures the dog, while the second recognizes its absence. As mentioned earlier, among the nonequivalencies in the canine-human relation is the imbalance that the untimeliness of the dog's death creates. It is always too soon, before our own. To be sure, all deaths are premature and before our own, but this shock is especially experienced in the case of the brief canine life. This untimeliness is registered in the keen desire to resurrect the dog, willingly to suspend disbelief in order to imagine it still alive. At the same time, awareness of mutability forces one to come to terms with the fact that the pet is "no longer."

Let me first elaborate the implications of the "not yet." In the autobiographical work, to write the story of the dog's life means keeping it alive and endowing it with a future. While composing the story, it seems as if the dog were still living, which is also the effect upon reading it. Paradoxically, then, the memoir is an act of forgetting the death, of going back in time and writing as if there were no death at the end. It celebrates reunion. The narrative, although based on actual occurrences, inhabits the self-consciously fictive space of the "as if." The story line thus serves against discontinuity, the previously mentioned untimeliness, that death brings with it. Moreover, the author must trust that, by rehearsing the dog's life and showing what leads up to death, the shock will be softened.

Calling the dog back to life suggests that one fears the dog will disappear again if he is not invoked. In the case of the prosopopeia in

Charles Siebert's *Angus*, this invocation of the absent dog even entails giving him a voice as the first-person narrator. This fear of disappearance operates according to a complex temporal scheme. It is both retroactive—a reaction to death—and a rehearsal of anxieties prior to the dog's death—an anticipation that the dog could be dead if it is lost. Countless narratives in literature and film stage the dog missing so that it may return—from the cinema classics *Lassie Come Home* (1943) and *Homeward Bound: The Incredible Journey* (1993) to the recently published *Timoleon Vieta Come Home: A Sentimental Journey* (2003) by Dan Rhodes. In the second half of this utterly heartless, sardonic novel the dog is depicted as returning to its owner after having been abandoned, only to be murdered on the final leg of its months-long journey. In general, such narratives imagine the dog gone, to be preemptively dead, so as to perform its reappearance: they thus repeat the psychological impetus behind writing the dog's life after its death, namely, to enact its coming back to life. In both cases, the attempt is to anticipate the trauma of loss and thereby mitigate the full impact of its shock. Rhodes, by contrast, sadistically destroys the reader's longing for a gentle end by ruthlessly killing off the dog just before it reaches its destination.

Key to the logic of the "not yet" is the belief in the power of resurrection in signs. As Kristeva writing on melancholia states, "language starts with a *negation* (*Verneinung*) of loss" (*Black Sun* 43): one recovers the lost essential object again in signs, "or rather since I consent to lose her I have not lost her (that is the negation), I can recover her in language" (43). Indeed, the autobiographical rendition of a dog's life marks this consent to rehearse the loss, to re-traverse it in the telling, so as to recover the dog in re*present*ation. The writer tries to regain the intensity of their relation through language. If language is always haunted by its own uncertainties and imprecision, especially with regards to a species who does not share it, at least in bringing a dead pet back to life through signs, language can seem to triumph.

The converse of this celebration of resurrection through language is the resigned acceptance that the tale of the canine life will necessarily differ from the original. Writing retrieves a life, gives meaning to it, but also signals that it is different from its real-life model. The representation is invariably an inadequate substitution. It thus betokens renunciation and relinquishment. Peter M. Sacks, in studying the self-reflexive intricacies of language in the elegy, notes how "only the object *as lost*, and not the object itself, enters into the substitute sign, and the latter is accepted only by a turning away from the actual identity of what was lost" (6). In the act of writing the bereaved acknowledges that he or she grasps the sign of what was lost and that the dog and self, in the auto-biographical narrative, acquire a fictional identity, something other than the original, at one remove from it. This recognition of difference entails an acceptance of loss.

According to the "no longer" vector, then, writing serves to recognize the actuality and magnitude of the bereavement, rather than deny it. It repeats and reinforces the awareness of the loss, rather than erase it. Paradoxically, however, this reinforcement is not a means of enhancing the grief but of controlling it. As Abraham and Torok observe, commu-nication via language is the first step in "successful replacement of the object's presence with the self's cognizance of its absence" (128). As cen-tral to this process of mourning, the emptiness is filled with words and the dog becomes the creation of the writer's imagination. But rather than a token of narcissistic melancholic self-absorption, this move must be seen as a process of healing, whereby the psychic energy is redirected away from the lost object and toward the self, as Freud outlines in his description of the work of mourning. In other words, by assimilating the loss into one's own product, into one's own biography (as in Eliza-beth von Arnim, Colette Audry, and Rhoda Lerman), one undergoes a process of detachment from the loved object and a restorative reposi-tioning of the self. To put it another way, one needs to keep the dead dead, so that it does not return to haunt one. To represent something is to bury it: although representation commemorates the dead, it also defends against its return, so that the living can continue to live.

In sum, despite the melancholic attachment to the departed love object, these autobiographical stories that both start and culminate in the dog's death work through the process of mourning by giving voice to the loss. They countervail depressive muteness and avenge against the passivity one experiences in the face of death. Writing here serves both as a testimony to the dog's life and as a gift to the departed. It offers a farewell that acknowledges the departure of the beloved. But it also insists on sharing the testimony of loss with others in a bid to reverse the social foreclosure of grief. For instance, what makes the sim-ple, even sentimental *La nécrologie de Joffre* so rich is that Pedrick is actu-ally fighting an internalized suppression of bereavement that mirrors the societal disparagement of and injunction against the mourning of animals. Rather than accept the disavowal of loss society requires of him, he verbally acknowledges his bereavement. This putting words to his grief signals mourning as a therapeutic counterdirection to depres-sive silence. Rather than claiming that the loss is so painful and unique that it cannot be communicated and that it needs to be entombed away and silenced within one, writing emphasizes that the mourning needs to be witnessed.

I now turn to four autobiographical works on the death of a pet dog: Marie Bonaparte's *Topsy: The Story of a Golden-Haired Chow* (1940), Colette Audry's *Behind the Bathtub: The Story of a French Dog* (1962), Michael Field's *Whym Chow: Flame of Love* (1914), and Sally Mann's *What Remains* (2004). The first takes place in the time of the "not yet" but imagines the time of the "no longer," for Topsy has been diagnosed with cancer. The second, by contrast, is written during the "no longer" but depicts a highly ambivalent relationship to the "not yet," for the author constantly wishes her troublesome dog were no longer part of her life. Both works, by highly gifted intellectuals of their day, display a subtly complex range of emotions toward their companions, testifying to how tortuous and fraught with guilt the thought of their death is, precisely because of the authors' inability to disentangle themselves from a specular relation to the beloved pet. The pairing of the next two selections juxtaposes the hallucinatory resurrection of the pet in the exuberant, ornate elegies of Katherine Bradley and Edith Cooper (a.k.a. Michael Field) with a very different resurrection—the actual exhuming of a beloved dog bordering on the morbid. By photographing the remains of her beloved greyhound, Sally Mann visually renders her profound bereftness and gives full witness to her desolation. In utter contrast to the attachment to which these women testify, I conclude with analysis of two works that explore societal disavowal of grief over animal loss. As investigations into the intentional killing of dogs, Alejandro González Iñárritu's film *Amores Perros* and J. M. Coetzee's novel *Disgrace* depict the repercussions of the refusal to mourn. They therewith also become moving testimonials to the intricacies of bereavement.

Marie Bonaparte

Princess Marie Bonaparte, great-granddaughter of Napoleon's brother Lucien, wife of Prince George of Greece, and cousin to Christian X, king of Denmark, possessed not only impeccable titles but a brilliantly sharp mind as well. She began psychoanalytic therapy with Freud in 1925 and soon became one of his most devoted disciples, publishing, among other studies, *The Life and Works of Edgar Allan Poe: A Psycho-Analytic Interpretation* (1933); a two-volume autobiography *To the Memory of the Departed* (1952); *Chronos, Eros, Thanatos* (1952); and the collection of

essays, *Female Sexuality* (1953). She was, moreover, Freud's prime bene-
factor as well as a close family friend, who played an instrumental role
in helping him gain permission to leave Vienna after the *Anschluss*. During this time while waiting for their exit visas, Freud and his daughter
Anna distracted themselves by translating into German Bonaparte's
story about her chow Topsy. Freud himself was deeply attached to his
own succession of chows, who would sit at the foot of the analytic
couch during sessions. Jo-fi had been a gift of Marie Bonaparte to Freud
in 1930, and one of her puppies, Lun-yu replaced her when she died.
Not surprisingly given her connection to psychoanalysis, Bonaparte's
tribute to her dog offers a rich study of her affective ties, though she
refrains from outright analyzing her anxieties about Topsy's illness,
uncannily mirroring Freud's oral cancer, from which he was to die in
1939.

Topsy was written between March 1935 and June 1936. The short
chapters are parceled into even briefer reflections, each a jewel, suggesting that the work was composed in diary-like entries. The published version displays several photos of Topsy, adorned with such captions as "In
the Meadow" or "Topsy Sleeping." As no human is present, one can
imagine Bonaparte herself photographing her companion, with the
result that the photos, like their accompanying text, bespeak the solitary, deep bond between dog and mistress. After briefly narrating how
she came to chows and mentioning that three of them already lie
buried, Bonaparte tells of one winter morning, on a day when coinci-
dentally she herself was ill, detecting a small growth under five-year-old
Topsy's right lip. The tumor proves to be cancerous and the dog is taken
to the "God of the Rays." Belying her owner's constant fear of loss,
Topsy is healed by the radiation therapy. Yet once beset by anxieties,
Bonaparte continues to be haunted by worries that the cancer might
return. The story ends with Topsy, the "talisman of life" by her bedside,
during another spell of illness, barring the "entrance of my room to a
worse ill, and even to death" (79). Since Topsy is in fact cured, the question arises as to what motivates these recurrent fantasies, about not only
the dog's death but her own as well.

In this final chapter Bonaparte narrates how as a child she was reas-
sured, when sick, by her nurse Mimau that the malady would be tran-
sient and would not take her life away, as death had taken her mother.
Mimau, she continues, now lies buried close to her parents, yet despite
the passing of time she still harbors the same irrational childhood dread
that a chance illness could lead to death. Like Mimau, Topsy serves to
comfort and protect her. Endings and beginnings thus intertwine: just

as the close circles back to childhood recollections of bereavement, so too does the prologue begin with Bonaparte's memory of losing, as a young girl, her beloved fox terrier. As an adult recalling this loss, for the longest time Bonaparte would not allow her children to adopt a pet, for "why thus squander my heart away?" (9). When Bonaparte does relent, it is when her sixteen-year-old daughter suffers from a protracted illness, a detail that gains full significance only at the close, namely, that the nearness of the dog will stave off, like an amulet, the threat of abandonment, sickness, and death.

The beginning and ending of *Topsy* thus highlight that the anxieties about the chow's cancer diagnosis are deeply interwoven with other memories of loss; the dog's presence, after all, is to mitigate against such pain. Bonaparte remarks that she loves her pet more now that it is ill, an odd confession that can perhaps be explained by the fact that, because Topsy has stood in for other losses, her imminent death renders her all the more precious. For instance, the author writes that Topsy takes the place of her daughter once she left home (11) and that "dogs are children that do not grow up, that do not depart" (55). As we have seen, Topsy also substitutes for the deceased parent or caregiver, but she also guards against their vampiric return: "Under the nocturnal trees seem to roam the ghosts of those that are gone—my mother, my dead mother, who wants her child back; my dead father come back to claim me. When you are gone, Topsy, who will guard me from these ghosts?" (27). Conversely, Bonaparte dreams of a future reunion in paradise, not only with Topsy, who will welcome her into the beyond, but with her mother whom she never knew. Further collapsing canine and human parentage, Topsy's radiation treatment recalls that of the author's father, the latter being unsuccessful. And, although decorously left unmentioned, Bonaparte must anticipate the worsening of the cancer of her mentor and paternal substitute, Freud.[3] Indeed, in a 1948 essay entitled "De l'essentielle ambivalence d'Éros," Bonaparte narrates how in 1937 she brought Topsy to Vienna so that her "spiritual father" could meet her "child" (*Chronos* 68). What this overdetermination, this intricate interweaving of Topsy with various family members going back to Bonaparte's childhood suggests is that what is mourned is actually her own bereft, abandoned self, herself as forlorn child. Indeed, the collapsing of differences includes, above all, the melancholic, narcissistic confusion of self and other. As indicated, Bonaparte frequently fantasizes her own death and afterlife: "A same death, one evening of ultimate weariness, will lay us into the earth" (22).

To imagine Topsy greeting her in paradise is to imagine the chow already dead. Bonaparte anticipates the full range of stages leading from the present illness to the beyond, including tranquilizing Topsy before the trip to the veterinarian, the lethal injection, her burial in the garden, and decay of her body. These steps are fantasized in elaborate detail, pictured "with fearful intensity" (35). Moreover, when Bonaparte reflects on the dog's present life it is retroactively, from the perspective of her death, in the future anterior: "What will Topsy have loved when death comes to take her away?" (55–56). In sum, the pet is revered and idealized as if it were already being commemorated.

Psychoanalytically speaking, there are two possible reasons for this fantasy of Topsy's death. The first explanation is Freud's own: when Bonaparte visited him in Vienna with Topsy and continued her sessions with him, she spoke extensively of her worries over her pet but surprised herself by suddenly blurting out to Freud that she wished Topsy were dead. Freud responded that because she loves Topsy so much, and because every violent sentiment is ambivalent, she turns her desires against her adored pet (*Chronos* 69). Bonaparte later expands on his interpretation with the profound observation that the strange love between creatures of different species was so replete with a painful tension (*tension douloureuse* [83]) that she wished it would end. A second explanation for the fantasy of Topsy's death comes to mind when one brings into play the complicated temporal structure of anticipation and retrospection, namely, that Bonaparte can be said to be so afraid of future loss that she separates herself earlier. In fact, she can cast the dog as departed because it has already become totally introjected. Once the dog is protected and held safe in this melancholic psychic entombment, the external object can safely be imagined dead. In short, she loves Topsy to death.

The paradox of this spectralization and hollowing out of the present is that the dog itself is ignorant of impending death and lives solely in the moment, an irony that does not escape Bonaparte: "I love this tiny life which deems itself eternal, since its running paws so cheerfully deny their inevitable stop, one day" (63–64). This contrast between the present moment as full *and* as vanishing also informs the function of the photographs that accompany the text: although they capture an instant from life—Topsy among the daisies or enjoying the warm spring sun—for the reader they commemorate a life now departed. The momentary exists only ephemerally in the photo. As Roland Barthes writes about the "melancholy of Photography," "by shifting this reality to the past ('this-has-been'), the photograph suggests that it is already dead"

(*Camera Lucida* 79). Thus, although the photos depict Topsy's gaiety and beauty, they also preserve her in effigy.

The most telling sign of the author's melancholia, however, is that it is not only the external object that is cast as dead (though kept entombed alive in the loving heart). In the specular attachment called love, the self is imagined as dead as well. Abraham and Torok write: "The bereaved become the dead for themselves" (111). Although she may seem "an eternal goddess" to Topsy (51), Bonaparte anticipates herself growing old and dying. In a strange reversal of whom is most likely to perish first, Bonaparte imagines being memorialized in Topsy's mind. It is she who becomes the revenant who returns to haunt the chow: "Topsy, should I die before you, my image, an uncertain phantom, will haunt you when you sleep. . . . I should not be altogether dead if, in the memory of some few creatures . . . my spectre would thus survive" (72). Her imagination carries her so far along this path of self-obliteration that she claims that, were Topsy to have puppies, they would be forever ignorant of her existence!

To the same effect, rather than hoping that her writings endow her with immortality, Bonaparte, in the self-chastisement that characterizes melancholia, refers to the "vain signs on this paper" (71), "a worthless heap of cellulose which men call paper" (73). She even self-consciously reflects on how writing is instrumental in Topsy's death: "It is only with ink and paper that she has been killed" (46). Something vampiric indeed pervades the text, as if the author wished Topsy dead so that the dog could return in her writing. To the same effect, Bonaparte endeavors to fill the anticipated absence with the fullness of spoken address, for the most striking rhetorical device in the story is that of apostrophe. It is as if, by calling out Topsy's name, invoking it repeatedly, the dog fantasized as departed can become alive again. Or, in a variation of this desire, the dog survives precisely so that she can repeatedly imagine it dead.

This complicated temporal structure of preemptive and retroactive mourning can also be elucidated in terms of psychoanalytic theories of trauma. In addition to coping with the shock of the diagnosis, Bonaparte is clearly trying to forestall the trauma of the dog's imminent death. But, as indicated, via Topsy she is also working through previous, perhaps unvoiced, traumas of childhood separation. She can conceivably be fearful of future bereavement because of her painful experience with prior ones. Freud explains in *Beyond the Pleasure Principle* how psychic protection is often not in place at the time a trauma occurs, hence the blow occurs suddenly and without forewarning. No defenses have been built up against harmful stimuli from the exterior. It is only subsequently that the survivor erects the defenses that should have been present in the first place to protect the self. This fortification after the fact (in the belated operation Freud terms *Nachträglichkeit*) occurs via an unconscious repetition compulsion: the victim imagines reconfronting the stimulus, which is retrospectively mastered by developing the anxiety that was previously omitted. Involuntary disturbing fantasies also surface with the psychic purpose of preventing or postponing future trauma. *Angst*, in other words, protects against *Schreck*. Trauma theory thus clarifies Bonaparte's otherwise inexplicable fantasies concerning Topsy's death even after the dog is cured: she returns to the thought of the pet dying because the initial shock came so unexpectedly, never allowing her to master its acceptance. The repetition compulsion morphs as well into the fantasies she has about the ghosts of her parents returning and about herself as a specter returning to haunt Topsy. It also explains the unintentional recollection of childhood fears of illness and her need to have the dog serve as a talisman against such recurrence. Sadly, the fear of repetition itself—of yet another loss projected far into the future—makes her vow never to get another dog after Topsy.

If the dog serves as our companion during waking hours, we hope it will also ease us into death and accompany us into the beyond. Thus, Bonaparte envisions her and Topsy sharing the same death. Yet, as talisman, Topsy also guards against visitations by family ghosts and wards off fears of abandonment. Marie Bonaparte's autobiographical story thus taps into the mysterious powers attributed the dog by world religions from time immemorial. In Greek mythology, Cerberus guards the entrance to Hades, keeping the living out and the dead in. Anubis was the hound- or jackal-headed Egyptian god of the tomb and protector of the deceased. And in one of the two great Hindu epics, the *Mahabharata*, King Yudhishthira refuses to enter into heaven without his dog, at which point the dog is transformed into Dharma himself, the God of Righteousness. To see the dog either as an emissary to the other world or as a protector of the tomb are ways of counteracting the inconceivable notion that our passage into death must occur without them.[4] However fanciful Bonaparte's imagination and blithe her affection, her narrative delves into these ancient apprehensions regarding the loneliness of death and the longing for the dog to continue its companionship and protection into the unknown life beyond. Moreover, although in order to write a luminescent tribute to her dog she refrains from plodding self-analysis, she casts these primal fears with all the acuity and sensitivity to detail that her psychoanalytic training can advance.

Colette Audry

Another work of profound psychological insight and laborious mourning is Colette Audry's *Behind the Bathtub* (*Derrière la baignoire*), a bestseller in France that won the Prix Médicis in 1962. Audry, in addition to being a novelist and playwright, was a politically active socialist, feminist, and lycée professor. *Behind the Bathtub* is a remarkable autobiographical text that will have no truck with trite, cute, or even half-way sentimental anecdotes about one's pet. Instead the novel details the author's constant irritability, humiliation, and heartbreak over a dog with a nervous and excitable temperament. It is a work infused with Bonaparte's notion that this strange, intense love between species is characterized by ambivalence. Admitting that she did not even want a dog, Colette Audry acquires an Alsatian (or, as it is known today, a German shepherd) with little forethought or preparation. Although a loyal creature, it brings out her impatience and even meanness, for it is agitated and uncontrollable in many social situations. Indeed the bitch so suffers from intense loyalty and fear of abandonment that she cannot be left with friends or in a kennel when Audry travels. Nor can her owner take Douchka with her in the car on vacations, for the dog barks incessantly. *Behind the Bathtub* is a story that candidly portrays the painful tensions between the species.

Audry writes with startling frankness about her resentment toward what she calls not the faults but "vices" of Douchka (39). She is shackled to Douchka as if to a "ball and chain" (40); she witnesses "the transformation of [her] holiday freedom into a species of slavery" (42); and because of Douchka she is "obliged to perform innumerable tiresome chores, take countless precautions" (184). With no other recourse in sight she repeatedly contemplates putting her dog to sleep. Yet, although the love she bears Douchka is a "sickly, resentful emotion . . . forever taking back what it had given" (184), it is a profound attachment nonetheless. Thus, what Audry calls her "slavery" or "ball and chain" must be seen not only as frustration at Douchka's bad behavior but as a reflection of a deep emotional bond. The vassalage in the human-canine relationship, Audry reminds us, is reciprocal. Indeed, on Douchka's death Audry is weighed down by a guilt that seems heavier than the responsibility she bore toward the dog while it was alive, as if she needed to compensate for the previous resentment.

When chastised as a puppy Douchka would crawl away and hide in a cramped spot behind the bathtub. Although she quickly outgrew this refuge and the protection it offered, it still remained "a kind of penitential corner" (29) to which she would withdraw. Three-quarters of the way through the novel Douchka suddenly falls ill with a severity Audry fails to realize. Overnight she dies and the author, looking for her in the morning, discovers her in the same corner behind the bathtub. At this point in the novel the title starts accruing major significance, intimating retrospectively that the entire story must be a coming to terms with this death. The spot "behind the bathtub" seems to symbolize all that is shameful and abject in the dog, all that Audry despised and rejected but later realizes she must spell out in her writing in order to begin to comprehend and accept.

Whereas the days of routine care previously seemed tediously endless, now the days of missing Douchka seem achingly countless (258). Audry devotes the last quarter of the novel to reflections on Douchka's palpable absence and ends with the painful self-indictment: "In her final moments she felt so wretchedly at odds with life, so alien to her own nature, so changed and broken and desperate, that she could only assume she had *done something wrong*. An unknown and imaginary crime loomed over her. So she crawled away to her penitent's corner, bitterly ashamed, and died. And I was not there with her" (307). The intriguing question the novel poses is: given the irritations Douchka caused, why would Audry's bereavement be so intense, especially because what she desired—to be relieved of an onerous burden—actually occurs? In other words, what does mourning Douchka's death have to do with the litany of frustrations enumerated during her lifetime? In brief, how does the "no longer" inform the "not yet"?

Immediately on Douchka's death the author starts jotting down notes in order to map out the boundaries of her grief (250) and to win back "a little territory from this devouring void" (260). She wants to prolong Douchka's presence with memories, to fill the void with writing, for words stave off the involuntary tears (260). Audry soon becomes obsessed with the task and refuses to leave anything out of her inventory (289). She wants "to conduct a final summing-up of [Douchka] from every aspect" (280), though as a result she comes to realize that she is reassembling this period of her own life. We recall that, according to Freud, the process of mourning involves detaching the emotional cathexis from the lost object and redirecting the psychic energies back toward the self. In *The Ego and the Id* (1923) he further notes how loss is reconfigured as a means of constituting the ego: "The character of the ego is a precipitate of the relinquished object-investments [*Objektbesetzungen*] that contains the history of these object-choices" (13:257). In order for this recuperation to occur, Audry must avow and record traces of Douchka as an integral part of herself. What her writing accomplishes is the expression of herself as a subject with affective, desirous ties to Douchka, rather than one who repudiates the bond. But the process is an arduous one that has to struggle against prior disavowal. The complete imbrication of self and other, which Audry tried earlier to deny in wishing Douchka dead, is now realized with such intensity that she can claim that Douchka's death "will only end with the termination of my life" (305). She now admits that she was so close to Douchka and had adopted her so absolutely into her life that no other dog could satisfy her as a replacement. The voicing of such attachment, previously disowned, marks her first step in the act of mourning. Thus the whole novel, the collection of articulated emotion, can be seen as Audry's long farewell, as a protracted process of mourning. As befits the "no longer" paradigm, the empty sadness is filled with words that acknowledge the loss.

The story begins with the author riding in the car with Douchka and her son Jean-François. So annoyed are they by the dog's incessant barking that they consider turning her loose and abandoning her on the road. It had happened once before, when two miles from home, they let her out, only to have the dog limp back with raw pads, exhausted and bewildered. The novel thus begins with the recollection of a cruel deed made all the more shameful because of the dog's loyalty. As if to publicly display her petulance and to chastise herself openly before her readers, Audry narrates several instances of her hostility toward Douchka, resulting in the dog's humiliation and confusion. She also tells how the dog suffered from being boarded and mistreated in a kennel and, later, from being tranquilized in the car so that its riders could have some peace. Yet although these episodes are narrated without compunction—similar to Audry confessing her wish to be rid of Douchka—they beg to be aligned with the end of the novel, namely, that Audry cannot shake off the fear that she abandoned Douchka at the point of her death. Together these episodes serve, in retrospect, as reminders of her guilt at having left her companion desperately alone; they culminate in the manner and place of the dog's death. That this guilt lurked, repressed, in the back of Audry's mind during Douchka's life can be seen in her fantasy that, were the dog to wander off and become lost, it would be the dog's own fault, thankfully not her own (221). She thus earlier tries to dispel thoughts of remorse and any shame associated with it. Yet they come back to haunt her, as if self-incrimination and self-indictment were part of the vigil, the watch she keeps over the dead.

It is curious that the death of Douchka occasions the narration of sadistic impulses toward her. Melanie Klein explains, however, that "every objectal loss entails a manic sadistic triumph over the object" (cited in Abraham and Torok 120). This aggression stems from the ambivalence toward the object—the melancholic rejoices on having conquered the object on which he or she feels to have squandered psychic investment. Such libidinal fantasies, however, are also accompanied by remorse, as if one's sadism had caused the loss of the good object. Thus Audry closes the novel in contrition and self-reproof. Perceptive and self-critical of her emotions as she is, Audry realizes the extent of the projection of her own negative characteristics onto the dog. Douchka's agitation and excitability correspond to Audry's brusqueness and irritability. For instance, when the Alsatian snarls at irksome children, the author admits to being "just as aggressive as she was, in my own way; her behavior gratified me, there was more of the wild beast in me than in her" (106–7). Consequently, scolding the dog is "like becoming exasperated with oneself" (173). "Quite unconsciously," she continues, "I had come to identify our two personalities" (173). Thus, projection and identification can be diagnosed as parallel symptoms of Audry's melancholia: she identifies with the lost object toward which she bears anger.

After the death, signs of Audry's melancholia—her interminable mourning—become more readily detectable in the ways in which she tries to hold onto the ghost of Douchka. For instance, she calls grieving a way of staving off the death: "The day when I ceased to grieve for her she would be finally dead, but not before" (260). She even registers the dog's absence as a physical and tangible presence: "But she was *there*, she remained there all the time. This too-palpable absence, this brooding void lurking behind the wall, was her latest device for prolonging her existence in my personal life" (276). Like the owner of Pedro, she wants to move elsewhere because the reminders of Douchka are scattered everywhere in her apartment (262). Audry, moreover, remains fiercely loyal to Douchka even after, or more properly, especially after her death. Thus she claims to live not just *with* her grief but *by* it (290). Finally, this need to reverse the damage of her neglect and now protect Douchka safely within a solicitous self can be seen in Audry's reference to the "cramped haven of [the] heart" where the departed Douchka retreats to dwell (276).

But although one can identify and label these moments of prolonged melancholic attachment and identification, it must be emphasized that Audry is also actively trying to disengage herself from the tie that she so keenly feels in bereavement. The anger that she voices can thus also be read as the attempt to withdraw from the intensity of her affection. By disparaging Douchka and reminding herself of how much she wanted to get rid of her, Audry can begin to release herself from the painful ties to the lost object. Thus, however counterintuitive it may seem, her very petulance can be read as a sign of the inordinate devotion from which she is attempting to break away. As Freud notes: "Thus in melancholia an inordinate number of individual battles spring up around the object, in which hate and love fight with each other, the former trying to release the libido from the object, the latter trying to maintain the libido's position against the assault" (10:444). Ambivalence, he notes, arises from the threat of loss: this oscillation between love and hate ostensibly lies at the heart of Audry's conflict with Douchka.

Another way in which she tries to detach herself is to be wary of the trivial anthropomorphization with which owners commonly treat their pets. The pathos of this novel indeed resides in its respect and appreciation of Douchka's difference and unapproachability. Audry admits that the attachment grows because, in endeavoring to understand Douchka's behavior, she humanizes her: "Day by day the thorny complexities of our relationship steadily deepened, but somehow we managed to adapt ourselves to them. The more I fell in with her ways, the more I tended, despite everything, to humanize her in my imagination; and the more complex our relationship became, I suppose, the deeper grew my attachment to her" (89). Yet Audry also admits: "What *she* was I shall never know: how can one penetrate to the soul of a dog?" (65). Such observations express her constant frustration with Douchka but also how this consternation folds into love.

Part of the mourning process that Audry undergoes, then, is that, in accepting death, she accepts that Douchka was always only "a figment of my imagination" (253), a "baffling creature . . . of whom I understood so little" (94). Audry acknowledges that she "tended to confuse, hopelessly, the real Douchka and my imagined projection" (306). "She was never able to tell me, openly, what *she* thought of my verdict on her, and indeed of the way I had treated her, because our whole range of thought was, beyond any doubt, a closed book to her, of which she knew nothing" (305). The humility that underlies this confession marks a renouncing of control over the other and, by extension, of a relinquishing of the beloved, a farewell to her. However painful the reminder of her having misinterpreted Douchka is, however inconsolable she becomes when she recalls the rift between them, Audry's bereavement is also a letting go of Douchka and, hence, a sane refusal to cling to the falsifications and sentimentalizations that projection and anthropo-morphization create. In sum, through the act of autobiographical self-analysis, Audry recognizes the irreconcilable separation between herself and the Alsatian, which is part of her acceptance of loss.

Shortly after Douchka dies, the author's father passes away and, four months after that, her mother as well, but it is the animal for whom she weeps. Although Audry realizes that this displacement of grieving may shock many, she frankly admits that the response of oth-ers matters little to her (285). It is this honesty with which Audry records her emotions that make *Behind the Bathtub* such a revealing work. For, it must be stressed, it is not that her attachment to Douchka is pathological or abnormal, nor, as every dog owner knows, are her frustration and anger with an unruly pet unusual. But the candor with which she expresses her irritability, on the one hand, and her intense grief, on the other, *are* unconventional and extraordinary. As stated at the beginning of this chapter, mourning of the dead pet in contempo-rary Western society tends to be silent and fleeting, reflecting the dis-avowal of the affective tie that joins human and canine, a bond that often fits the lofty description of what Barthes called "a mystic impulse," the "exaltation of loving *someone unknown*" (*A Lover's Discourse* 135), but that is rarely declared as such. Colette Audry joins Marie Bonaparte, Elizabeth von Arnim, Sue Coe, and Rhoda Lerman as women writers and artists who chronicle this attachment, both its flashes of exaltation as well as the weightiness of sadness at the animal's pitifulness and incomprehension.

Michael Field

In sharp contradistinction to both *Topsy* and *Behind the Bathtub*, there is no ambivalence about the love for the pet dog in the collection of thirty ardent poems that comprise Michael Field's *Whym Chow: Flame of Love* (written 1906 and published 1914 in a terra cotta suede limited edition): they form an impassioned eulogy to an eight-year-old chow. Where the ambivalence arises is in the mind of the reader, for the dog is brought so vividly back to life that he or she is uncertain whether these poems could ever have been written following its death. They are an example of a tri-umphal resurrection and making present through language: they bestow the utter illusion of the "not yet," as Whym Chow reappears with greater clarity. In Kristevean terms, they are a veritable *Verneinung* or negation of loss: I have not lost my pet, for it is recovered through poetry. The collection begins with the epithet, "Leave the fire ashes, what survives is gold." Mourning is left behind as the chow, with its regal leonine mane, golden flame of fur and "beauty—that of action born, / . . . / An apparition of exceeding fire" (poem 11, "Dei Dono"), is conjured back to life in all his magnificence.[5] The gold is thus not only the treasured dog but also the poetry that survives and purifies the grief.

Even more remarkable is the authorship. Michael Field is the nom de plume of Katherine Bradley and her niece Edith Cooper, a lesbian couple who prodigiously wrote poetry and drama at the turn of the century. They saw in the love and loyalty their dog had for them the passion and commitment they bore each other. The puppy, a three-month-old with long red-gold hair, was a birthday present to Edith on 26 January 1898 and was named after a family friend, Edward Whymper. The chow came to fill an absence in Katherine and Edith's household, for he arrived shortly after the death of latter's father. The dog's own death ushered in another major transition in the couple's life, for the year following it they converted to Catholicism. Biographer Emma Donoghue remarks that the women "claimed that the intensity of [Whym's] love had caused his life to be 'consumed' after only eight years, and that he was now their 'guardian angel' or spirit guide" (122). She explains the conversion as inevitable: "The Michaels were so lonely and isolated after their dog's death that they needed a new kind of ready-made family" (26). In their religiosity the poems only partially lead the way to the conversion, for they are blasphemous enough both in their lesbian passion and association of the dog with Christ that they would necessarily predate a strict assumption of Catholic doctrine.

To illustrate this heresy, consider the fifth poem in the series, "Trinity," cited here in full.

I did not love him for myself alone:
I loved him that he loved my dearest love.
O God, no blasphemy
It is to feel we loved in trinity.
To tell Thee that I loved him as Thy Dove
Is loved, and is Thy own,
That comforted the moan
Of Thy Beloved, when earth could give no balm
And in Thy Presence makes His tenderest calm.

So I possess this creature of Love's flame,
So loving what I love he lives from me;

Not white, a thing of fire,
Of seraph-plumèd limbs and one desire,
That is my heart's own, and shall ever be:
An animal—with aim
Thy Dove avers the same. . . .
O symbol of our perfect union, strange
Unconscious Bearer of Love's interchange.

The pronouns are initially confusing and need to be paid close attention. The addressee of the poem is the Godhead; "he" refers to the chow, who loves "my dearest love," thus the female partner. The act of loving traverses various vectors: the dog is loved, for loving the other woman, who is loved in turn by the speaker. In "so loving what I love" the chow doubles the "I" ("he lives from me"). And, giving a whole new dimension to the phrase, "flaming creatures," insofar as the dog is "this creature of Love's flame," he resembles the Holy Spirit of the Trinity, iconographically depicted either as a flame or a dove. Although the phrasing "this creature of Love's flame" might suggest the offspring of heterosexual union, it is precisely not a child but something more spiritual (though obedient to the dualities in this poem, still of flesh and blood).

If it is recalled that "Trinity" belongs to a collection that commemorates a deceased pet, Whym Chow can also be read as the Paraclete whose purpose is to comfort the living. As recalled alive in these poems, his presence acts as a solace to his owners and helps them surmount their grief. Through the joint composition of the elegies, Edith and Katherine write the "we"—they speak in a unified tongue. In other words, through the death of Whym, they renew their poetic inspiration. Now that he is gone they "meet / Still together in the sweet / Company of close-drawn breath" (poem 22). Thus their love for each other is strengthened and intensified by remembering Whym Chow. Any loss of the reciprocity they enjoyed in daily communion with their dog is overcome by their renewed togetherness. Whym, so to speak, flames and illuminates their love and their poetry and, to continue the metaphor of divine fire, serves as the eternal torch to both. Katherine and Edith's love is the continuation of Whym's life, a transfiguration of the meaning of his presence, with the result that the couple is freed from extended grieving.

Envisaged as resurrected, Whym acquires Christ-like resonances. The third poem, for instance, beginning "Crowned with wine-steeped / Daphne-bough" in an allusion to Dionysus, whose rebirth is celebrated in the Eleutherian mysteries, ends with the invocation to Whym, as if pleading for his intercession, "Nay, be with us such / As by holiest grace / Spirits have been made / Wayfarer with men, fired through to bless!"[6] Earlier in the poem, Edith and Katherine intone and pray: "By the blood, the wine, / O beloved, our Want, our hidden Soul, / Be our daemon, be Guardian-angel near." Perhaps the most blasphemous poem, though one spoken in the spirit of utter devotion, is the thirteenth entitled "My Cup," alluding to the sleeping draught the women gave the dog to relieve its pain. Like Christ, Whym Chow drinks the bitter, sacramental chalice of death and, like Christ, is both the embodiment of Love and dies in love: "Chow thou hast drunk the bitter cup— / Love unto death, / That makes love free and lifts it up." If Whym Chow flames the fire of ardor between the two women, one can also say their love is sanctified by a death that assumes sacrificial overtones.

This love, forged as it is at the juncture of heterospecies and homoerotic desire, is doubly transgressive. In dissolving so completely the boundaries between species in the unity and symmetry of love that "Trinity" envisages, Katherine and Edith challenge the boundaries that define what proper and natural love is, whether it be directed to a canine or human being. The intensity of the dog's devotion becomes a model for their own fervor toward each other. For instance, in the ninth poem, which begins "My loved One is away from me / Whom thou dost love," when her partner is gone, the speaker is solaced by her joint undeterred vigil with Whym: "By the unbounded pressure of one yearning / Vaster than we, no pause in it, no turning!" She then enjoins her pet, now that he is in heaven: "O Chow, my little Love, you watch above her / Watch still beside me, be with me her lover." The description of the love the dog holds toward them thus serves to illuminate the passion they bear each other and that might not otherwise find voice. Moreover, now that Whym is the one to have left, the women reciprocate his love in the common vigil that is their poetry.

The Fields' love has two contradictory facets to it: it provocatively mixes both innocence and daring, and this ambiguity is what links their devotion to Whym and to each other. In praising the quotidian life with their pet, they claim that dog love is natural and pure; so too the personal intimacy between the two women creates its own genuineness. Both conservatively dressed late Victorians who would never dare to wear pants to signal the gender invert, they use innocent, unsullied animal love to portray what they regarded as an uncomplicated, natural commitment to each other. And yet it is also a transgressive love that requires a degree of allegorical couching. It is significant that nowhere in the entire series is the word dog used. The poem "Trinity" only mentions that "he" is "an animal" like the dove of the Godhead. Just as the species goes unnamed, so too is their companionship not overtly identified as homosexual. And, of course, the authors camouflage themselves under the pseudonym Michael Field, although at this late date in their publishing career they had been already outed as two female authors. This indirectness deflects the labeling or admittance of moral impropriety. Yet, although, as in "Trinity," the Fields repudiate the heretic nature of their triangular passion by calling it sacred, the very words, "no blasphemy / It is to feel" betray that they are in fact acutely aware of their transgression. They combine utter sincerity with clearsighted ironic self-consciousness about both their religious and societal sacrilege.

Poem 27 can be read as an example of this allegorical veiling, whereby it is significant that the Fields chose to write in the florid, highly wrought, dissimulative style that characterizes allegorical discourse in general. It begins: "Full of the passions nurtured in the wild / And virgin places of the world. Whym Chow, / Thou camest to thy Mistress, as a child." As Katherine also knew her niece Edith as a child, she could be said to have molded the girl's "untranslatable, / And native being" and to have lit in her "heart a star / First love." To then call Whym's love "infinite and savage," divulging "recesses never shown," and "a new / Compulsion from . . . Eros" could also be to name the powerful erotic desire that drew the two women together. Friends of Oscar Wilde, the Fields allude to him when they ask "What is the other name of Love? / Has Love another name?" (poem 6), here, too, brilliantly conjoining dog love with the "Love that dare not speak its name." In yet another veiled erotic allusion, in poem 22 that begins "Sleeping together: Sleep," the dog is described as leaping into their common bed in a stanza that begins with an echo of the first, "Loving together, love." The mystic *trans*cendence and *trans*port that this triangular love embodies hence also signifies its *trans*gression. So intensely to love either a dog or a member of the same sex is to explore a passion veering from the societal norm.

To speak of the Fields' erotic, physical language is to return to how Whym Chow is hallucinated as immediate and present. In other words, the *Verneinung* or negation of the loss is effective because it is so vividly sensual. In some poems, such as "Introit," it is explicitly stated that "The dead comes back again, the dead, our dead, / . . . . / O Chow, my little Love, thou art come home."[7] In others, the resurrection is implied by the lush, resplendent verse employed to bring him back to life. In poem 4, for instance, the Fields recall Whym's vivacious energy: "He loved thy torch of vivid flame, / He loved the breath of life, the rush, the glance / Of eyes from inmost happiness." These poems mark an effort to regain through representation the intensity lost on his death. They fill the emptiness with an abundance of words.

An especially sensuous passage conjures the intimacy of contact with the warmth and depth of his coat: "Dearer would that fur beguile / Than the pillow's tenderest fold; / Deeper than the turf, its pile, / Warmer and more manifold / In its lulling magic spell / Than the seashore's golden hum" (poem 24). The speaker finds the fur even "Sweeter of its yielded balm" than a human breast, for confiding in the dog allows "absolution whole— / Sorrow buried, joy revealed." With the dog's "wondrous fur" becoming a "loved confessional," once again the allusion to Catholic practice is blasphemous in its eroticism, yet simultaneously the trope appears natural and apt precisely because of its sensuality. As in the religious experience of absolution, the forgetting of oneself in a furry body allows the boundaries to one's being to be dissolved and extended. These memories of expansion also allow the Fields to forget the dog's demise and to counteract any feeling of self-depletion in bereavement. Indeed, in this elegiac collection mannered, ornate, sensuous language manically covers up the loss of the pet. Sadness is exalted and grief stylized into a worship of the deceased that beatifies the love between the two women.

Sally Mann

A year after her beloved greyhound Eva died, renowned American photographer Sally Mann mustered enough courage to exhume her corpse in order to examine the remains. She was curious, out of a love that was still present, about what had "finally become of that head I had stroked, oh, ten thousand times, those paws she so delicately crossed as she lay by my desk, rock-hard nails emerging from the finest white hairs" (*What Remains* 6). Sally Mann was then surprised to see "how elegantly the remains had turned into the earth" (video clip from "Sally Mann"), for all that was left were Eva's bones, the pelt of indigestible hair, and clumps of adipocere, with the skeleton appearing "like a constellation in a rich black sky" (*What Remains* 6). In the exhibition catalog the artist describes what she then did: "After bagging the larger bones, I reverently picked out the tiny pieces that remained—tail bones, teeth, claws, brushing the fragrant humus as an archaeologist might. Back on the floor in the studio I reassembled her, head to tail; bone by bone" (6). Using the technique

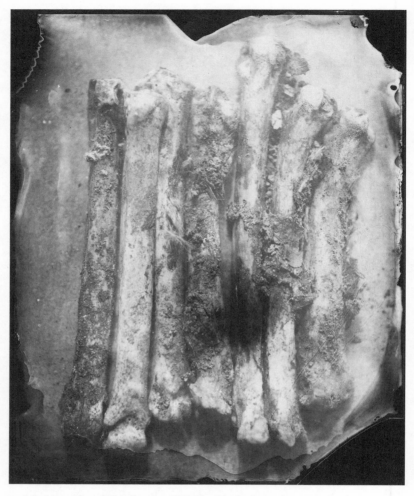

13 Sally Mann, from *What Remains*, 2003. Varnished gelatin silver. 8 × 10 inches. Copyright Sally Mann. Courtesy Gagosian Gallery.

developed in 1851 called wet-plate collodion process, Sally Mann proceeded to photograph arrangements of the hide and bones. She refrained from portraying the entire skeleton as if it would be reminiscent of an anatomy class prop but instead aligned the bones gently and reverently side by side (fig. 13) or isolated a single rib or claw on which to focus her lens. The series of photos appeared in the 2004 Corcoran Gallery exhibition entitled *What Remains* under the subtitle "Matter Lent."

The phrase "matter lent" hails from a poem by seventeenth-century writer Jacques-Bénigne Bossuet entitled "On Death, a Sermon":

All things summon us to death;
Nature, almost envious of the good she has given us,
Tells us often and gives us notice that she cannot
For long allow us that scrap of matter she has lent . . .
She has need of it for other forms,
She claims it back for other works. (11)

As Eva, lent briefly as a gift in life, was never to be possessed or mastered, Mann must relinquish her back to the earth. A comfort must have resided for the bereaved in knowing of that return, which is to say, of a kind of resurrection through "other forms." The phrase "matter lent," though, also suggests that the photographer wishes, in a gesture of humility, to preempt the charge that she was instrumentalizing the dead in performing the sacrilege of disinterment and turning a beloved pet into intellectual and artistic property. One is suspicious of such a possible appropriation in large part because of what could be construed as the sensationalism of another section of *What Remains*, photos taken at a forensic study site of bodies in various stages of decomposition. But rather than seeing Sally Mann as a grave robber, the Eva photographs suggest that she is involved in a necessary mourning process in a drive to come to terms with the "no longer," the utter finality of the greyhound's death, in marked contrast to the autobiographical works previously analyzed that attempt to conjure the dog back to life in a full narrative of its life or through florid verse. And although Sally Mann might be accused of uncovering and publicly displaying what is intensely personal, namely, the remains of a loved one, by representing finitude and loss she militates against how grief over a pet is socially foreclosed.

Despite Mann's words on "the existence of beauty where [one] would never expect to find it—in death," there is much emptiness in these photos. Although she discovers uncovered in the earth a "celebration of [Eva's] splendid anatomy and splendid structure," the minimalism of the photos bespeak a tremendous loss. Sally Mann, that is, creates a tension between beauty and nothingness, between the affirmation of the natural processes of disintegration and rebirth and the display of bereavement. Indeed, despite the written preface and the interspersing of poetry in the catalog and exhibition, the photographs themselves suggest an unutterable, choking grief that can only put on display but not verbally express what is essentially a void—the next to nothingness that is left to one after a loss. In the sparsity and in the blackness that surrounds, say, a single toenail, one is reminded of the silence of photography and hence of how one could not possibly find the words to articulate one's sorrow. Unlike *Whym Chow: Flame of Love*, no apostrophe is conceivable.

Eva, no longer even a corpse, is reduced to her remains—is irremediably gone—and the photos are a gesture of farewell to her. Although the exhuming suggests a desire bordering on necrophilia to be close again to the dog—to be near "that head I had stroked, oh, ten thousand times"—the barrenness of the remains emphasizes the impossibility of this desire. The striking images of decay, in fact of the residue left after decay, override any memories of togetherness with the dog. If it can be said that photography maintains the memory of the dead as dead, Sally Mann devotedly complies with the exigencies of her medium. Moreover, realization of the irreversible course of death is brought home by the factuality inherent in the medium: the camera documents the sheer reality of bone and pelt. What is gone, too, in these photos is any index of the rest of the world, for, with the demise of the cherished companion, the world disappears from view. This reduction of representable material forces Mann to the edges of asymbolia, in other words, to a bleak Kristevean *Verleugnung* in contrast to the plenitude and artificiality of hyperbole that characterizes *Verneinung*. *Verleugnung*, it may be recalled, is a negation of the disavowal of loss: one returns back to the loss, which is precisely what Mann does in revisiting the gravesite.

But there is a different impulse at work here as well. Sally Mann also tries to wrest herself away from dwelling at the site of loss. Instead of melancholically interiorizing loss or, in the words of Abraham and Torok, encrypting it away, it is telling that she literally engages in a work of public mourning, namely, instead of burying she unearths the loved object and then exhibits it, imparting and sharing her grief. The stages and difficulty of this process demonstrate Mann's efforts to gain control over her sorrow, to perform detachment, and to restore and reposition her self. First, the disinterment suggests a kind of searching rather than a melancholic hiding away. Second, she minutely collects, cleans, and reassembles the bones, as she says, like an archeologist. The reassembling or resurrection of the original, though, is clearly impossible. Instead what transpires is a process of diminution as Mann culls tiny pieces of bone, the fragments from the remains. Via this process of fragmentation, she marks or signifies her own falling apart at the loss, at the same time that she tries to restore the wounded self through creating an artifact that is witness to a natural process of dissolution that she calls beautiful. Third and finally, the collodion procedure itself is arduous, being both physically demanding and potentially dangerous given the chemicals used. To labor with the technique is to labor with one's mourning.

According to *A Guide to Early Photographic Processes*, collodion negatives were produced when a "sheet of glass was hand-coated with a thin film of collodion (guncotton dissolved in ether) containing potassium iodide, and was sensitized on the spot with silver nitrate. The plate had to be exposed while still wet, and developed immediately. Collodion negatives gave a very high resolution of detail; exposure times normally ranged from some seconds to a minute or two" (Coe and Haworth-Booth 18). Sally Mann speaks of the sensuality of the procedure in an interview: "It's a lovely process to work with. I like the making of the negative. You start with a glass plate, pour the colloid on the plate, and it shivers, it's alive. It actually does shiver when it hits the glass and then it gels. It's really exciting" ("Sally Mann"). The result, too, retains the imprint of the artist's tactile involvement. Since where one holds the plate the collodion is removed, Mann's actual physical presence is signified in the final product.

The production of the collodion negative also reflects back on Mann's subject matter: given that the entire process must be enacted quickly, it mirrors the transitoriness and ephemerality of life. Moreover, given that it is so exacting, blemishes and imperfections are bound to occur, lending a worn, distressed quality to the photos, which thus also index the passage of time. The glass plate, for instance, must be thoroughly cleaned and polished so that no markings are left in the final image, which appear as spots of light. Sweep lines can also appear when the developer does not cover the plate. Above all, a ghosting, the coating of poured collodion can be seen at the edges of the photo. The result is that the photographs from *What Remains* look so fragile, worn, and handled—as if they too were in the process of decomposition. If André Bazin sees in photography "a preservation of life by a representation of life" (10), with Sally Mann the opposite occurs. Instead of preserving in the sense of embalming life, what Bazin also refers to as the "mummy complex" (9), Mann records disintegration and decay and instrumentalizes the wet-plate collodion technique to enhance this display of physical corruption.

In terms of temporality, it is important to note that death in "Matter Lent" is not represented as a final moment, nor can it be conventionally reiterated that photography captures a fleeting moment in time, for

Mann underscores how death is an ongoing process. We are witness to decay after death and a prolonged labor of mourning demonstrated via the stages the artist goes through in working with the remains. This process stretches even into the time preceding the dog's death. A greyhound is, after all, only skin and bones filled out by musculature. In recollecting the "rock-hard nails emerging from the finest white hairs," Mann seems to anticipate retroactively the death that is to come, that is, how the bones will emerge in a beautiful constellation out of the earth. Conversely, the loveliness of the bone structure is what she finds again. Life itself leads to death, and death continues the activities of life.

Although Sally Mann's work of mourning bears offsetting from that of Katherine Bradley and Edith Cooper, nonetheless a certain Catholicism links them. To begin, the title "Matter Lent" recalls the Christian season of contrition, self-denial, and mournfulness. Yet the representation of the dog's remains is by no means exclusively somber and lugubrious but infused with a certain mystic incandescence. The photo of the inside of the hide, in particular, due to the shimmering, ghostly paleness of the skin is hallucinatory and reminiscent of the Shroud of Turin. Bazin, in fact, in "The Ontology of the Photographic Image," notes that the Holy Shroud "combines the features alike of relic and photography" (14). The respect bestowed in fidelity on each bone does indeed make them appear as saints' relics. In some photos their resplendent white leads them to resemble precious pieces of ivory or mother of pearl. Their painstaking recovery and photographing are performed meticulously as if in a ritual. Moreover, the random spots of light left from the specks of dirt on the glass plate before the collodion is poured evoke the flickerings from some sort of transcendent luminosity.

Most important, one walks away from Sally Mann's collection struck by the singularity of *this* beloved dog and of *this* bone. "Matter Lent," after all, is a variation on the family photo as keepsake, as memento of a deceased loved one. Her art thus sharply contrasts with the anonymity, "fear of the familiar" (Steve Baker), and the undercurrent of violence in the taxidermic installations on display at London's Saatchi Gallery—works by Berlinde de Bruyckere and the Young British Artists Damien Hirst, Mark Dion, and Jordan Baseman. Sally Mann's focus on the individuality of Eva, even in the ravagements of death, helps her to escape a melancholia that would disavow the import of loss and thus fail to recognize, respect, and delineate the separation between the surviving self and lost other, between human and animal.

What occurs, though, when abjection and destitution are disavowed, when one disowns the animal and refuses to grieve its suffering or death, in fact hastens them? How does one articulate the loss of that which is presumed insignificant? I turn now to two works that graphically depict callousness toward animal misery and the resulting implications of this resistance to mourning—Alejandro González Iñárritu's film *Amores Perros* and J. M. Coetzee's novel *Disgrace*. In grappling to find meaning in a dog's unwantedness, they explore issues of sacrifice and expiation, indeed, like Sally Mann, of ritual. They come to recognize that even in its degradation and vulnerability, in fact precisely because of them, man shares a kinship with the animal.

Alejandro González Iñárritu

"Am I my brother's keeper?" The Lord meets Cain's self-defense with the response, "The voice of your brother's blood is crying to me from the ground." As Abel's death was the inaugural taking of human life, the Lord's anger has been interpreted as an injunction not only against fratricide but against all murder. Brotherly love cannot be restricted to blood ties. Curiously, though, it is Cain who brings the nonviolent offering of fruit to the Lord, whereas Abel slaughters the first sheep of his flock. In a symbolic move that characterizes sacrifice, killing is condoned, though precisely only of nonhuman animals.[8] If propinquity is extended beyond immediate family, must it perforce exclude animals? According to the surrogate logic of sacrifice (whereby the sacrificed object stands in for and diverts from another), the answer must be ambiguous: propinquity with animals can be both affirmed and denied through the substitutive ritual of the consecrated offering.[9]

In Alejandro González Iñárritu's acclaimed film *Amores Perros* (*Life's a Bitch* [2000]) a businessman named Gustavo arranges to murder his half-brother Luis. The hit man he employs to do the job is one of the main protagonists, El Chivo (the goat). Rather than finish the task, El Chivo clandestinely brings the rival brothers together, whom he nicknames Cain and Abel, in order to have them decide their own fate, as they struggle for the gun he leaves behind. In an intricate narrative replete with symbolic parallels between various strands, González Iñárritu suggests that this fratricidal revenge is similar to the dogfights witnessed earlier in the movie. As one critic writes about this scene, the two brothers "determined to kill one another are chained to either side of a room and strain at their binds like dogs held in check before a fight" (Lawrenson 28). By thus juxtaposing the suffering and death of humans and canines, González Iñárritu rethinks propinquity in relation to the dog. Indeed, the constellation of issues here—biblical allusion, symbolic exchange, and wanton killing—begs one to address the religious question of sacrifice. In other words, how can the senseless deaths of dogs be made meaningful? Given the complex narrative structure and system of metaphoric substitutions and relays in the film, what do the dogs come to represent, what is forfeited in their deaths, and what awareness, if any, does their loss bring?

The opening scenes of *Amores Perros* are shocking in their violence and gore, which show the cheapness and waste of both human and canine life. As the camera pulls back from a rear window of a speeding car, it reveals a rottweiler bleeding to death in the backseat. The high velocity chase soon ends as the vehicle careens into another at a stoplight. The rest of the film shows the three narratives that lead up to and interconnect at this moment of the crash. The first of these begins with another scene of spilt canine blood: caged dogs, mostly pit bulls, line a bloody corridor along which are dragged the corpses of those who have been maimed in dogfights. Throughout the rest of the film dogs are repeatedly set upon each other and, once dead, heaved into pickup trucks and hauled away as sheer inert matter; they are dead waste receiving no burial and no mourning. Yet, in this film, characters who do not grieve such loss of life, be it human as well as canine, reap the consequences of refusing to go through the emotions of guilt, sorrow, and suffering.

The first story in this intricately woven triptych revolves around illegal dog fighting, and, as in the rest of the film, where the high and mighty are repeatedly brought low, the dogs represent the degradation to which one can descend. A slight young man named Octavio becomes involved in the gambling arena once he hears that his brother's Rottweiler, Cofi, successfully defended himself against an attack by the current favorite. He enters Cofi in the ring so as to raise money with which to escape with his brother's abused wife, Susana, with whom he has fallen in love. Trying to revenge Ramiro's brutality toward Susana, satisfy his jealousy, and take the opportunity to seduce her, Octavio arranges for thugs from the dog fighting world to beat up his brother. In the denouement, a bloodied Ramiro disappears with his wife, their newborn, and the money; Cofi is shot during a fight in the ring; Octavio stabs his competitor El Jarocho in retaliation; Octavio tries to escape in the car that ends in the crash.

The other vehicle involved in the accident belongs to the high fashion model Valeria Amaya. In contrast to the poverty and degradation of the previous protagonists, she has just appeared on a television talk show, landed a lucrative position as the poster girl for a perfume company, and moved into a new apartment with her wealthy lover. In the sudden turn of events that result from the crash she is confined to a wheelchair, her sole preoccupation now being her beautifully groomed toy dog Richi, whom in the television interview she had called her son. While playing fetch with him, the dog falls through damaged floorboards and cannot get out. Just as Valeria is sequestered in her darkened flat, as if buried alive in her immobility, so too is Richi trapped in a rat-infested hole. Although it seems, in contrast to the cavernous corridors of the dog fights, that Valeria lives far above destitution in her high-rise, Richi's entrapment beneath the floor suggests that the life below will take its revenge. Indeed, Valeria's fate worsens as gangrene sets into her leg, prompting its amputation. Although she finally regains her dog, it is a double-edged consolation: the recovery poignantly contrasts with her irredeemable loss of career, beauty, and mobility.

The third narrative concentrates on the itinerant El Chivo, who once abandoned wife, daughter, and professorial career in order to become a leftist guerrilla. After being captured and interned for twenty years, he now earns occasional money through contract killing and lives in a squalid setting with a retinue of dogs, his substitute for a family. Witnessing the car crash, he takes Cofi, who has been abandoned for dead, into his care, tends his gunshot wound, and nurses him back to health. In the most moving scene of the film, however, he returns home to find that Cofi, conditioned to fight, has slaughtered all his other dogs, including the one he calls his baby. About to shoot Cofi in despair, he desists, a turn that instigates a series of reversals in his life, including the decision not to murder Luis.

As the first and third narratives suggest, González Iñárritu symbolically links fratricide with animal sacrifice. The first to arrive at the car crash, El Chivo steals the wallet of the unconscious Octavio, in which he finds first a photo of the two brothers smiling and then another, cut out of a larger one, where Octavio embraces Cofi. The dog comes to stand in for absent brotherly relations. In this fatherless society, Cofi substitutes for the affection and protection an older brother ideally gives.[10] As fraternal enmity builds, so too are canine lives destroyed. Octavio arranges for his brother to be beaten up by the same people with whom he gambles on Cofi's life. Then, shortly after Cofi is shot and abandoned for dead at the car crash, his brother is gunned down. Above all, the metaphor of dog fighting, where like kills like, graphically signifies the sibling rivalry and fantasies of fratricidal revenge.

When brotherhood is not recognized, trafficking in dogs and women result instead. Octavio disregards the fraternal bond in coveting both his brother's wife and dog. That he and Ramiro vie over the right to ownership of Cofi can be seen most clearly when Ramiro threatens to knock off Cofi unless Octavio splits the winnings with him. In this world dogs are commodities, valuable only insofar as they bring in money, otherwise they are disposable and replaceable. Similarly, just as Valeria's looks are bought and sold, so too is Susana regarded as a sex object by both brothers. Though in different ways, both brothers disregard her timidity and use her as a pawn for their own misguided desires. The dog, in addition, can be used to signify machismo. Octavio, who is nicknamed Princess by El Jarocho and dwarfed by the brutal Ramiro, uses Cofi to substitute for his lack of physical strength. He usurps the Rottweiler in a ploy to steal his brother's superior position in the family. Just as he proclaims Cofi as his own because he feeds him, so too does he pride himself in taking over the role of provider for Susana's baby. When Cofi brings home the winnings, Octavio can thus rise in symbolic power over his brother.

Fratricide, the killing of dogs, and, this time, also mourning are brought together in alignment to mark the turning point in El Chivo's life. When the Rottweiler kills his family of dogs, El Chivo restrains himself from shooting him in revenge, as if he realized the implications of unrestrained, repetitive killing. In fact, he begins to mourn his own losses, starting with the death of his beloved dogs. At the only point in the film where a dog's passing is commemorated, El Chivo lights a pyre to immolate the bodies of his pets. In the logic of exchange and justice that governs this film, acquiring Octavio's dog means sacrificing the others. This sacrifice is solemnized, as it were, in a burnt offering. Underscoring the religious overtones of El Chivo's conversion González Iñárritu explains in an interview: "So it's not just love that redeems The Goat, it's also the dog. Man redeemed by a beast; this idea fascinates me" (Lawrenson 30). In other words, only by first admitting to himself the devastation of the loss of canine life is El Chivo able to realize what he has been repressing all his life—the repercussions of the loss of human life.

The closing dedication of the film reads: "To Luciano, because we are also what we have lost." The psychoanalysts Abraham and Torok have written that melancholic "incorporation is the refusal to reclaim as our own the part of ourselves that we placed in what we lost" (127). *Amores Perros* insists on recognition of identification with that which we have forfeited, especially when such mourning involves the loss of kin, whether it be of brother or dog. Unless we recognize this logic of "because we are also what we have lost," we too are dead, as is El Chivo before he finally comes to vocalize his grief over not just his dogs but his former existence. Admission of loss is paradoxically his first step in regaining a sense of self and coming back to life. Octavio, by contrast, in failing to grieve for his brother and to abandon his desire to possess his sister-in-law, is not just physically but emotionally crippled after the car crash.

In González Iñárritu's subsequent film *21 Grams* (2003), Sean Penn's character, after receiving an organ transplant, wants to meet the widow of the man whose heart beats in place of his own, as if he wanted to share in the mourning. He acknowledges that he is another person because of what another has lost. He moreover recognizes that the sacrifice (that he lives thanks to another's passing) demands of him a sacrifice on behalf of the grieving widow, whose revenge he assumes as his own. The characters in this similarly tripartite narrative do come into contact with each other, unlike in *Amores Perros*, where the overall sense of loss and pathos is augmented because the characters never learn of their connections to each other. We are what we have lost, but in the commonalty of life, we are also what others have lost. More to the point, in *Amores Perros* this shared mortality does not exclude the animal, to whose loss we must also testify in mourning. Rather than separate human from animal lives, González Iñárritu encourages us to recognize how the passing of a mere animal defines who we are. Indeed, the stories of Valeria and El Chivo intimate that among the deepest emotional and physical daily attachments are with one's dogs, as if they were one's flesh and blood. Thus the ethical impulse in the film does not solely respond to the question "Am I my brother's keeper?" but involves extending kinship and reciprocity to the canine species.

Was, though, the reception of *Amores Perros* indicative that its audience was willing to recognize such an ethic? Public controversy arose concerning the treatment of animals on the set, as Paul Julian Smith reports in his monograph on the film: *Amores Perros* "hit censorship problems in Germany and the UK because of its subject matter. Although the Royal Society for the Prevention of Cruelty to Animals filed a complaint to the British Board of Film Classification, *Amores Perros* was passed without cuts after the distributor . . . convinced the board that the dogs were not harmed" (13). In the United States the film received a rating of "Questionable" from the American Humane Association (AHA), which was not in a position to monitor the production and had to rely on a submitted behind-the-scenes video for reassurances that animals were not abused. Moreover, AHA guidelines prohibit the risky use of tranquilizers, which were administered during production (*Guidelines for the Safe Use of Animals in Filmed Media*).

Such ratings and censorship are curious insofar as it could be argued that the film confronts the viewer with the depravity of placing bets over dogs howling in pain and fighting to the death. Since the film militates against brutality toward animals rather than fomenting it—and moreover aligns this killing with that of human lives—one wonders why humane societies would not embrace its ethical stance. The exclusive focus of media attention on whether animals were harmed during production thus suggests that a different form of censorship is being camouflaged. Highly paradoxically, this focus disavows the film's dramatic portrayal of the consequences of animal death and hence the necessity of recognizing propinquity with the dog. One could extrapolate from this disavowal that the public discourse on animals, here reflected in AHA guidelines, has become so limited, legislated, and reduced to facticity (in this case to what happened on the set) that, in its censorship, it diverts attention from its own shortcomings, namely, its incapacity to engage in meaningful ethical debate on the magnitude and profound implications of animal loss.

J. M. Coetzee

In closing I want, in terms of death, to return to the issue of shame addressed in a previous chapter. The dog is said to be without shame, without the self-consciousness of chagrin, shamefulness, or dirtiness. If dogs are a reminder of the uncleanly world, then they are especially so in their death and even more so when this death is deemed necessary because they are unwanted and forsaken. The fate of the homeless, superfluous dog is to be euthanized or, in the words of J. M. Coetzee in his novel *Disgrace* (1999), to be disposed of, made to disappear, be dispatched to oblivion (142). To die like a dog, as Josef K. does in Kafka's *The Trial*, is to die in shame. The demise of the abandoned dog is vastly different, of course, from the passing of a beloved pet as discussed earlier; yet here too, indeed especially because it can be so easily dismissed, mourning is necessary.

Another reason why one associates dogs with shamelessness is because they can be pleading: they are not afraid to show their desperation. David Lurie, the main protagonist in *Disgrace*, who is "convinced the dogs know their time has come," observes that "they flatten their ears, they droop their tails, as if they too feel the disgrace of dying" (143). His daughter Lucy also notes of a neglected dog she rescued: "Poor old Katy, she's in mourning. No one wants her, and she knows it" (78). If the dogs indeed know the dishonorable state of their own unwantedness, then perhaps they do experience shame. Shame carries with it a sense of isolation from one's community, an isolation that dogs would keenly feel and that would be strongest when they are locked in a pound and destined to lethal injection. One wonders whether one could possibly begin to imagine such desperation, to fathom the despondency of being so unloved and superfluous as to have to die. What would it be like to sense that one's own life is so poor that it merits being eradicated, that one's own death is disgraceful?[11]

In words that could have governed the making of *Amores Perros*, Jacques Derrida called mortality "the most radical means of thinking the finitude that we share with animals, the mortality that belongs to the very finitude of life, to the experience of compassion, to the possibility of sharing the possibility of this non-power, the possibility of this impossibility, the anguish of this vulnerability and the vulnerability of this anguish" ("The Animal" 396). Derrida seems to advocate neither merely that we be conscious of the mortality we share with all living things nor simply that we be conscious how we wield power over the vulnerable but that we need to be open as well to the possibility of actually sharing the experience of "this non-power." But how could one bodily apperceive to the same degree the "anguish of this vulnerability and vulnerability of this anguish"? Would the temptation not be to delude oneself into an all too easy anthropomorphized specularity? For how can one even "share" in mortality, for how could we know what death means for a dog? Would the dog not be most foreign to us in its experience of death? Or, as Derek Attridge questions apropos *Disgrace*, "If a dog is an absolute other, what is a dead dog, and what response does it demand?"

In J. M. Coetzee's *The Lives of Animals* (1999), the main character, Elizabeth Costello, has been invited to deliver two honorific college lectures, mirroring the occasion for which Coetzee wrote the work, namely, an invitation to present the 1997–98 Tanner Lectures at Princeton University. A novelist and animal rights advocate, Costello maintains that "there is no limit to the extent to which we can think ourselves into the being of another. There are no bounds to the sympathetic imagination" (35). But as just questioned, is it indeed possible so totally to share an animal's experience? Surely there must be impasses to knowing a radical other, especially given the disempowering nonequivalencies between man and beast that would need to be overcome. Perhaps Costello means to speak prescriptively, namely, that there should be no bounds to the sympathetic imagination. Or perhaps Derrida and Costello are suggesting that one can attempt to atone for subjugating dependent creatures, for not being able to command that limitless sympathy and compassion, and for not being able truly to share in their degradation. Perhaps at the very least, though that in itself is a large step, we can be mindful not to disavow their vulnerability and shame. And perhaps, to return to the earlier chapter, it is possible, in the words of Silvan Tomkins, to feel a vicarious shame "at the indignity or suffering of . . . [an] animal to the extent to which I feel myself identified with . . . the animal kingdom, and have reverence for life as such" (Sedgwick and Frank 160). Another psychologist on shame, Karen Hanson, offers the notion that "shame may sometimes be a required element of atonement . . . because of the way in which feeling shame requires attention to and the *incorporation* of the viewpoints of others" (169). In his novel *Disgrace*, winner of the 1999 Booker Prize, J. M. Coetzee raises the question of the grounds for identification with the lowly dog. He struggles with the problem of how to cope with shame and guilt over others' suffering, for when the main character attends to abandoned, suffering, and dying dogs, he seems to reach for atonement.[12]

David Lurie, through whose consciousness the third-person narrative is filtered, is a fifty-two-year-old university professor who, after sleeping with an unwilling young student, Melanie Isaacs, is dismissed from his position in the wake of a sexual harassment hearing. He goes to the eastern provinces of South Africa to visit his grown daughter, Lucy, who lives on a small farm, where she tends a dog kennel and raises vegetables for local sale. During his stay, while he is locked up by local black men, she is gang-raped and left pregnant with a child she then voices the intention to keep. In the political sea change of postapartheid South Africa, she sees this violation as a fate she must accept. In the meantime, Lurie has taken to volunteering at a local animal shelter where he helps one of Lucy's friends, Bev Shaw, euthanize and dispose of unwanted dogs. As in Lucy's acceptance of the rape and decision to carry the pregnancy to term, it is suggested that this type of menial work, so far removed from his former existence, involves some sort of reparation, though for what is left unspecified. In the following, I shall concentrate on the sections in the novel dealing with dogs, leaving aside but mindful of the larger question, as Derek Attridge puts it: "Do these elements of the novel constitute a response to the private and public events that it so powerfully and dishearteningly presents in its central narrative?" Without attempting to see how it might elucidate either the two rapes in the novel or larger postapartheid issues, I believe Lurie's response to canine death is overwhelming enough in its implications to merit sole focus.

At the animal welfare clinic people bring in dogs who "suffer from distempers, from broken limbs, from infected bites, from mange, from neglect, benign or malign, from old age, from malnutrition, from intestinal parasites, but most of all from their own fertility. There are simply too many of them. When people bring a dog in they do not say straight out, 'I have brought you this dog to kill,' but that is what is expected" (142). Were it not that such disposal of sick dogs and new litters occurs everywhere regardless of wealth, one would be tempted to attribute such easy euthanasia to poverty. More encompassing as an explanation of the clinic's function is that animals are considered, as Lurie himself earlier lectures his daughter, as simply of "a different order of creation" from humans (74). This hierarchy of creation to which Lurie alludes has an extended tradition in Western theology and philosophy and has justified an interpretation of animal death as categorically different from that of the human. Lurie himself mentions that the "Church Fathers had a long debate about them, and decided they don't have proper souls. . . . Their souls are tied to their bodies and die with them" (78). As Derrida and Agamben have more fully detailed, man has felt the need to "recognize himself in a non-man in order to be human" (Agamben 27), whether the delimitation be said to lie in the possession of a soul, language, consciousness, or anticipation of death, for, as Derrida points out, this list is as endless as it is arbitrary ("And Say the Animal" 137). Or, to refer to Elizabeth Costello's own passionate response when confronted with the comment that animals "live in a vacuum of consciousness": "They have no consciousness *therefore*. Therefore what? Therefore we are free to use them for our own ends? Therefore we are free to kill them? Why? What is so special about the form of consciousness we recognize that makes killing a bearer of it a crime while killing an animal goes unpunished?" (*The Lives of Animals* 44). Costello thus spells out with her characteristic scrappiness the murderous consequences of this systematic demarcation of animal from human.

Outside of any immediate religious context, the allusion to the soul resurfaces at the end of *Disgrace* in reference to the killing of "the old, the blind, the halt, the crippled, the maimed, but also the young, the sound—all those whose term has come" (218). Lurie speculates: "Something happens in this room, something unmentionable: here the soul is yanked out of the body; briefly it hangs about in the air, twisting and contorting; then it is sucked away and is gone" (219). He imagines the unsuspecting dogs entering the room and sniffing "the soft, short smell of the released soul" (219).[13] And again in a brief, unelaborated, and therefore puzzling reference to Christian belief, Lurie carries the one dog to whom he has become attached into this room "like a lamb" (220). There is no spiritual consolation in this sacrifice, though the allusion carries a weightiness, a portent of meaning now unidentifiable in an secular age.

On the topic of sacrifice, Joseph de Maistre has written that the "animals that are the most valuable because of their utility, the gentlest, the most innocent, those nearest to man because of their instincts and habits . . . the most *human* victims in the animal kingdom were chosen" (358–59). Indeed, this particular dog whom Lurie, in the final words of the novel, is "giving up" (220), was most human in his attentiveness to music and in the affection and trust he showed Lurie. Accordingly, he would be less "like a lamb" than like a human, though the very differences at this point are in the process of collapsing. What is important is that, true to the ritual of sacrifice, it is someone else than the guilty party who is offered up.[14] In the economy of exchange that sacrifice sets into motion and yet intends to halt, Coetzee seems to ask whether reparations can be made for this substitutive animal sacrifice, especially when one participates in it directly, as does Lurie, though it is a necessary job no one else but he and Bev Shaw will take on. Indeed, rather than attribute a sense of shame to the animals in their unwanted death, Lurie says that they can smell his own shame at the task he is committing. Can one begin, then, to weigh the responsibility and guilt that comes from spilling innocent blood? And what would be the appropriate protest of an individual to that overwhelmingly long tradition of justifying the human by denigrating the nonhuman and to the omnipresence of animal suffering in the here and now? How is the loss of animal life to be mourned?

David Lurie does more than assist Bev Shaw in what he euphemistically calls *Lösung* (solution; sublimation), a phrase that recalls the *Endlösung* (final solution) of the Jews by the Nazis.[15] He also disposes of the remains by taking the animal corpses to a nearby incinerator, where, instead of leaving them with the rest of the waste, he loads them up into the trolley to the furnace. He does this because if he leaves the bodies to rigor mortis, the workmen will have to beat the bags and break the limbs of the animals before they will ride up the trolley without being caught in its bars. Lurie asks himself, as does the reader, why he has taken on this job. At first he says that he does not want to inflict the dishonor on the dogs of having their corpses broken and beaten but then admits that they are dead "and what do dogs know of honour and dishonour anyway?" (146). He declares that "there must be other, more productive ways of giving oneself to the world" than "offering himself to the service of dead dogs" (146). And, in similarly sober self-deprecation, he admits no one else would be "stupid enough to do it. That is what he is becoming: stupid, daft, wrongheaded" (146).

The emphasis here on nonutilitarian purposelessness is significant. If we ask the question of a possible reparation, expiation, a reckoning of human guilt vis-à-vis the animal, the answer would have to be that Lurie's gesture is meaningless. Similarly, when he comforts the dogs before their deaths, he acknowledges that it is a gesture that is "little enough, less than little: nothing" (220). There is no way to make good the death of the animal, just as one cannot speak of purification or transcendence through its sacrifice, though the dog is "like a lamb." Lucy earlier makes the comment that dogs "do us the honour of treating us like gods, and we respond by treating them like things" (78). If indeed we are like gods demanding their sacrifice, there is no redemption in return. The infinite separation between species becomes absolute in the dogs' death.

There are contrasting critical assessments of this ending. Isidore Diala maintains that in letting the dog die that has adopted him Lurie demonstrates his "abiding abdication of responsibility" (58), while Lucy Graham calls his care for the dead dogs "ineffectual, even self-indulgent" (11). Michael Marais, by contrast, names it his "acceptance of the impossibility of death and also the transformation of his desire for the Other [as in the case of Melanie] into self-substituting responsibility" (178). Is his refusal to save the young dog, then, a betrayal and act of callousness, or is it a relinquishing of the selfish desire to keep the dog a bit longer? If this is indeed a sacrificial gesture of giving up, then perhaps it can be read alongside the other gesture of humility and servitude of giving the dogs an honorable immolation. This act is not done "out of simple generosity," because it is "admirable," or because he "feel[s] guilty or fear[s] retribution," all motives Lurie had previously attributed to the "animal-welfare people" as he called them (73–74). It is an exercise outside any economy of exchange, performed in a humility that is not born of self-chastisement or penance but out of humble affiliation with the unwanted.

To be involved in the dogs' death is to share in their shame; and to insist on the mourning process, even if it is merely the ritual of accompanying them to the incinerator, is a way of articulating the loss of what had been belittled and presumed to be insignificant. Thus, although the dogs may be considered worthless and his presence at the incinerator beyond any use value, still his act, a kind of vigil, indicates that their lives are incommensurable. If people bring their dogs to the clinic unable to mention, despite their intention, that they want the dogs to be killed, he wants to restore some measure of dignity. Unlike the previous owners, he refuses to disavow the shamefulness and difficulty of their disposal. Most important, his gesture, however insignificant because personal, is a protest against the mechanization of animal death, against "a world in which men do not use shovels to beat corpses into a more convenient shape for processing" (146). This resistance is not only directed against mechanization but a logic of "rationality and measured productivity." I would hence agree with Attridge that the very essence of Lurie's act lies in its purposelessness. "Coetzee strips away all the conventional justifications for kindness to animals— implying not that these are empty justifications but that they are part of the rational, humanist culture that doesn't get to the heart of the matter." In denying this rational logic of exchange and expiation, Attridge is also perceptive in assessing that "Lurie's commitment to the dead dogs can't be thought of as an attempt to counterbalance the sexual wrong that began the sequence of events it culminates."

To come back to the line of questioning with which I opened this section: "How [is it] possible to care for the other if that other is infinitely unknowable" (Graham 11)? Lucy Graham correctly points out that Coetzee is aware of the limits of sympathy and of the extent to which one can identify with the abject, which can be seen in how he resists depicting the scenes of sexual violation via the perspective of the victim. Mindful of these restrictions, I think it is still possible to say that he also proposes that, in Derrida's words, we can and do share with animals mortality and vulnerability. Lucy tells her father: "This is the only life there is. Which we share with animals. That's the example that people like Bev try to set. That's the example I try to follow. To share some of our human privilege with the beasts" (74). She indeed later comes to experience this humble commonalty when she is about to lose her property and speaks about the humiliating situation in which she finds herself: she admits that she must accept living with nothing, "no property, no rights, no dignity . . . like a dog." But she also affirms that "perhaps that is a good point to start from again" (205). Elizabeth Costello similarly speaks in terms of sharing "the substrate of life" with other living beings (*The Lives of Animals* 35). Lurie's servitude to the dead canine bodies must be seen in conjunction with such passages, which suggest that the menial task he performs is an expression of sharing in the dogs' own abjection. This communion is prefigured when earlier in the novel he finds that he has fallen asleep on the concrete floor next to Katy in her cage.

If shame wants to be kept hidden, then this sharing would be a way to turn shame inside out. In other words, that which was interiorized and kept secret becomes embodied and represented with the result not only that one's own abjectness is acknowledged and mourned but that it does not separate one from others. Thus, after the episode when Lurie falls asleep in Katy's pen, "a shadow of grief falls over him: for Katy, alone in her cage, for himself, for everyone" (79). Lurie's grieving—which includes his humble gesture of properly mourning the dogs by giving them a less disgraceful termination to their lives—is a way to insist on identifying and sharing with the otherwise despised and disowned. In contrast, as was saliently illustrated in Thomas Mann's story "Tobias Mindernickel" and in Sue Coe's *Pit's Letter*, degradation can often be projected onto the dog so as to disavow it in oneself.[16] As Stephen Webb succinctly puts it, it is easy "to disown and project our worst impulses onto those who are close enough to us to suffer but far enough away so that their complaints can be ignored. Animals, after all, represent instinct, and thus they are the perfect receptacles for the disposal of human instinct in its most vulgar and immediate forms" (154). As an antidote to such disavowal Coetzee suggests that the embodiment of shame in the other can serve as a point of identification and empathy, perhaps even for the expression of compassionate love: as Lurie and Bev Shaw concentrate all their "attention on the animal they are killing" he gives it "what he no longer has difficulty in calling by its proper name: love" (219).

Notes

1. In *Simulacra and Simulation* (137–41), Jean Baudrillard responds
    to Deleuze and Guattari's notions of "becoming-animal" and
    "deterritorialization" by observing that animals actually tend
    to display a keen sense of territory. Yet because the animal is
    silent, Deleuze and Guattari can instrumentalize it and put it
    into the category of the indecipherable and savage.
2. Ecofeminist intervention has found the animal rights phi-
    losophy of Peter Singer and Tom Regan limiting, insofar as
    it excludes emotions and sympathy as central to ethical the-
    ory. As an alternative, writers such as by Josephine Donovan
    and Carol J. Adams stress the need for an ethics of caring for
    the suffering and shamed.
3. The essay has been translated by David Wills in *Critical
    Inquiry* as "The Animal That Therefore I Am." The citations
    from this essay are from Wills's translation, unless I also
    make reference to the French original.
4. In the same spirit of acknowledging the ethical import of
    how we talk about pets closest to us, theologian Stephen
    Webb writes: "Something powerful resides in the very
    inconsistencies of our attachments, which enables caring to
    overflow the particular and thus challenge general customs
    and habits" (64).
5. This history of defining the essence of humanity in con-
    tradistinction to the animal in abjection has been brilliantly
    traced and criticized not only by Derrida but also by Giorgio
    Agamben, David Clark, Aaron Garrett, Andrew Linzey,
    Richard Sorabji, and Stephen Webb, among others.
6. I discuss Kristeva's *Black Sun: Depression and Melancholia* in
    more detail in the first chapter.

7. This inability to declare or concede closeness furthermore explains the "fear of the familiar" among the postmodern artists Steve Baker discusses and it informs the abjection with which they display the body of the dead animal (as with Jordan Baseman, Mark Dion, and Damien Hirst), as if trying to exorcise any conceivable tie to it as an individual, living being.

8. Baudrillard brilliantly draws out the implications of animals not being "intelligible to us either under the regime of consciousness or under that of the unconscious. Therefore, it is not a question of forcing them to it, but just the opposite of seeing *in what way they put in question this very hypothesis of the unconscious, and to what other hypothesis they force us*. Such is the meaning, or the non-meaning of their silence" (138).

9. I am thinking here of Adam Phillips's characterization of psychoanalysis as "essentially a transitional language, one possible bridge to a more personal . . . idiom. It is useful only as a contribution to forms of local knowledge, as one among the many language games in a culture" (8). I thereby acknowledge that at different times I deploy different psychoanalytic models that can compete with each other, for instance, in chapter 3 I turn to Jessica Benjamin, whereas in chapter 1 to Julia Kristeva. I have opted, however, not to take on the task of sorting out their differences.

10. For an excellent overview and assorting of the various theories of melancholia from Aristotle to Kristeva, see Radden's introduction to her collection of excerpts from these various thinkers.

11. I wish to echo the words of Elizabeth Costello in J. M. Coetzee's *The Lives of Animals*: "That is the kind of poetry I bring to your attention today: poetry that does not try to find an idea in the animals, that is not about the animal, but is instead the record of an engagement with him. . . . That is why I urge you to read the poets who return the living, electric being to language" (51, 65).

12. I here borrow throughout this discussion from the masterful exegesis by Raymond Klibansky, Erwin Panowsky, and Fritz Saxl. They examine the philosophic, astrological, medical, and art historical traditions, leading back to the Ancients, that informed Dürer's etching.

13. Taking this medical-philosophical tradition into consideration, one finds much in Lucian Freud's oeuvre that would signal the melancholic humor. The somber tones characteristic of his canvases seem to reflect a certain malaise. In the spirit of the melancholic, Freud shuns ceremony and paints a drab reality. Mostly composed in his studio and adopting unsettling angles, the works emit a sense of claustrophobia; the space is eerily barren and littered with used paint rags, which art historian David Cohen called "overt symbols of mortality" and "symbols of the passage of time, of waste and decay" (35). In the sparseness of the decor, it was as if Freud, like Dürer's Melencolia herself, wanted to see beyond materiality and uncover the truth behind appearances.

14. See the collection of illustrations in Schuster, vol. 2.

15. Dürer also painted the sighthound in his engraving of Saint Eustache. According to legend, the saint was hunting when he discovered a stag with the crucifix mounted on its antlers and instead of shooting it, knelt down in prayer. The dogs stop their coursing as well and look on with awe or respectfully lie down. The dogs participate in experiencing the miracle and regard nature as a manifestation of the sacred, of which they too are part. Here then, again, the dog can represent the reverse facet of melancholia—instead of regarding the world as empty, nature is idealized and sublimated.

16. Unless I specify another source, all translations are my own.

17. The page reference is to the German edition, *Sämtliche Erzählungen*, while the translation is from *Kafka's Selected Stories* (New York: W. W. Norton, forthcoming). I thank Stanley Corngold for sharing his translation with me before it went to press.

18. Could Kafka here be alluding to the fable by Jean de La Fontaine where the wolf says to the dog that he prefers to keep his freedom, even though he is starving, rather than be subservient to a master?

19. Compare Deleuze and Guattari, who maintain that all resemblances between man and dog are "energetically eliminated. Kafka attacks 'the suspect temptations of resemblance that imagination proposes'; through the dog's solitude, it is the greatest difference, the schizo difference that he tries to grasp" (*Kafka* 14) and that "it is no longer a question of a resemblance between the comportment of an animal and that of a man; it is even less a question of a simple wordplay. There is no longer man or animal, since each deterritorializes the other, in a conjunction of flux, in a continuum of reversible intensities" (22).

CHAPTER ONE

1. Rilke's first *Duino Elegy* inverts this claim: "die findigen Tiere merken es schon, / daß wir nicht sehr verläßlich zu Haus sind / in der gedeuteten Welt" (441). [The knowing animals know / we are not very securely at home / in our interpreted world (5).] Now it is the humans who are estranged from the world because they interpret it. I shall return to the *Duino Elegies* in the conclusion of this chapter.

2. Derrida further discusses Heidegger's essay in *Of Spirit: Heidegger and the Question*. Lippit investigates Derrida on Heidegger (55–66). See also Agamben's lengthy analysis of Heidegger in *The Open*.

3. That nature is in need of salvation after the Fall is also reflected in Rom. 8:19: "For the creation waits with eager longing for the revealing of the sons of God." Rilke similarly posits the need for salvation for the animal when, referring to the story of Jacob and Esau in Genesis 27, he writes at the close of the sixteenth sonnet that he shall present the dog to God for a blessing: the dog is Esau in his hide (*Esau in seinem Fell*), for his coat actually disguises his humanness, which is evident in his loyalty and willingness to

share man's company. Contrast this with Milan Kundera's observation in *The Unbearable Lightness of Being* (1982) that the longing for Paradise is man's longing not to be man and that dogs were never expelled from Paradise: "No one can give anyone else the gift of the idyll; . . . The love between dog and man is idyllic. It knows no conflicts, no hair-raising scenes; it knows no development" (298).

4. Cary Wolfe, in an analysis of Lyotard on language, goes one logical step further and says that to deny animals the capacity to phrase also means that the "'silence' and 'feeling' of the mute or unspoken are not available to the animal" (16).

5. Compare the feminist-inspired short story by Ursula K. Le Guin, "She Unnames Them" (1985), where the animals in the world decide to abandon their names. As a result, the female speaker says: "They seemed far closer than when their names had stood between myself and them like a clear barrier" (27).

6. Wolfe aligns Derrida's interrogation of this philosophical tradition with biologists involved in animal language studies, such as Humberto Maturana and Francisco Varela, who look at how the linguistic patterning among animals is not dissimilar to human language-building systems.

7. In his 1980 novel *Loin (Far Away)*, French psychoanalyst J.-B. Pontalis has his narrator dream that he is writing at his desk, while his dog is growing impatient, wanting to go out. He tells him, "I promise, in just a moment." Astonished to see the dog in response moves its lips, he bends down to him, only to hear in soft but clear words the rebuke, "I don't believe you" (148).

8. See Ziolkowski's treatment of this tradition in his essay "Talking Dogs: The Caninization of Literature."

9. Cf. the concluding words of Marian Scholtmeijer in *Animal Victims in Modern Fiction*: "In their very being, animals repudiate our efforts to subjugate them to cultural purposes. When we ask them to affirm the importance of human existence, their silence is more articulate than any of the words we impose upon them" (297).

10. Compare Lippit's related questioning: "Given the openness of animals, what Lyotard refers to as their 'passivity,' one must ask whether human beings have learned to read or decipher such animal disclosures. And to the extent that animals are incapable of maintaining secrets, mustn't one question not only the nature of their expression but also its figurative modalities, its expressive form? For if animals are indeed incapable of language, as most traditional philosophers argue . . . , then mustn't one be attentive to the possibility that another communicative medium may in fact be operative in nature's animal provocations?" (22).

11. In discussing Hearne's response to Wittgenstein, Wolfe perceives that she actually takes a hint from his notion of a shared language game. He points out, that, according to Wittgenstein, "*a* world emerges from building a shared form of life through participation in a language game. And

indeed, this is the direction in which Hearne has taken Wittgenstein's cue in her writings on how the shared language of animal training makes possible a common world between beings with vastly different phenomenologies" (5). But Wolfe then goes on to say that Hearne thereby limits her very attempt to open up transspecial dialogue: "It is not at all clear, of course, that we have any ethical duty whatsoever to those animals with whom we have not articulated a shared form of life through training or other means" (8).

12. Clark similarly observes that Levinas "reminds us that the animalization of animals is in its own way also deadly, and thus worthy of our concern. How are animals animalized by humans? Levinas's answer is at once complex and brutally simple: *we eat meat*" (169).

13. Clark is more skeptical: "Levinas continues to feel as if his account could, at any moment, fall into mere fabulation, or worse, sentimentality. Throughout, the thought of the animal is always somehow too anthropomorphic, always vanishing beneath the surface of its humanistic interpretations" (173).

14. Because of its compensatory function, the presence of a dog will always mitigate against the psychotic state of *Verwerfung* where no substitute or language is allowed, and which explains why elderly patients and autistic children will unexpectedly communicate with a therapy dog; they abandon the mutism of *Verwerfung*.

15. There is some ambivalence in Kristeva whether fetishism functions as a cure or symptom of melancholia. She writes that the fetish "appears as a solution to depression and its denial of the signifier" (45); at the same time, like melancholia, fetishism operates via disavowal of loss and adherence to the object.

16. Revealing this melancholia to be operative on a mass scale (though hardly expressive of the beauty of sublimation!) is the pervasive "disnification" (Steve Baker) of the animal. John Berger, in particular, has pinpointed how in industrial and postindustrial societies the existence of the household pet itself compensates for how animals have otherwise disappeared from daily life: pets are thus themselves a sign of bereavement.

17. Compare Lippit on animals, affect, and the absence of words: "The other side of thought . . . appears in the animal's visage—a countenance that, for Giorgio Agamben, 'always seems to be on the verge of uttering words.' On the verge of words, the animal emits instead a stream of cries, affects, spirits, and magnetic fluids" (166). He also observes that the animal marks "a limit of figurability, a limit of the very function of language" (163). Lippit examines how Lewis Carroll, Franz Kakfa, and Akutagawa Ryunosuke dynamically stretch the limits of language in their treatment of the animal. In this chapter I am looking more at melancholic linguistic breakdown, which is empathetic with the animal's imputed muteness.

18. Since contact with canine somatic communication can prevent humans from falling into *Verwerfung* (see n. 14 above), where can one look to find a suitable illustration of the third Kristevean category? William Wharton's *Birdy* (1978)

takes as its subject the melancholic desire to communicate with the beast, resulting finally in the loss of ability to speak with one's own species. *Birdy* demonstrates the mania possessing one boy to chirp, fly, and even mate as a bird. The main protagonist, nicknamed Birdy, psychotically tries to imagine away the barrier between himself and the canaries as well as between dream and reality. By the end, which is where the narrative begins, he is housed in a mental institution fully incapable of human speech. He thus moves from the *Verneinung* of difference (between the species) to the catatonic extreme of *Verwerfung*. Yet despite the psychosis into which he descends, Birdy's capability for empathy and compassion is also portrayed by Wharton. The boy melancholically senses his separation from his comely pets: "I'm yearning to shift my finger through the bars of the cage and touch her foot. I feel caged out of her cage" (45) or "I feel like an awkward giant; the bird is only a bit of feathers beating and struggling in my hand" (204). Birdy lyrically expresses admiration for the gracefulness of the canaries, the longing to share in the beauty of flight, and the effort to imagine their existence. But the desire to be part of the animal world, the tragedy of human exile from it, is ambiguously sullied by the teenager's alienation from his own body: "They don't recognize me at all. . . . It makes me feel rejected, alone. I spend my days watching different birds with the binoculars because it gets me close, blocks everything else; the birds fill my whole vision. . . . I'm getting to hate taking my eyes from the binoculars and looking at myself and everything around me. My hands, my feet, are grotesque. I'm becoming a stranger in myself" (203). The melancholic feels unworthy, for the loss of closeness to the desired object translates as a sense of his own deserted, devalued self.

19. "Mumu," *Faithful Ruslan*, and *Niki* are political allegories, but inner censorship can also structure masquerade in dog stories that allude to homosexuality. For more on this topic, see my article "Literary Fiction and the Queer Love of Dogs," in particular the discussion of Jean Dutourd's novel, *A Dog's Head* (1951).

20. I borrow the term "cynomorphic" from Theodore Ziolkowski. Cynomorphic tales are ones narrated from a dog's perspective in the third person or by a dog in the first person. On language and animals in literature, see also Margot Norris, *Beasts of the Modern Imagination: Darwin, Nietzsche, Kafka, Ernst, and Lawrence*. For her, the beasts are these writers themselves, "who create *as* the animal—not *like* the animal, in imitation of the animal—but with their animality speaking" (1). She calls such writers "biocentric."

21. For a lengthy discussion of this matter see my article, "A Higher Language: Novalis on Communion with Animals."

22. Note the difference here to the highly anthropomorphic arguments of Temple Grandin, the autistic woman who has designed humane devices for cattle being led to slaughter. She argues that her autism, her thinking in pictures rather than words, allows her to perceive how animals see the world.

NOTES TO PAGES 56–60

What she does share with the writers discussed here, however, is an awareness of the limitations of human language. And she cautions: "Animal
researchers take a lot for granted: 'animals don't have language,' 'animals
don't have psychological self-awareness'—you find blanket assertions like
this sprinkled throughout the research literature. But the truth is, we don't
know what animals can't do any better than we know what they can do"
(Grandin and Johnson 283).

23. Neumann argues that the portrayal of the dog in art and literature is
    devoted to holding up a mirror to the human being—for instance, the dog
    becomes the symbol of idealized human loyalty or fidelity. In the play
    between man and animal, nature and culture, talking dogs represent the
    artist's desire for spontaneous, natural speech.

24. Lest one also assume that animals have no artistic sense, see the fascinating
    collection of photographs in Vicki Mathison, *Dog Works: The Meaning and
    Magic of Canine Constructions.*

25. Compare Scholtmeijer's general comment about the animal in fiction: "But
    since fiction does not close off the world, it is in a unique position to give
    material representation to the inadequacies of language and thus to sustain
    without finality the multi-sided and conflicted being of the animal. Fiction
    elicits the reality of the animal by revealing the fragmentariness of human
    responses" (*Animal Victims* 91).

26. Compare Norris: "Speaking as the animal requires the abolition of human
    speech and the repeal, if not entirely of the intention to communicate,
    then certainly of the intention to mean and signify. But the solution to this
    dilemma could not simply be silence: it had to be silence with a difference,
    silence that signaled the renunciation (not merely the absence) of speech.
    Only Kafka and perhaps [Max] Ernst, in their repeal of reason and logic and
    in the strategies to frustrate meaning and communication, approximated
    this condition" (225).

27. The majority of works in the popular cynomorphic genre (which I would set
    in opposition to the philosophic tradition Ziolkowski uncovers) banally
    reduce what could transpire in a dog's mind to fixation on a bone, anticipa-
    tion of the next walk, or preoccupation with scents on the roadside. Nagel's
    point is that we cannot know that their inner consciousness is so simplistic.

28. In "Our Friend, the Dog" (1903), which is similarly an homage to a dead
    pet, Belgian writer Maurice Maeterlinck also muses on how arduous the task
    must be for a young dog to adapt to the arbitrary strictures of human life.

29. The epilogue in which the author assumes back his own voice is flat and
    mundane. Here he narrates how they found Angus and took him to the
    veterinarian, where he dies.

30. To appreciate Siebert's uniqueness, contrast his depiction of Angus with
    Norris's characterization of animal behavior: "The animal's desire is direct
    and appropriative while the human's is mediated and directed toward the
    recognition of the 'other.' . . . The animal is autotelic and lives for itself in

the fulness of its being while the cultural man lives in imitation of the desire of the 'other,' driven by his *manque à être*; the animal surrenders to biological fate and evolutionary destiny while the human disregards the physicality of what is and reads his fate in the gaze of the 'other'" (4).

31. To speak through the dog in the cynomorphic narrative is to incorporate the dog into one's own body, to become one with its voice. It is thus an inherently melancholic genre. Martin Buber, who often speaks of the "melancholy of our fate" in *I and Thou*, refers to his cat's glance as a "speech of disquietude" and, much like Siebert, sees in this glance an array of pressing questions that the cat poses to him about their precarious interdependence, that for that moment of the glance becomes an I-Thou relational event: "The beginning of this cat's glance, lighting up under the touch of my glance, indisputably questioned me: 'It is possible that you think of me? Do you really not just want me to have fun? Do I concern you? Do I exist in your sight? Do I really exist? What is it that comes from you? What is it that surrounds me? What is it that comes to me? What is it?'" (97). As in Siebert, this ventriloquized rhetoric of questioning stems from a melancholic desire to be closer to the animal.

32. Although they share a fascination with sleeping hounds, the two artists could not be more different: Thormann is preoccupied with the intangibility and enigma of their dreams, while Hockney focuses on the immediacy of their dormant bodies.

33. In an essay wonderfully entitled "Iphigenie als Hund," Johannes Langner argues that the pose of the dog recalls Anselm Feuerbach's 1871 painting *Iphigenie*, which Marc's own Exlibris lithograph also resembles with a seated woman posing pensively, her chin propped up by her hand. I would add that this iconography traces back to Dürer's *Melencolia I*, with the result that Marc could be collapsing into one figure the white hound of Dürer's engraving and Melencolia herself!

34. Compare Rilke's notion of gazing into the dog discussed at the end of my introduction.

35. Gerhard Neumann, in an article on the motif of the dog and ape in literature, argues that the gaze of the dog functions as a mirror to the human: it authenticates or guarantees his identity and bestows a false sense of the true and natural. Neumann's insight would apply to Maeterlinck's Pelléas but not to Tulip, who, precisely because she signifies a natural authenticity, serves to expose Ackerley's disingenuousness.

CHAPTER TWO

1. Wills mistranslates *pudeur* as "immodesty" (372), hence I cite the French original.

2. See Morrison and Stolorow.

3. Jack Katz writes: "Literature has suggested that shame is the primary social emotion, in that it is generated by the virtually constant monitoring of

the self in relation to others. Such monitoring . . . is not rare but almost continuous in social interaction" (210).

4. Donald Nathanson, in his introduction to his edited volume *The Many Faces of Shame*, writes: "The human being is not the only animal that displays shame affect. One of the reasons dogs have been the favored companion of so many people for so many generations is the general resemblance of the canine facial affect system to that of the human; Darwin drew many of his analogies from pictures of dogs. It is hard not to smile when a beloved dog, made aware of its transgression, responds to verbal censure with bowed head, averted eyes, generally decreased body tonus, and drooping tail" (30–31).

5. Rego is one of the leading figurative artists today. Starting with her first major piece, *Stray Dogs (The Dogs of Barcelona)* (1965), canines populate her works. Almost as if they were her familiar, they figure alongside women from the *Girl and Dog* series (1986) to *Betrothal* (1999).

6. The impurity of the mongrel mix between human and canine haunts several examples of contemporary science-fiction novels. Neither human nor animal, the figures in Carol Emshwiller's *Carmen Dog* (1988), Kirsten Bakis's *Lives of the Monster Dogs* (1997), and Jeff Noon's *Pollen* (1995) represent awkward, provisional bodies. In Emshwiller's feminist novel, females of all species start to metamorphose and are subject to degrading experiments and persecution by the male members of society. The heroine Pooch develops from the household pet into a lovely woman who still carries with her the subservient modesty and self-uncertainty of a downtrodden dog. In Kirsten Bakis's novel, the dogs are the actual result of cruel operations that embedded voice boxes in their throats and substituted prostheses for hands. Having taken up abode in New York City, they are the object of "amusement and revulsion" (7). The main character, Ludwig von Sacher, is sensitive to the shame of being "ugly parodies of humans . . . caricatures of human beings" (8) and recognizes that "there is no place for monsters in this world" (8). In *Pollen*, the character Clegg exclaims: "Shit, there's too much dog in me, I guess. . . . You humans don't know what it's like. The dog in my veins is a slave to love" (150). If Rego's dog-women seek to release the instinctual in themselves, the cyborg dog is ashamed of its animal residue.

But if Bakis's cyborg dogs dress in nineteenth-century garb and sequester themselves away from the shaming gaze of humans, in Noon's postmodern world, hybridity and fluidity are inescapable and everywhere: "Every combination was there. Not many pure dog or pure human, but hundreds of crazy messed-up mutants in-between. Evil-looking creatures for the most part; bits of dog sprouting from human forms, scraps of humanity glimpsed in a furry face" (95). When, at the end of the novel, the canine-human mutant Coyote dies, he springs from the grave again: "His body is a compound of flora and fauna; flowers and dog-flesh. And humanity. Somewhere in that bouquet, a tiny trace of the human" (239). Contamination becomes a cause for reveling in a polymorphous perversity, for Jeff Noon's shape-shifters celebrate a Deleuzean nomadism and becoming-animal.

    Other novels that contain mutant or cybernetic dogs are Mikhail Bulgakov's *The Heart of a Dog* (1925), Clifford Simak's *City* (1952), Ray Bradbury's *Fahrenheit 451* (1953), Richard Adams's *The Plague Dogs* (1978), Dean Koontz's *Watchers* (1987), and Bruce Sterling's *Holy Fire* (1996).

7.   Rego notes: "With pastel you don't have the brush between you and the surface. Your hand is making the picture. It's almost like being a sculptor. You are actually making the person. It's very tactile . . . and there's a lot of physical strength involved because it's overworked, masses and masses of layers changed all the time. It takes a lot of strength. But it's wonderful to do, to rub your hand over" (quoted in McEwen 215).

8.   The woman becoming dog similarly expresses a visceral self-abandon in Djuna Barnes's novel *Nightwood* (1936). At the close, Robin, who has left Nora, her devout lover, returns to a decaying chapel on the latter's property. When Nora's dog, suspicious of an intruder, runs into the church, Robin goes down on all fours and challenges the beast. "The veins stood out in her neck, under her ears, swelled in her arms, and wide and throbbing rose up on her fingers as she moved forward. . . . Then she began to bark also, crawling after him—barking in a fit of laughter, obscene and touching" (169–70). Robin's becoming-dog resonates on multiple levels. Her ferociousness betokens the animality and instinctiveness of her inarticulate desires, yet also confirms the wayward innocence and unreflectedness of her remorseless deserting of husband, son, and lover in order to pursue her nocturnal adventures. In adopting the pose of another creature, she demonstrates her decenteredness as a human being. Yet in returning close to Nora she also, despite her wild abandon, suggests an unvoiceable loyalty. Nora herself is doggedly devoted to Robin and embodies the degradation of loyal, spurned love. That Robin's encounter with the dog and with the animal in herself occurs in a church also marks the profanity and yet intensity bordering on spirituality that characterizes Nora's and Robin's lesbian relation.

9.   Ruth Rosengarten offers a reading of the series that focuses on abandonment rather than abandon. Basing her reading primarily on *Bad Dog*, she writes that the series "evoke the hurt and humiliation, the poignant combination of eroticism and violence that happen within conditions of great intimacy; the expectation, the vertigo, the abdication of self that are at the heart of the lover's affliction. . . . And love's object, an implicit though physically absent male, remains insistent in these works" (88).

10. *Two Girls and a Dog* possibly alludes to Watteau's *Fête in a Park* (circa 1718), where two girls are playing with a dog on a leash, tugging at it. On the other side of the painting, three women sit with men, attracting their attention. Like Watteau, Rego points to the connection between dogs and lovers, or sex and control.

11. Jack Katz writes: "When there is a moment of revelation to others, the ashamed person often cannot or will not lift his or her head to perceive the others' regard, and so he or she maintains a phantomlike sense of the 'others' whose knowledge brings shame. In these cases, it is not actually seeing others seeing oneself that brings shame, since one may never quite catch their gaze. What brings shame is taking toward oneself what one presumes is the view that others would have were they to look" (234).

12. Other animals in *Animal Portraits* include sheep, mice, pigs, rabbits, frogs, vipers, cats, and roosters.

13. Compare the shame of the dog-human hybrid in Jean Dutourd's novel *A Dog's Head* (1951).

14. William Wegman, e-mail message to the author, July 13, 2005.

15. With reference to Sartre, Beth Bjorkland analyzes the workings of *le regard* in this story.

16. Locating Ulrich Seidel on the broader spectrum of postmodern art, one can say that the visceral, the abject, or the Lacanian Real (think of David Lynch or Damien Hirst) can never be as wholly unmediated as its artists pretend it to be or want it to appear.

CHAPTER THREE

1. Compare Donna Haraway's proclamation: "I resist being called the 'mom' to my dogs because I fear infantilization of the adult canines and misidentification of the important fact that I wanted dogs, not babies. My multispecies family is not about surrogacy and substitutes; we are trying to live other tropes, other metaplasms. We need other nouns and pronouns for the kin genres of companion species, just as we did (and still do) for the spectrum of genders" (96).

2. On the topic of bestiality, see Midas Dekkers.

3. Dekkers notes: "Compared with reality, in which it is virtually always men who actually copulate with animals, in art the roles are completely reversed. Since most artists over the centuries have been men, the reason for this role-reversal is obvious, because it corresponds with male fantasies. . . . [A] man identifies with the active party: the animal" (154–55).

4. My approach sets itself apart from Gerhard Neumann's claim that the dog frequently symbolizes a "Mit-sich-Eigenseins in der unwandelbaren Treue zu sich selbst" (108). He gives as examples of how the dog functions as guarantor of human identity the self-portraits of artists with their dogs (Hogarth, Courbet, Dali) or the dog in family portraits. As to the dogs who accompany women in paintings (Fragonard, Boucher), they serve as substitutes for the male, voyeuristic gaze. Without denying these art-historical traditions, I call into question that the dog merely indexically references fidelity to oneself, i.e., that authenticity is necessarily phantasmic and certified by recourse to "nature." In the following works by women, I claim

that authenticity is an achievement attained through intersubjective communication with the dog.

5. See the section "Denying Animal Subjectivity" in Brian Luke.

6. See, in particular, Carol Adams's *Neither Man nor Beast: Feminism and the Defense of Animals* and the two books she edited with Josephine Donovan, *Beyond Animal Rights: A Feminist Caring Ethic for the Treatment of Animals* and *Animals and Women: Feminist Theoretical Explorations*.

7. Among the essays in Adams and Donovan's collection is Marian Scholtmeijer's, "Animals in Women's Fiction." She concludes that "seeking community with animals, these stories [by women authors] create whole worlds in defiance of obdurate conceptions of reality" (256).

8. For a fine article on the television series, see Jenkins.

9. The recent film *Because of Winn-Dixie* (2005), about a girl and the dog who adopts her, reverses this trend of focus on the juvenile male protagonist.

10. Might this definition of "repetition" counter its association with trauma and anxiety in Freud's psychoanalytic notion of the "repetition compulsion"? I thank the anonymous reader from the University of Chicago Press for this insight.

11. See Carol Adams's chapter "Examining the Arrogant Eye" in *Neither Man nor Beast*.

12. A former Guggenheim fellow, Pamela Stewart has written numerous books of poetry and has published in several national magazines and anthologies.

13. The third photo depicts one of the prostitutes, again in her undergarments, but this time in black shoes and stockings, posing on an ironing board set up outdoors. Lying on her stomach, she pulls a white toy dog up onto its hind legs. The dog is delighted at the attention and both appear engrossed in each other in a scene of domestic merriment.

14. Howie intriguingly compares Bellocq's photographs of prostitutes in the company of dogs with other early pornographic shots where the woman poses with the dog close to her genitals: in the latter, the relationship between woman and dog appears strained and uncomfortable for both (32–34). On the art historical tradition of associating the courtesan with the dog, see both Posner and Thomson.

15. When Sontag writes, "How touching, good natured, and respectful these pictures are" (8), or Goldin, "With the women's obvious trust, warmth, and ease, these pictures transcend the normal customer-to-prostitute relationship" (91), I think they mistake the ease that comes from cool self-distantiation for naturalness. As Howie and I indicate, one needs to differentiate between photos.

16. Joseph Sandler notes that, in psychoanalytic terms, the phenomenon of some people resembling their dogs is most likely to be the consequence of narcissistic object choice (1103).

17. Natalie Kusz is the author of the memoir *Road Song*, published by Farrar Straus and Giroux, which has been released in British, German, and

Chinese editions. She teaches at Eastern Washington University and was previously the director of creative writing at Harvard University.

18. Woolf wrote in her diary (April 29, 1933): "That silly book Flush,— o what a waste of time" (*Diary* 153). See Caughie on the function of mocking and silliness in *Flush*.

19. On the woman's position (mirrored in the dog) in a patriarchal society, see the chapter "Flush's Journey from Imprisonment to Freedom" in Squier.

20. See also Kathleen Kete on nineteenth-century French pet fancy.

21. For documentation on the Victorians' championing of animal rights, see Rod Preece, *Awe for the Tiger, Love for the Lamb*.

22. Gertrude Stein also wrote a novel *Ida* (1941) about a woman and her succession of dogs, one of whom was named "Love." Stein tells of how Ida and her dog would hold hands together.

23. Derrida responds to Descartes's "Cogito ergo sum" similarly to Stein: "The animal looks at us, and we are naked before it. Thinking perhaps begins there" ("The Animal" 397).

24. Taking Benjamin's notion of intersubjectivity as a model for human-canine interaction goes beyond seeing the dog solely as a transitional object—to use Winnicott's term—that substitutively prepares one for interhuman relations. Winnicott refers to dolls and stuffed animals as instruments the child uses to substitute for human interactions; in playing with the toy, the child works through imaginary and emotional human situations. Marjorie Garber deploys the notion of transitional objects to refer to the dog as a "fantasy companion" (131). But to speak of the dog as a preparatory device for social adjustment, however apt when parents deliberate whether to acquire a pet for their children, is to infantilize human-canine connections.

25. Lerman's novels include *Animal Acts* (1994) and *God's Ear* (1989). She has also rewritten her 1979 novel *Eleanor* for the stage and television with Jean Stapleton playing Eleanor Roosevelt.

26. Similarly, in Ingeborg Bachmann's tale "Das Gebell"(The barking [1972]) an old woman starts imagining she hears dogs barking. They represent the unvoiced anger she harbors toward her callous son.

27. Similarly, "The dogs sit on my face and eat my brains" (75).

28. This fear mimics an attitude in scientific research. According to a CNN.com article on "Many Scientists Unwilling to Study Dogs" (November 21, 2002), "There are more studies on the call of the red winged blackbird than on what different dog barks mean. And there's more data on the head movements of some lizards than on what a dog's tail wagging means. This dearth of details on humans' most loyal companion might have something to do with scientists distancing themselves from anything that goes beyond cold, hard facts, said zoologist Patricia McConnell. 'Science has always been uncomfortable with emotions, so there's a real bias against studying domestic animals,' said McConnell."

29. Although I have here concentrated on works by and about women, the implications for the representation of men and dogs are considerable. For instance, the realist tradition of black-and-white photography of the dog is replete with examples both of tough working- or lower-class men softened by the presence of the dog (Richard Billingham, Shelby Lee Adams) and of nubile naked boys with dogs (from the late nineteenth-century Wilhelm von Gloeden to Sally Mann). André Kertész's 1928 "Marché aux animaux" and Danny Lyon's 1967 "Knoxville TN" each depict a boy looking warily while guarding a puppy as if clutching to the last vestiges of innocence. Roland Barthes wrote of Kertész's picture: "That lower-class boy who holds a newborn puppy against his cheek . . . looks into the lens with his sad, jealous, fearful eyes: what pitiable, lacerating pensiveness! In fact, he is looking at nothing; he *retains* within himself his love and his fear" (*Camera Lucida* 113). Contemporary Japanese photographer Yasushi Kanazawa has a collection entitled *Tom and His Dog Banzai* (1998) that ironically juxtaposes macho, tattooed Tom with his fat little terrier. The Spanish photographer Baylón included among his many shots of street dogs, one of a homeless man and his dog sleeping on the cement ("Perros con amo" [1987]). Similarly, the homeless American writer Lars Eighner has written movingly yet nonsentimentally on caring for his dog Lizbeth during times in which he could not extend this care to himself.

CHAPTER FOUR

1. As we shall also later see in the works by Michael Field, Marie Bonaparte, and Colette Audry.
2. Freud speaks of the melancholic's "open wound" (10:439).
3. For a reading of *Topsy* as an allegory of the relations between Bonaparte and Sigmund and Anna Freud, see Reiser. She suggests that "*Topsy* may well have served as a way simultaneously to avoid and to express (indirectly) thoughts and concerns that all three shared. Freud wrote to Jones in May 1938, just as the translation was finished that 'between beloved friends much should be obvious and remain unexpressed'" (685). Reiser also addresses Bonaparte's relationship to her own father, as does, more extensively, Thompson.
4. On dogs as envoys to the afterlife, see the powerfully haunting story of a bed-ridden boy, his dog, and a revenant in Ray Bradbury's short story, "The Emissary" (1947).
5. All excerpts, citing poem number and/or title, are from the *Chadwyck-Healey English Poetry Full-Text Database*.
6. Note, also, the fourth poem that begins, "O Dionysus, at thy feet," as if comingling Christ and Dionysus as the "tragic god": "Receive him, tragic god of tendrilled fire— / Our sweetest . . . / Leave us not lonely!" Whym Chow was buried on 1 February 1906 under an altar to Dionysus in the garden.

7.   In contrast, there are isolated moments of profound, inconsolable bereavement, as in poem 26: "thou art in a little grave, deep, deep, / Scooped in my heart." Edith wrote the day Whym died: "Today I have had the worst loss of my life—yes, worse than that of beloved Mother or the tragic father" (Field, *Music and Silence* 173).

8.   Compare René Girard:

> One of the brothers kills the other, and the murderer is the one who does not have the violence-outlet of animal sacrifice at his disposal. This difference between sacrificial and nonsacrificial cults determines, in effect, God's judgement in favor of Abel. To say that God accedes to Abel's sacrificial offerings but rejects the offerings of Cain is simply another way of saying—from the viewpoint of the divinity—that Cain is a murderer, whereas his brother is not. . . . According to Moslem tradition, God delivered to Abraham the ram previously sacrificed by Abel. This ram was to take the place of Abraham's son Isaac; having already saved one human life, the same animal would now save another. (4)

9.   In the interview "Eating Well," Derrida addresses this "*sacrificial* structure" underlying discourses about the animal, stating that "the 'symbolic' is very difficult, truly impossible to delimit in this case, hence the enormity of the task, its essential excessiveness, a certain unclassifiability or the monstrosity of that *for which* we have to answer here, or *before* which (whom? what?) we have to answer" (112). He then goes on to acknowledge the need to "*sacrifice sacrifice*" (113). Compare Stephen Webb: "The pet relationship is the opposite of scapegoating. . . . Pets give us a sacrifice that is antieconomical, based on a surplus of emotions and affection in which we give up something for the other in order to let the other become more than it otherwise would be rather than asking the other to give up its life so that we can benefit from it. What pets are for is, decisively, the end of the reign of animal sacrifice—the sacrifice of sacrifice" (154). Drawing out the implications of Christ's own sacrifice to end all sacrifices he cites Carol Adams: "A Christology of vegetarianism would affirm that no more crucifixions are necessary" (161). Webb further argues regarding a vegetarian eucharist: "To eat in memory of the sacrificed Jesus is to acknowledge our role in inflicting pain on others, while it is also to state our intentions not to participate in such cruelty in the future" (163).

10.   Although we see the mothers of Ramiro, Octavio, and Susana, there is no mention of the fathers. Similarly, Valeria requests that Daniel not contact her father in Spain, who would only say she brought her misfortune on herself. And, of course, El Chivo is the absent father of Maru, who takes him for dead. The absence of good internal objects from the family, to speak with Melanie Klein, results in the projection of hatred outward, onto the dog.

11.   One may debate whether dogs can sense, as Lurie says, that their time has come. But why could they not? In visiting abbatoirs for her work *Dead*

Meat, Sue Coe repeatedly observed the horror and fear of animals watching as, in front of them, their fellows are stunned and have their throats slit.

12. Wurmser differentiates between shame as stemming from the violation of self and guilt from the violation of others (17). See Lewis's helpful table on the differences between guilt and shame (113).

13. See also Elizabeth Costello's words in *The Lives of Animals*: "To be alive is to be a living soul. An animal—and we are all animals—is an embodied soul" (33).

14. See Joseph de Maistre: "The innocent can pay for the guilt . . . a less valuable life can be offered and accepted for another" (358).

15. In *The Lives of Animals*, Elizabeth Costello compares the killing of animals in the meat industry to Treblinka.

16. See Derrida: "I situate disavowal at the heart of all these discourses on the animal" ("And Say the Animal" 128).

Works Cited

Abraham, Nicolas, and Maria Torok. *The Shell and the Kernel.*
Translated by Nicholas Rand. Vol. 1. Chicago: University of
Chicago Press, 1994.

Ackerely, J. R. *My Dog Tulip.* New York: Poseidon Press, 1965.

Adams, Carol. *Neither Man nor Beast: Feminism and the Defense of
Animals.* New York: Continuum, 1994.

Adams, Carol, and Josephine Donovan, eds. *Animals and Women:
Feminist Theoretical Explorations.* Durham, N.C.: Duke
University Press, 1995.

————, eds. *Beyond Animal Rights: A Feminist Caring Ethic for the
Treatment of Animals.* New York: Continuum, 1996.

Adams, Robert. *I Hear the Leaves and Love the Light: Sally in the
Back Yard.* Tucson: Nazraeli, 1999.

Adamson, Joseph, and Hilary Clark, eds. *Scenes of Shame:
Psychoanalysis, Shame, and Writing.* Albany, N.Y.: SUNY Press,
1999.

Agamben, Giorgio. *The Open: Man and Animal.* Translated by
Kevin Attell. Stanford, Calif.: Stanford University Press, 2004.

American Humane Association. *Guidelines for the Safe Use of
Animals in Filmed Media.* American Humane Association,
Film and Television Unit, Sherman Oaks, Calif. http://www.
americanhumane.org/site/DocServer/pa_FilmGuidelines0604.
pdf?docID=1821. October 2003.

Amores Perros. DVD. Directed by Alejandro González Iñárittu. 2000;
Marina Del Rey, Calif.: Studio Home Entertainment, 2001.

Arnim, Elizabeth von. *All the Dogs of My Life.* London: Virago,
1995.

Attridge, Derek. "Age of Bronze, State of Grace: Music and Dogs
in Coetzee's *Disgrace.*" *Novel: A Forum on Fiction* 34 (Fall
2000): 98–121. http://search.epnet.com/direct.asp?
an=5847403&db=afh.

Audry, Colette. *Behind the Bathtub: The Story of a French Dog*. Translated by Peter Green. Boston: Little, Brown, & Co., 1963.

Baker, Steve. *Picturing the Beast: Animals, Identity, and Representation*. Urbana: University of Illinois Press, 2001.

———. *The Postmodern Animal*. London: Reaktion Books, 2000.

Bakis, Kirsten. *Lives of the Monster Dogs: A Novel*. New York: Warner Books, 1997.

Barnes, Djuna. *Nightwood*. New York: New Directions, 1961.

Barthes, Roland. *Camera Lucida: Reflections of Photography*. Translated by Richard Howard. New York: Hill & Wang, 1981.

———. *A Lover's Discourse: Fragments*. Translated by Richard Howard. New York: Hill & Wang, 1978.

———. *Roland Barthes by Roland Barthes*. Translated by Richard Howard. New York: Hill & Wang, 1977.

Baudrillard, Jean. "The Animals: Territory and Metamorphoses." Pages 129–41 in *Simulacra and Simulation*. Translated by Sheila Faria Glaser. Detroit: University of Michigan Press, 1994.

Bazin, André. "The Ontology of the Photographic Image." In *What Is Cinema?* Edited and translated by Hugh Gray. Berkeley: University of California Press, 1967.

Benjamin, Jessica. *Shadow of the Other: Intersubjectivity and Gender in Psychoanalysis*. New York: Routledge, 1998.

Benjamin, Walter. *Gesammelte Schriften*. Frankfurt am Main: Suhrkamp, 1980.

Berger, John. "Opening a Gate." Pages 1–6 in *The Shape of a Pocket*. London: Bloomsbury, 2001.

———. "Why Look at Animals?" Pages 1–26 in *About Looking*. London: Writers & Readers Publishing Cooperative, 1980.

Berke, Joseph H. "Shame and Envy." Pages 318–34 in *The Many Faces of Shame*, edited by Donald Nathanson. New York: Guilford Press, 1987.

Binder, Hartmut. *Kafka-Kommentar zu sämtlichen Erzählungen*. Munich: Winkler, 1975.

Bjorkland, Beth. "Thomas Mann's 'Tobias Mindernickel' in Light of Sartre's 'Being-for-Others.'" *Studies in Twentieth-Century Literature* 2, no. 2 (Spring 1978): 103–12.

Böhme, Hartmut. *Dürers "Melencolia I": Im Labyrinth der Deutung*. Frankfurt: Fischer, 1989.

Bonaparte, Marie. *Chronos, Eros, Thanatos*. Paris: Presses Universitaires de France, 1952.

———. *Topsy: The Story of a Golden-Haired Chow*. Translated by Princess Eugenie of Greece. London: Pushkin, 1940.

Bradbury, Ray. "The Emissary." Pages 115–23 in *The October Country*. New York: Ballantine, 1955.

Brown, Rebecca. *The Dogs: A Modern Bestiary*. San Francisco: City Lights, 1998.

Browning, Elizabeth Barrett. "To Flush, My Dog." Pages 347–48 in *Poetical Works*. New York: T. Y. Crowell, 1891.

Buber, Martin. *I and Thou*. Translated by Ronald Gregor Smith. 2d ed. New York: Charles Scribner's Sons, 1958.

Butler, Judith. *The Psychic Life of Power: Theories in Subjection*. Stanford, Calif.: Stanford University Press, 1997.

Canetti, Elias. *Über Tiere*. Munich: Hanser, 2002.

Carter, Keith. *Bones*. San Francisco: Chronicle Books, 1996.

Caughie, Pamela. "*Flush* and the Literary Canon: Oh where oh where has that little dog gone?" *Tulsa Studies in Women's Literature* 10, no. 1 (Spring 1991): 47–66.

Clark, David. "On Being 'The Last Kantian in Nazi Germany': Dwelling with Animals after Levinas." Pages 165–98 in *Animal Acts: Configuring the Human in Western History*, edited by Jennifer Ham and Matthew Senior. New York and London: Routledge, 1997.

Coe, Brian, and Mark Haworth-Booth. *A Guide to Early Photographic Processes*. London: Hurtwood, 1983.

Coe, Sue. *Dead Meat*. New York: Four Walls Eight Windows, 1995.

———. *Pit's Letter*. New York: Four Walls Eight Windows, 2000.

Coetzee, J. M. *Disgrace*. New York: Penguin 1999.

———. *The Lives of Animals*. Princeton, N.J.: Princeton University Press, 1999.

Cohen, David. "Freud's Probity." In *Lucian Freud's Etchings from the Paine Webber Art Collection*. New Haven, Conn.: Yale Center for British Art, 1999.

Dekkers, Midas. *Dearest Pet: On Bestiality*. Translated by Paul Vincent. London: Verso, 1994.

Deleuze, Gilles, and Félix Guattari. *Kafka: Toward a Minor Literature*. Translated by Dana Polan. Minneapolis: University of Minnesota Press, 1986.

———. *A Thousand Plateaus: Capitalism and Schizophrenia*. Translated by Brian Massumi. London: Athlone, 1988.

Derrida, Jacques. "And Say the Animal Responded?" Pages 121–46 in *Zootologies: The Question of the Animal*, edited by Cary Wolfe. Minneapolis: University of Minnesota Press, 2003.

———. "'Eating Well,' or the Calculation of the Subject: An Interview with Jacques Derrida." Pages 96–119 in *Who Comes after the Subject?* edited by Eduardo Cadava, Peter Connor, and Jean-Luc Nancy. New York: Routledge, 1991.

———. "L'animal que donc je suis (À suivre)." Pages 251–301 in *L'animal autobiographique: Autour de Jacques Derrida*. Edited by Marie-Louise Mallet. Paris: Galilée, 1999. Translated by David Wills as "The Animal That Therefore I Am (More to Follow)." *Critical Inquiry* 28, no. 2 (Winter 2002): 369–418.

———. *Of Spirit: Heidegger and the Question*. Translated by Geoffrey Bennington and Rachel Bowlby. Chicago: University of Chicago Press, 1989.

Dery, Tibor. *Niki: The Story of a Dog*. Translated by Edward Hyams. London: Secker & Warburg, 1958.

Diala, Isidore. "Nadine Gordimer, J. M. Coetzee, and André Brink: Guilt, Expiation, and the Reconciliation Process in Post-Apartheid South Africa." *Journal of Modern Literature* 25, no. 2 (Winter 2001–2): 50–68.

Donoghue, Emma. *We Are Michael Field*. Bath: Absolute Press, 1998.

Donovan, Josephine. "Attention to Suffering: Sympathy as a Basis for Ethical Treatment of Animals." Pages 147–69 in *Beyond Animal Rights: A Feminist Caring Ethic for the Treatment of Animals*, edited by Carol Adams and Josephine Donovan. New York: Continuum, 1996.

Drexler, Rosalyn. *The Cosmopolitan Girl*. New York: M. Evans, 1974.

Duve, Karen. "Besuch vom Hund." Pages 47–52 in *Keine Ahnung*. Frankfurt am Main: Suhrkamp, 1999.

Eighner, Lars. *Travels with Lizbeth*. New York: St. Martin's Press, 1993.

Emshwiller, Carol. *Carmen Dog*. London: Women's Press, 1988.

Faustina, Helen. *Read My Autobiography: I Am the Great Pedro, the Wisest Dog in the World*. New York: Knickerbocker Press, 1930.

Field, Michael. *Music and Silence: The Gamut of Michael Field*. Compiled by Ivor Treby. Bury St. Edmunds, Suffolk: De Blackland, 2000.

———. *Whym Chow: Flame of Love*. London: Eragny Press, 1914. Chadwyck-Healey English Poetry Full-Text Database. Cambridge, 1992. http://gateway.proquest.com/openurl?ctx_ver=Z39.88-2003&xri:pqil: res_ver=0.2&res_id=xri:ilcs-us&rft_id=xri:ilcs:ft:ep2:Z000374011:0

Freud, Lucian. Interview by William Feaver. BBC Radio 3, 10 December 1991.

Freud, Sigmund. *Gesammelte Werke*. 18 vols. London: Imago, 1940–52.

Galsworthy, John. "Memories." Pages 139–62 in *The Inn of Tranquillity: Studies and Essays*. London: Heinemann, 1912.

Garber, Marjorie. *Dog Love*. New York: Touchstone, 1996.

Gauß, Karl-Markus. *Von nah, von fern: Ein Jahrbuch*. Vienna: Paul Zsolnay Verlag, 2003.

Girard, René. *Violence and the Sacred*. Translated by Patrick Gregory. Baltimore: Johns Hopkins University Press, 1977.

Goldin, Nan. "Bellocq Époque." *Art Forum* 35, no. 9 (May 1997): 88–91, 142.

Graham, Lucy. "'Yes, I am giving him up': Sacrificial Likeness with Dogs in J. M. Coetzee's Recent Fiction." *Scrutiny: Issues in English Studies in Southern Africa* 7, no. 1 (2002): 4–15.

Grandin, Temple, and Catherine Johnson. *Animals in Translation: Using the Mysteries of Autism to Decode Animal Behavior*. New York: Scribner, 2005.

Greer, Germaine. "Paula Rego." *Modern Painters* 1, no. 3 (Autumn 1988): 28.

Grenier, Roger. *On the Difficulty of Being a Dog*. Translated by Alice Kaplan. Chicago: University of Chicago Press, 2000.

Hanson, Karen. "Reasons for Shame, Shame against Reason." Pages 155–79 in *The Widening Scope of Shame*, edited by Melvin R. Lansky and Andrew P. Morrison. Hillsdale, N.J.: Analytic Press, 1997.

Haraway, Donna. *The Companion Species Manifesto: Dogs, People, and Significant Otherness*. Chicago: Prickly Paradigm Press, 2003.

Hearne, Vicki. *Adam's Task: Calling Animals by Name*. Pleasantville, N.Y.: Akadine, 2000.

———. *The White German Shepherd*. New York: Atlantic Monthly Press, 1988.

Henry, O. "Memoirs of a Yellow Dog." In *The Four Million*. New York: Doubleday, 1903.

Hockney, David. *Dog Days*. London: Thames & Hudson, 1998.

Hofmannsthal, Hugo von. *Gedichte und Lyrische Dramen* and *Prosa*, vols. 1 and 2. In *Gesammelte Werke*. Frankfurt: Fischer: 1950–52.

Howie, Mary Elizabeth. "Dogs, Domesticity, and Deviance in the Storyville Portraits of E. J. Bellocq." Master's Thesis, University of North Carolina, Chapel Hill, 2000.

Jenkins, Henry. "'Her Suffering Aristocratic Majesty': The Sentimental Value of *Lassie*." Pages 69–101 in *Kids Media Culture*, edited by Marsha Kinder. Durham, N.C.: Duke University Press, 1999.

Kafka, Franz. *Der Prozeß*. Frankfurt am Main: Fischer, 1972.

———. *Kafka's Selected Stories*. Translated and edited by Stanley Corngold. New York: Norton, forthcoming.

———. *Sämtliche Erzählungen*. Frankfurt am Main: Fischer, 1970.

Katz, Jack. "The Elements of Shame." Pages 231–260 in *The Widening Scope of Shame*, edited by Melvin R. Lansky and Andrew P. Morrison. Hillsdale, N.J.: Analytic Press, 1997.

Keats, John. *Selected Poems and Letters*. Edited by Douglas Bush. Boston: Houghton Mifflin, 1959.

Kemp Ross, Margaret. "I Married My Dog." The Back Page by William Steig. *New Yorker* (June 19 and 26, 2000), 190.

Kete, Kathleen. *The Beast in the Boudoir: Petkeeping in Nineteenth-Century Paris*. Berkeley: University of California Press, 1994.

Kierkegaard, Søren. "The Lilies of the Field and the Birds of the Air." Pages 313–56 in *Christian Discourses*. Translated by Walter Lowrie. Oxford: Oxford University Press, 1939.

King, Betty Lim. *Girl on a Leash: The Healing Power of Dogs: A Memoir*. Lenoir, N.C.: Sanctuary Press, 1998.

Klibansky, Raymond, Erwin Panofsky, and Fritz Saxl. *Saturn and Melancholy: Studies in the History of Natural Philosophy, Religion and Art*. London: Nelson, 1964.

Kristeva, Julia. *Black Sun: Depression and Melancholia*. Translated by Leon Roudiez. New York: Columbia University Press, 1989.

———. *Powers of Horror: An Essay on Abjection*. Translated by Leon Roudiez. New York: Columbia University Press, 1982.

———. *Tales of Love*. Translated by Leon Roudiez. New York: Columbia University Press, 1987.

Kundera, Milan. *The Unbearable Lightness of Being*. Translated by Michael Henry Heim. New York: Harper & Row, 1984.

Kusz, Natalie. "Retired Greyhound, II." Page 100 in *Unleashed: Poems by Writers' Dogs*, edited by Amy Hempel and Jim Shepard. New York: Crown, 1995.

Kuzniar, Alice. "A Higher Language: Novalis on Communion with Animals." *German Quarterly* 76, no. 4 (Fall 2003): 426–42.

———. "Literary Fiction and the Queer Love of Dogs." *Sexualities* (forthcoming).

Lacan, Jacques. *Le séminaire de Jacques Lacan*. Vol. 20, *Encore, 1972–1973*. Paris: Seuil, 1975.

Lamartine, Alphonse de. *Joceyln*. Paris: Garnier-Flammarion, 1967.

Langner, Johannes. "Iphigenie als Hund: Figurenbild im Tierbild bei Franz Marc." Pages 50–73 in *Franz Marc, 1880–1916*. Munich: Städtische Galerie im Lenbachhaus, 1980.

Lawrence, D. H. *Phoenix: The Posthumous Papers of D. H. Lawrence*. London: Heinemann, 1936.

Lawrenson, Edward. "Pup Fiction." (Includes interview with Alejandro González Iñárritu by Bernardo Pérez Soler). *Sight and Sound* 11, no. 5 (May 2001): 28–30.

Le Guin, Ursula K. "She Unnames Them." *New Yorker* 49 (January 21, 1985): 27.

Lerman, Rhoda. *In the Company of Newfies: A Shared Life*. New York: Henry Holt, 1996.

Levinas, Emmanuel. "The Name of a Dog, or Natural Rights." Pages 151–53 in *Difficult Freedom: Essays on Judaism*. Translated by Seán Hand. Baltimore: Johns Hopkins University Press, 1990.

Lewis, Helen Block. "Shame and the Narcissistic Personality." Pages 93–132 in *The Many Faces of Shame*, edited by Donald Nathanson. New York: Guilford Press, 1987.

Lippit, Akira Mizuta. *Electric Animal: Toward a Rhetoric of Wildlife*. Minneapolis: University of Minnesota Press, 2000.

Lisle, Leconte de. *Oeuvres*. Vol. 2, *Poèmes Barbares*. Paris: Société d'édition, 1976.

Llewelyn, John. "Am I Obsessed by Bobby? (Humanism of the Other Animal)." Pages 234–45 in *Re-Reading Levinas*, edited by Robert Bernasconi and Simon Critchley. Bloomington: Indiana University Press, 1991.

Luke, Brian. "Taming Ourselves or Going Feral? Toward a Nonpatriarchal Metaethic of Animal Liberation." Pages 306–8 in *Animals and Women: Feminist Theoretical Explorations*, edited by Carol Adams and Josephine Donovan. Durham, N.C.: Duke University Press, 1995.

Maeterlinck, Maurice. "Our Friend, the Dog." Pages 11–43 in *The Double Garden*. Translated by Alexander Teixeira de Mattos. New York: Dodd, Mead, & Co., 1905.

Maistre, Joseph de. *St. Petersburg Dialogues*. Translated by Richard A. Lebrun. Montreal and Kingston: McGill-Queen's University Press, 1993.

Mann, Sally. *What Remains*. Boston: Bulfinch, 2003.

———. "Sally Mann." 1 November 2004. http://www.pbs.org/wnet/egg/301/mann/

Mann, Thomas. *Werke.* 12 vols. Frankfurt am Main: Fischer, 1967.

Marais, Michael. "'Little enough, less than little: nothing': Ethics, Engagement, and Change in the Fiction of J. M. Coetzee." *Modern Fiction Studies* 46, no. 1 (Spring 2000): 159–82.

Marc, Franz. *Schriften.* Edited by Klaus Lankheit. Cologne: Du Mont, 1978.

Marks, Ben. "William Wegman: Putting on the Dog." *Artspace* 14, no. 5 (July–August 1990): 54–56.

Mathison, Vicki. *Dog Works: The Meaning and Magic of Canine Construction.* Photographs by Tim Dodgshun and Trudy Nicholson. Berkeley: Ten Speed Press, 2000.

McEwen, John. *Paula Rego.* London: Phaidon, 1992.

Miller, Sandra. "People by Lucian Freud." *Artforum International* 26 (October 1987): 113–18.

Metz, Christian. "Photography and Fetish." *October* 34 (1985): 81–90.

Morrison, Andrew P. "The Eye Turned Inward: Shame and the Self." Pages 271–91 in *The Many Faces of Shame,* edited by Donald Nathanson. New York: Guilford Press, 1987.

Morrison, Andrew P., and Robert D. Stolorow. "Shame, Narcissism, and Intersubjectivity." Pages 63–87 in *The Widening Scope of Shame,* edited by Melvin R. Lansky and Andrew P. Morrison. Hillsdale, N.J.: Analytic Press, 1997.

Muir, John. *"Stickeen" and the Lessons of Nature.* Edited by Ronald H. Limbaugh. Fairbanks: University of Alaska Press, 1996.

Nagel, Thomas. "What Is It Like to Be a Bat?" *Philosophical Review* 83, no. 4 (October 1974): 435–50. http://members.aol.com/NeoNoetics/Nagel_Bat.html.

Nathanson, Donald. "A Timetable for Shame." Pages 1–63 in *The Many Faces of Shame,* edited by Donald Nathanson. New York: Guilford Press, 1987.

Neumann, Gerhard. "Der Blick des Anderen: Zum Motiv des Hundes und des Affen in der Literatur." *Jahrbuch der deutschen Schillergesellschaft* 40 (1996): 87–122.

Nietzsche, Friedrich. *Sämtliche Werke in 12 Bänden.* Stuttgart: Kröner, 1964–65.

Noon, Jeff. *Pollen.* Manchester: Ringpull, 1995.

Norris, Margot. *Beasts of the Modern Imagination: Darwin, Nietzsche, Kafka, Ernst, and Lawrence.* Baltimore: Johns Hopkins University Press, 1985.

Novalis. *Werke, Tagebücher und Briefe Friedrich von Hardenbergs.* Edited by Hans-Joachim Mähl and Richard Samuel. 3 vols. Munich: Hanser, 1978–87.

Owens, Craig. "William Wegman's Psychoanalytic Vaudeville." *Art in America* 71, no. 3 (March 1983): 100–109.

Pedrick, William Robert. *La nécrologie de Joffre.* New York: Harper & Brothers, 1922.

Phillips, Adam. *On Kissing, Tickling, and Being Bored: Psychoanalytic Essays on the Unexamined Life.* Cambridge, Mass.: Harvard University Press, 1993.

Pontalis, J.-B. *Loin.* Paris: Gallimard, 1980.

Posner, Donald. *Watteau: A Lady at Her Toilet.* New York: Viking, 1973.

Preece, Rod. *Awe for the Tiger, Love for the Lamb: A Chronicle of Sensibility to Animals.* New York: Routledge, 2002.

Radden, Jennifer, ed. *The Nature of Melancholy: From Aristotle to Kristeva.* Oxford: Oxford University Press, 2000.

Reiser, Lynn Whisnant. "*Topsy*—Living and Dying, a Footnote to History." *Psychoanalytic Quarterly* 56, no. 4 (1987): 667–87.

Rhodes, Dan. *Timoleon Vieta Come Home: A Sentimental Journey.* Edinburgh: Canongate, 2003.

Richter, Jean Paul. *Ideengewimmel: Texte und Aufzeichnungen aus dem unveröffentlichten Nachlaß.* Edited by Kurt Wölfel and Thomas Wirtz. Frankfurt: Eichborn, 1996.

Rilke, Rainer Maria. *Duino Elegies.* Translated by Patrick Bridgwater. London: Menard Press, 1999.

———. *Rilke and Benvenuta: An Intimate Correspondence.* Edited by Magda von Hattingberg (Benvenuta). Translated by Joel Agee. New York: Fromm, 1987.

———. *Sonnets to Orpheus.* Translated by M. D. Herter Norton. New York: Norton, 1992.

———. *Werke in drei Bänden.* Vol. 1. Frankfurt: Insel, 1966.

Ritvo, Harriet. *The Animal Estate: The English and Other Creatures in the Victorian Age.* Cambridge, Mass.: Harvard University Press, 1987.

Rosengarten, Ruth. "Home Truths: The Work of Paula Rego." Pages 43–118 in *Paula Rego.* London: Tate Gallery Publishing, 1997.

Ruddick, Sara. *Maternal Thinking: Towards a Politics of Peace.* Boston: Beacon, 1989.

Sacks, Peter M. *The English Elegy: Studies in the Genre from Spenser to Yeats.* Baltimore: Johns Hopkins University Press, 1985.

Sammallahti, Pentti. *Sammallahti.* Tuscon: Nazraeli Press, 2002.

Sandler, Joseph. "On Communication from Patient to Analyst: Not Everything Is Projective Identification." *International Journal of Psycho-Analysis* 74 (1993): 1097–1107.

Sartre, Jean-Paul. *Being and Nothingness.* New York: Washington Square Press, 1956.

Schels, Walter. *Animal Portraits.* Preface by Dennis C. Turner. Zurich and New York: Edition Stemmle, 2001.

Scholtmeijer, Marian. *Animal Victims in Modern Fiction: From Sanctity to Sacrifice.* Toronto: University of Toronto Press, 1993.

———. "The Power of Otherness: Animals in Women's Fiction." Pages 231–62 in *Animals and Women: Feminist Theoretical Explorations*, edited by Carol Adams and Josephine Donovan. Durham, N.C.: Duke University Press, 1995.

Schuster, Peter-Klaus. *Melencolia I: Dürers Denkbild.* 2 vols. Berlin: Gebr. Mann, 1991.

Sedgwick, Eve Kosofsky, and Adam Frank. *Shame and Its Sisters: A Silvan Tomkins Reader*. Durham, N.C.: Duke University Press, 1995.

Shell, Marc. "The Family Pet." *Representations* 15 (Summer 1986): 121–53.

Siebert, Charles. *Angus: A Memoir*. New York: Crown Publishers, 2000.

Smith, Paul Julian. *Amores Perros*. London: British Film Institute, 2003.

Smyth, Ethel. *Inordinate (?) Affection*. London: Cresset, 1936.

Sontag, Susan. Introduction to *Bellocq: Photographs from Storyville, The Red-Light District of New Orleans*. New York: Random House, 1996.

Squier, Susan M. *Virginia Woolf and London: The Sexual Politics of the City*. Chapel Hill: University of North Carolina Press, 1985.

Starobinski, Jean. "L'encre de la Mélancholie." *La Nouvelle Française* 123 (1963): 410–23.

Stein, Gertrude. *Ida*. New York: Random House, 1941.

———. *What Are Master-pieces*. Los Angeles: Conference Press, 1940.

Stewart, Pamela. "Newfoundland Praise." Pages 214–15 in *Dog Music: Poetry about Dogs*, edited by Joseph Duemer and Jim Simmerman. New York: St. Martin's Press, 1996.

Thompson, Nellie L. "Marie Bonaparte's Theory of Female Sexuality: Fantasy and Biology." *American Imago* 60, no. 3 (2003): 343–78.

Thomson, Richard. "'Les quat' Pattes': The Image of the Dog in Late Nineteenth-Century French Art." *Art History* 5, no. 3 (September 1982): 323–37.

Thormann, Otmar. *Low Moral; Dreaming Dogs: Zwei Fotomappen*. Introduction by Kurt Kaindl. Salzburg: Edition Fotohof im Otto Müller Verlag, 1990.

Tierische Liebe (Animal Love). DVD. Directed by Ulrich Seidel. 1995; Chatsworth, Calif.: Image Entertainment, 2004.

Tuan, Yi-Fu. *Dominance and Affection: The Making of Pets*. New Haven, Conn.: Yale University Press, 1984.

Turgenev, Ivan. "Mumu." Pages 355–406 in *The Torrents of Spring, etc*. Translated by Constance Garnett. New York: Macmillan, 1920.

Webb, Stephen H. *On God and Dogs: A Christian Theology of Compassion for Animals*. Oxford: Oxford University Press, 1998.

Wegman, William. *Fashion Photographs*. New York: Harry N. Abrams, 1999.

———. *Fay*. New York: Hyperion. 1999.

———. *Hardly Gold*. New York: Picture Ray Video. 1997.

———. *My Town*. New York: Hyperion, 1998.

———. *Selected Video Works*. New York: Picture Ray Video. 1994.

Wharton, William. *Birdy*. New York: Knopf, 1978.

Winnicott, D. W. "Transitional Objects and Transitional Phenomena" (1951). Pages 1–25 in *Playing and Reality*. London: Tavistock, 1971.

Wittgenstein, Ludwig. *Philosophical Investigations*: Oxford: Basil Blackwell, 1958.

———. *Zettel*. Edited by G. E. M. Anscombe and G. H. von Wright. Translated by G. E. M. Anscombe. Berkeley: University of California Press, 1970.

Wolfe, Cary. "In the Shadow of Wittgenstein's Lion: Language, Ethics, and the Question of the Animal." Pages 1–57 in *Zoontologies: The Question of the Animal*, edited by Cary Wolfe. Minneapolis: University of Minnesota Press, 2003.

Woolf, Virginia. *The Diary of Virginia Woolf*. Edited by Anne Olivier Bell. Vol. 4, *1931–1935*. New York: Harcourt Brace Jovanovich, 1982.

———. *Flush: A Biography*. New York: Harcourt Brace & Co., 1983.

Wurmser, Léon. *The Mask of Shame*. Baltimore: Johns Hopkins University Press, 1981.

Ziolkowski, Theodore. "Talking Dogs: The Caninization of Literature." Pages 86–122 in *Varieties of Literary Thematics*. Princeton, N.J.: Princeton University Press, 1983.

Index